OpenFlow Cookbook

Over 110 recipes to design and develop your own OpenFlow switch and OpenFlow controller

Kingston Smiler. S

BIRMINGHAM - MUMBAI

OpenFlow Cookbook

First published: April 2015

Production reference: 1280415

Published by Packt Publishing Ltd.
Livery Place
35 Livery Street
Birmingham B3 2PB, UK.

ISBN 978-1-78398-794-8

www.packtpub.com

Credits

Author
Kingston Smiler. S

Reviewers
Renato Aguiar
Icaro Camelo
Praveen Darshanam

Commissioning Editor
Usha Iyer

Acquisition Editor
Subho Gupta

Content Development Editor
Susmita Sabat

Technical Editors
Madhunikita S. Chindarkar
Naveenkumar Jain
Vivek Pala

Copy Editors
Trishya Hajare
Vikrant Phadke
Aarti Saldanha

Project Coordinator
Milton Dsouza

Proofreaders
Safis Editing
Lesley Harrison
Paul Hindle
Kevin McGowan
Elinor Perry-Smith

Graphics
Sheetal Aute

Indexer
Priya Sane

Production Coordinator
Nitesh Thakur

Cover Work
Nitesh Thakur

About the Author

Kingston Smiler. S is a seasoned professional with 11 years of experience in software development and pre-sales, encompassing a wide range of skill sets, roles, and industry verticals. He has solid expertise in data communication networking, software-based switching and routing solutions, and virtualization platforms such as OpenStack, OpenDaylight Controller, Docker containers, CoreOS, and so on. He is currently working as an advisor and technical consultant for networking companies in the development of Layer 2 and Layer 3 IP protocols. Kingston also works on various technologies such as MVC-based web and Windows applications, e-commerce frameworks, open source IoT frameworks, single-board computers such as Raspberry Pi and Intel Galileo, and so on. He is active in various networking standard bodies such as IETF, IEEE, and ONF. He has proposed a couple of drafts in the MPLS working group of IETF. With the current surge in SDN, virtualization, and NFV, his primary focus is in these areas. Kingston completed a BE in computer science from Madras University.

First and foremost, I would like to thank the Lord for giving me the immense confidence and energy to start and complete this book successfully. I want to thank my kids, mother, brother, sister, and all my family members for their support. I would also like to thank all of my friends who supported me in writing, and encouraged me to strive towards my goal. Thanks to Subho and Susmita for their reviews and helping me to finish this book during my busy schedule. Finally, special thanks to my wife for her patience and support in writing this book, as most of this book was written during weekends, nights, vacations, and so on.

About the Reviewers

Renato Aguiar has more than 8 years of experience in software development, with a solid background in computer programming, algorithms, network protocols, and GNU/Linux. He has been working for the last 5 years mostly with software-defined networking (SDN), developing proof-of-concept software for HP's cutting-edge research and participating in academic publications. He is also interested in operations research, operating systems, functional programming, and computer security.

Icaro Camelo is an experienced software developer and has a master's degree in computer science (in the field of networking). He is trilingual (Portuguese, English, and French) and a problem solver, with more than 8 years of experience in IT as a system administrator and software developer.

Icaro is fond of cloud and software architecture, network programming, and software development best practices.

I would like to thank my wife, Anndreza Camelo, for supporting and inspiring me all the time.

Praveen Darshanam has approximately 8 years of experience in information security and telecoms as a security researcher, developer, and QA engineer. He has worked for companies such as Versa, Cisco, McAfee, and iPolicy Networks. His core expertise and passions are malware analysis, forensics, and application security, among others. Praveen has identified and disclosed vulnerabilities in enterprise-grade products and ICS software. He pursued his bachelor's and master's degrees in engineering from one of the premier institutes in India. He holds a number of industry certifications, such as CHFI, ECSA, and CEH. He is a well-known ethical hacking trainer in India and posts blogs at `http://blog.disects.com`.

I would like to thank my parents, sister, brother, wife, son, and friends for their everlasting love, encouragement, and support.

www.PacktPub.com

Support files, eBooks, discount offers, and more

For support files and downloads related to your book, please visit www.PacktPub.com.

Did you know that Packt offers eBook versions of every book published, with PDF and ePub files available? You can upgrade to the eBook version at www.PacktPub.com and as a print book customer, you are entitled to a discount on the eBook copy. Get in touch with us at service@packtpub.com for more details.

At www.PacktPub.com, you can also read a collection of free technical articles, sign up for a range of free newsletters and receive exclusive discounts and offers on Packt books and eBooks.

https://www2.packtpub.com/books/subscription/packtlib

Do you need instant solutions to your IT questions? PacktLib is Packt's online digital book library. Here, you can search, access, and read Packt's entire library of books.

Why Subscribe?

- Fully searchable across every book published by Packt
- Copy and paste, print, and bookmark content
- On demand and accessible via a web browser

Free Access for Packt account holders

If you have an account with Packt at www.PacktPub.com, you can use this to access PacktLib today and view 9 entirely free books. Simply use your login credentials for immediate access.

Table of Contents

Preface vii

Chapter 1: OpenFlow Channel Connection Establishment (Part 1) 1

- Introduction 2
- Connection setup on TCP and TLS 2
- Connection setup with multiple controllers 5
- Setting the role of the communication channel towards a controller 7
- Establishing an auxiliary connection to the controller 9
- Handling a handshake message from the controller 11
- Handling a switch configuration message from the controller 14
- Connection interruption procedures 16

(Part 2) 17

- Introduction 18
- Connection setup on TCP and TLS 18
- Multiple controllers managing a switch with different roles 21
- Setting the role of a controller's communication channel 22
- Auxiliary connection establishment 24
- Sending a handshake message to the switch 26
- Sending a switch configuration message to the switch 27

Chapter 2: Symmetric Messages and Asynchronous Messages (Part 1) 31

- Sending and processing a hello message 33
- Sending and processing an echo request and a reply message 35
- Sending and processing an error message 37
- Sending and processing an experimenter message 38
- Handling a "Set Asynchronous Configuration message" 39

Handling a "Get Asynchronous Configuration message" from the controller 40
Sending a packet-in message to the controller 41
Sending a flow-removed message to the controller 45
Sending a port-status message to the controller 47
Sending a controller role-status message to the controller 49
Sending a table-status message to the controller 51
Sending a request-forward message to the controller 52
Handling a packet-out message from the controller 53
Handling a barrier message from the controller 54
(Part 2) 57
Sending and processing a hello message 58
Sending and processing an echo request and a reply message 60
Sending and processing error message 61
Sending and processing experimenter message 62
Configuring the switch to send a list of asynchronous events the controller channel is interested in 64
Fetching the list of possible asynchronous events that can come from the switch to the controller channel 67
Processing a packet-in asynchronous message from the switch 68
Processing a flow removed asynchronous message from the switch 69
Processing a port-status asynchronous message from the switch 70
Processing the controller role-status message from the switch 70
Processing a table status asynchronous message from the switch 71
Processing a request forward message from the switch 72
Sending a packet-out message to the switch 73
Sending a barrier message to the switch 75
Chapter 3: Flow Table and Flow Entry Modification Messages (Part 1) 77
Introduction 77
Modifying a flow table with eviction enabled 92
Modifying a flow table with vacancy enabled 94
Adding a new flow entry to a flow table 95
Deleting a flow entry in a flow table 97
Modifying a flow entry in a flow table 98
Flow table synchronizations 99

(Part 2) 101
Introduction 101
Modifying a flow table with eviction enabled 102
Modifying a flow table with vacancy enabled 104
Adding a new flow entry to the flow table 106
Deleting an entry from a flow table 111
Modifying an entry in the flow table 112
Chapter 4: Group Table and Meter Table Modification Messages
(Part 1) 115
Introduction 115
Adding a new group entry in a group table 120
Deleting a group entry in a group table 122
Modifying a group entry in a group table 123
Adding a new meter in a meter table 124
Deleting a meter entry 125
Modifying a meter entry in a meter table 127
(Part 2) 129
Introduction 129
Adding a new group entry in a group table 130
Deleting a group entry in a group table 134
Modifying a group entry in a group table 135
Adding a new meter in a meter table 136
Deleting a meter entry 141
Modifying a meter entry in a meter table 142
Chapter 5: Handling Multipart Statistics Messages
(Part 1) 145
Introduction 145
Handling a multipart request message to get statistics
of an individual flow table entry 147
Handling a multipart request message to
get statistics of a group/aggregate of flow table entry 150
Handling a multipart request message to get statistics of flow table 151
Handling a multipart request message to get port statistics 153
Handling a multipart request message to get port queue statistics 158
Handling a multipart request message to get meter statistics 161
Handling a multipart request message to get group statistics 163

(Part 2) 167
Getting statistics of an individual flow table entry using multipart messages 169
Getting statistics of group/aggregate of flow table entries using multipart messages 171
Getting statistics of flow table using multipart messages 173
Getting port statistics using multipart messages 174
Getting port queue statistics using multipart messages 175
Getting meter statistics using multipart messages 177
Getting group statistics using multipart messages 178
Chapter 6: Handling Multipart State Information Messages
(Part 1) 181
Introduction 182
Getting information about the switch using multipart messages 182
Getting group description using multipart messages 183
Getting group feature using multipart messages 185
Getting meter configuration using multipart messages 186
Getting the meter feature using multipart messages 188
Getting the table feature using multipart messages 189
Getting port description using multipart messages 190
Getting table description using multipart messages 193
Getting queue description using multipart messages 194
Configuring Flow monitor using multipart messages 197
Experimenter multipart messages 202
(Part 2) 203
Introduction 204
Getting information about the switch using multipart messages 204
Getting the group description using multipart messages 205
Getting the group feature using multipart messages 205
Getting the meter configuration using multipart messages 206
Getting the meter feature using multipart messages 207
Getting the table feature using multipart messages 208
Getting the port description using multipart messages 217
Getting the table description using multipart messages 217
Getting the queue description using multipart messages 218
Configuring the flow monitor using multipart messages 219
Experimenter multipart message 223

Chapter 7: Handling Bundle Messages

(Part 1) 225

- Introduction 225
- Creation of a bundle 226
- Adding messages to a bundle 227
- Closing a bundle 229
- Committing or executing all the operations inside a bundle 230
- Discarding a bundle 231

(Part 2) 233

- Introduction 233
- Creation of a bundle 235
- Adding messages to a bundle 236
- Closing a bundle 238
- Committing or executing all the operations inside a bundle 239
- Discarding a bundle 240

Appendix: Common OpenFlow Headers, Structures, and Error Code 241

- Common OpenFlow headers 241
- Common OpenFlow structures 243
- Common OpenFlow error codes 248
- Common OpenFlow multipart message types 258

Index 261

Preface

With the tremendous growth in data traffic due to the increase in the number of devices connected to networks, and more and more applications moving into the cloud, service providers are moving towards virtualizing their infrastructure. With storage and computing virtualization, there is a clear necessity to provide virtualization in networks and a standardized way of programming network devices. With large data centers, there is also a clear necessity to change the traditional control plane and data plane paradigm to move towards flow-based switching, which is more generic and can be adapted for different avenues. Today's networks have evolved into complex proprietary systems, with little chance of offering any possibility to carry out experiments on new ideas or protocols. The Open Network Foundation (ONF) has come up with a specification to meet these requirements and has called it OpenFlow. The latest version of this specification is OpenFlow 1.4.

OpenFlow paves the way for the traditional network to be a programmable network, with standard interfaces between the controller (traditionally called a control plane) and the actual packet forwarding entity (traditionally called a data plane). OpenFlow was started as a means to try experimental ideas/protocols on large-scale networks by providing a standard, flow-based table called an OpenFlow table and separating the control plane from the data plane. This offers the possibility to program the forwarding decisions of those network devices supporting the OpenFlow specification in a flexible manner. There are two main components of the OpenFlow specification, the switch and the controller. This book describes in brief both the OpenFlow switch and controller, their operations, and so on.

An OpenFlow switch consists of one or more flow tables and group tables that perform packet lookups and forwarding. Each flow table in the switch contains a set of flow entries. Each flow entry consists of match fields, counters, and a set of instructions to apply to matching packets. The switch communicates with the controller and the controller manages the switch via the OpenFlow channel, using the OpenFlow protocol.

The OpenFlow controller is a software application that manages the switch using the OpenFlow protocol. The controller can add, update, and delete flow entries in flow tables, both reactively (in response to packets) and proactively.

This Cookbook provides an easy, more user-friendly and step-by-step approach to develop and understand OpenFlow switch and controller. Organized into two parts, part 1 explains OpenFlow from the switch point of view and part 2 explains it from the controller's point of view. You will see a 1:1 mapping between part I and part 2 chapters and recipes to provide a clear demarcation of the operations and responsibilities of the switch and controller.

What this book covers

Chapter 1, OpenFlow Channel Connection Establishment

Part 1 describes the various steps and mechanisms involved in establishing an OpenFlow channel from the switch. An OpenFlow channel is used to exchange an OpenFlow message between the switch and the controller.

Part 2 shows the various steps and mechanisms involved for the controller to establish a channel to the switch. An OpenFlow channel is used to exchange OpenFlow messages between the switch and the controller.

Chapter 2, Symmetric Messages and Asynchronous Messages

Part 1 covers the list of symmetric and asynchronous messages sent and received by the OpenFlow switch, along with the procedure for handling these messages.

Part 2 contains the list of symmetric and asynchronous messages sent and received by the controller and the procedure for handling these messages.

Chapter 3, Flow Table and Flow Entry Modification Messages

Part 1 describes in detail the flow table, flow table entries, and procedures for handling flow table messages and flow entry messages, such as adding a new flow, deleting an existing flow, modifying a flow, and so on.

Part 2 demonstrates the procedure to modify the flow table; add, delete, and modify a flow entry in the flow table; and handle the response message from the switch.

Chapter 4, Group Table and Meter Table Modification Messages

Part 1 explains the group table and its entries, the meter table and its entries, and the procedure for handling group and meter modification messages, such as add, delete, modify, and so on.

Part 2 explains the procedure to add, delete, and modify the group and a meter entry, along with the procedure to handle response messages from the switch after sending these messages.

Chapter 5, Handling Multipart Statistics Messages

Part 1 covers multipart messages, in particular multipart statistic messages to get flow statistics, port statistics, group statistics, meter statistics, and so on. This chapter also contains the procedure required for handling multipart statistics messages.

Part 2 shows the procedure to get statistical information, such as flow statistics, port statistics, group statistics, meter statistics, and so on from the switch using multipart statistics messages, along with the procedure for handling response messages from the switch after sending these messages.

Chapter 6, Handling Multipart State Information Messages

Part 1 illustrates multipart messages, in particular multipart state information messages used to get the port description, table description, queue description, and so on, and the procedure for handling multipart state information messages in the switch.

Part 2 describes in detail the procedure for getting state information, such as the port description, table description, queue description, and so on from the switch using multipart state information messages. This chapter also covers the procedure for handling response messages from the switch after sending these messages.

Chapter 7, Handling Bundle Messages

Part 1 describes in detail bundle messages and the procedure required for handling them in switch, such as creating a bundle, opening a bundle, adding a message to a bundle, and so on.

Part 2 illustrates the controller procedure for creating a bundle, opening a bundle, adding a message to a bundle, and so on, along with the procedure for handling the response messages from the switch after sending the bundle messages.

Appendix, Common OpenFlow Headers, Structures, and Error Code, talks about some common message headers, structures, and procedures defined in the OpenFlow specifications.

What you need for this book

As this book talks about the OpenFlow specification a in brief, the software or hardware requirements depend on the platform or the language in which you are trying to implement either the switch or the controller.

Who this book is for

This book is for network engineers who want to develop a new OpenFlow switch or understand an existing OpenFlow switch in terms of its OpenFlow-related message handling procedures. This book is also intended for application developers who want to develop an OpenFlow controller or want to understand existing controller operations to handle OpenFlow messages and events.

Sections

In this book, you will find several headings that appear frequently (Getting ready, How to do it, How it works, There's more, and See also).

To give clear instructions on how to complete a recipe, we've used these sections.

Getting ready

This section tells you what to expect in the recipe, and describes how to set up any software or any preliminary settings required for the recipe.

How to do it...

This section contains the steps required to follow the recipe.

How it works...

This section usually consists of a detailed explanation of what happened in the previous section.

There's more...

This section consists of additional information about the recipe in order to make you more knowledgeable about the recipe.

See also

This section provides helpful links to other useful information for the recipe.

Conventions

In this book, you will find a number of text styles that distinguish between different kinds of information. Here are some examples of these styles and an explanation of their meaning.

Code words in text, database table names, folder names, filenames, file extensions, pathnames, dummy URLs, user input, and Twitter handles are shown as follows: "If the role requested from controller is master or slave, then the switch must validate the `generation_id` value to check for stale messages."

A block of code is set as follows:

```
/* Switch features. */
struct ofp_switch_features {
struct ofp_header header;
uint64_t datapath_id; /* Datapath unique ID. The lower 48-bits are
                         for a MAC address, while the upper
                         16-bits are implementer-defined. */
uint32_t n_buffers;  /* Max packets buffered at once. */
uint8_t n_tables;    /* Number of tables supported by datapath. */
uint8_t auxiliary_id;/* Identify auxiliary connections */
uint8_t pad[2];      /* Align to 64-bits. */
        /* Features. */
uint32_t capabilities; /* Bitmap of support "ofp_capabilities". */
uint32_t reserved;
```

Warnings or important notes appear in a box like this.

Tips and tricks appear like this.

Reader feedback

Feedback from our readers is always welcome. Let us know what you think about this book—what you liked or disliked. Reader feedback is important for us as it helps us develop titles that you will really get the most out of.

To send us general feedback, simply e-mail `feedback@packtpub.com`, and mention the book's title in the subject of your message.

If there is a topic that you have expertise in and you are interested in either writing or contributing to a book, see our author guide at `www.packtpub.com/authors`.

Customer support

Now that you are the proud owner of a Packt book, we have a number of things to help you to get the most from your purchase.

Downloading the example code

You can download the example code files from your account at `http://www.packtpub.com` for all the Packt Publishing books you have purchased. If you purchased this book elsewhere, you can visit `http://www.packtpub.com/support` and register to have the files e-mailed directly to you.

Errata

Although we have taken every care to ensure the accuracy of our content, mistakes do happen. If you find a mistake in one of our books—maybe a mistake in the text or the code—we would be grateful if you could report this to us. By doing so, you can save other readers from frustration and help us improve subsequent versions of this book. If you find any errata, please report them by visiting `http://www.packtpub.com/submit-errata`, selecting your book, clicking on the **Errata Submission Form** link, and entering the details of your errata. Once your errata are verified, your submission will be accepted and the errata will be uploaded to our website or added to any list of existing errata under the Errata section of that title.

To view the previously submitted errata, go to `https://www.packtpub.com/books/content/support` and enter the name of the book in the search field. The required information will appear under the **Errata** section.

Piracy

Piracy of copyrighted material on the Internet is an ongoing problem across all media. At Packt, we take the protection of our copyright and licenses very seriously. If you come across any illegal copies of our works in any form on the Internet, please provide us with the location address or website name immediately so that we can pursue a remedy.

Please contact us at `copyright@packtpub.com` with a link to the suspected pirated material.

We appreciate your help in protecting our authors and our ability to bring you valuable content.

Questions

If you have a problem with any aspect of this book, you can contact us at `questions@packtpub.com`, and we will do our best to address the problem.

1

OpenFlow Channel Connection Establishment (Part 1)

In this chapter we will cover the following topics:

- Connection setup on TCP & TLS
- Connection setup with multiple controllers
- Setting the role of a communication channel towards a controller
- Establishing an auxiliary connection to a controller
- Handling handshake message from a controller
- Handling switch configuration messages from a controller
- Connection interruption procedures

Introduction

OpenFlow channel is a communication medium that is used to send and receive OpenFlow messages between the switch and controller. The switch must create an OpenFlow channel by initiating a connection to the controller. An OpenFlow switch can establish multiple connections to the same or different controllers in parallel, among which one of the controller's connections acts as master and the other controller's connections acts either as slave / equal. For detailed information regarding the controller roles, refer to the recipe, *Setting the role of a controller's communication channel* in *Chapter 1, OpenFlow Channel Connection Establishment (Part 2)*.

This chapter describes the steps and mechanisms involved in establishing an OpenFlow channel from switch to controller along with the handling of different messages related to OpenFlow channels and controller roles.

Connection setup on TCP and TLS

The switch must be able to establish communication with a controller at a configurable IP address, using either a user-specified transport port or a default transport port. The communication protocol can either be TCP or TLS and the default port for both of these protocols is 6653. The previous versions of OpenFlow used the default port of either 6633 or 976. However IANA has allocated port number 6653 to **Open networking foundation** (**ONF**) for OpenFlow protocol.

The connection from switch to controller is identified by the switch Datapath ID and an auxiliary ID. The Auxiliary ID of the main connection is always 0.

Getting started

To establish a communication channel with the controller, the user should configure the IP address, port number (optional) and the transport protocol (TCP/TLS) of the controller.The switch should provide a mechanism to configure these parameters via a standard **Command-line Interface** (**CLI**) or use a configuration file or other mechanism.

How to do it...

Based on the configured transport path protocol the switch should follow either the TCP procedure or the TLS procedure explained in this section for establishing connectivity to the controller.

TCP Procedure

Standard TCP/IP socket procedure should be used to establish the OpenFlow communication channel between the switch and controller. The switch should create a TCP socket and try to connect to the configured IP address and port number of the controller using the connect system call provided by the underlying operating system. The procedure in *C* on Unix-based operating systems is as follows.

```
struct sockaddr_in controller_address;
memset(&controller_address, '0', sizeof(controller_address));
controller_address.sin_family = AF_INET;
controller_address.sin_addr.s_addr =
  inet_addr("10.0.0.10");
controller_address.port = htons(6653);
if (socket (AF_INET, SOCK_STREAM, 0) < 0)
    {
        printf("\n Error : Could not create socket \n");
        return 1;
    }
if ((connect (s, (struct sockaddr*)&controller_address,
        sizeof(controller_address)) < 0))
    {
       printf("\n Error : Connect Failed \n");
       return 1;
    }
```

Downloading the example code

You can download the example code files from your account at `http://www.packtpub.com` for all the Packt Publishing books you have purchased. If you purchased this book elsewhere, you can visit `http://www.packtpub.com/support` and register to have the files e-mailed directly to you.

TLS Procedure

In order to establish a TLS connection, the switch and controller should authenticate each other mutually, by exchanging certificates which are signed using a private key. The switch must be configured with two certificates, one for authenticating the controller (for example, the controller certificate) and the other for authenticating the controller from the switch (for example, the switch certificate).

For establishing secure a communication channel across the controller and switch using TLS, OpenSSL library can be used. OpenSSL is an open-source implementation of basic cryptographic functions and utilities written in the *C programming language* and provides complete implementation of the SSL and TLS protocols.

As OpenSSL requires a TCP connection between the client and server, the first step is to create the TCP sockets as mentioned in the TCP procedure section of this recipe. Once the TCP connection is established, the procedure in C on Unix-based operating systems for establishing a secure communication channel using OpenSSL is as follows:

```
//Register the error strings libssl
  SSL_load_error_strings ();
// Register the available ciphers and digests
  SSL_library_init ();
// New context with mode as client and version as SSL 2 or 3
sslContext = SSL_CTX_new (SSLv23_client_method ());
if (sslContext == NULL)
  {
    printf("\n Error: Could not create SSL context\n");
      return 1;
  }

// Create a new SSL struct sslHandle = SSL_new (sslContext);
  if (sslHandle == NULL)
    {
      printf("\n Error: Could not create SSL handle\n");
        return 1;
    }
// Bind the SSL struct to the TCP connection
  if (!SSL_set_fd (sslHandle, socket))
    {
      printf("\n Error: Could not set socket \n");
        return 1;
    }
// Initiate SSL handshake
  if (SSL_connect (sslHandle) != 1)
    {
      printf("\n Error: Could not connect using SSL\n");
        return 1;
    }
```

There's more...

When the connection between the switch and controller is first established, either side of the connection must immediately send the hello message. The procedure to send and receive the hello message is explained in detail in *Sending and processing hello message* recipe of *Chapter 2, Symmetric Messages and Asynchronous Messages*.

The OpenFlow specification doesn't mandate any failure handling while establishing the communication channel. However it is recommended for the switch to re-initiate the connection periodically until the connection is successful. If the switch is unable to establish a connection with any of the configured controllers and the switch is a hybrid switch, then the switch can operate in non-openflow mode until the connection to any one of the controllers is successful.

See also

- For more information regarding the procedure to send and receive the `OFPT_HELLO` message, refer to the *Sending and processing hello message* recipe of *Chapter 2, Symmetric Messages and Asynchronous Messages*

Connection setup with multiple controllers

When a switch is configured to connect to more than one controller, then the switch should establish a communication channel with all the configured controllers. A switch may connect to multiple controllers for the following reasons:

- To improve the reliability of the system
- To provide load balancing across controllers depending on the role

When a switch is connected to more than one controller then the controller can take either the master role, slave role or the equal role. For more information regarding the controller role, refer to the recipe, *Multiple controllers managing switch with different roles* in *Chapter 1, OpenFlow Channel Connection Establishment (Part 2)*.

The switch maintains the role of the controller with respect to the controller's connection, as the switch identifies the controller with the channel ID, which is the combination of the Datapath ID and the Auxiliary ID.

A switch should be connected to only one controller in its master state. However it may be connected to multiple controllers in an equal state or in the slave state.

How to do it...

During the initialization of the OpenFlow switch, it should initiate a connection to all the configured controllers and should maintain the connectivity to all the controllers concurrently. The procedure to establish an OpenFlow communication channel to multiple controllers is similar to that of establishing a connection to a single controller as was explained in the *Connection setup on TCP & TLS* recipe. However, as the switch has to process requests concurrently from multiple controllers, the switch could employ mechanisms to read and process the message from multiple channels. This can be done, either by having different threads or different processes, each handling requests from multiple controllers, or should use some of the constructs provided by the operating system such as the `select()` system call.

How it works...

In a steady state, the switch should be able to send asynchronous message to all controllers through the channels associated with the controller. Similarly, the switch should be able to process the OpenFlow request message from any of the connected controllers. When a switch receives the OpenFlow request message from any one of the controllers, the switch should send the response only to the channel which is associated with that controller.

There's more...

The OpenFlow specification doesn't mandate any failure handling while establishing the communication channel. However, it is recommended for the switch to try to re-initiate the connection periodically until the connection is successful.

See also

- For more information about establishing the connection to a controller, refer to the previous recipe in this chapter. The next recipe describes how to set the role of the controller in detail

Setting the role of the communication channel towards a controller

Role-request messages are sent from the controller to set the role of its OpenFlow channel, or query that role. The controller's role in the switch is constantly changed as a result of a request from the controller. The switch cannot change the role of a controller channel on its own.

The controller may send the role request message to communicate its channel role at any time and the switch must remember the role of each controller connection

Refer to the *Setting the role of a controller's communication channel* recipe in *Chapter 1, OpenFlow Channel Connection Establishment (Part 2)* for more information on when and why the controller sends the role request message to the switch.

How to do it...

The message format used by the controller to send `OFPT_ROLE_REQUEST` messages is defined in the *Setting the role of a controller's communication channel* recipe in *Chapter 1, OpenFlow Channel Connection Establishment (Part 2)*. The switch should use the same message format for sending the reply message back to the controller.

If the role requested from the controller is master or slave, then the switch must validate the `generation_id` to check for stale messages. This is required because, if the stale messages are processed by the switch, then there is a possibility of one or more controllers and the switch might be out of sync with respect to the role.

Once the switch receives a role request message, it must return an `OFPT_ROLE_REPLY` message, if there is no error encountered while processing this role request message. The structure of this reply message is exactly same as the `OFPT_ROLE_REQUEST` message.

The field role should be set with the current role of the controller.

The field `generation_id` should be set to the current `generation_id` (the generation_id associated with the last successful role request). If the current `generation_id` was never set, the `generation_id` in the reply must be set to the maximum field value (the unsigned equivalent of *-1*).

If the validation of generation_id fails, the switch must discard the role request message and return an error message with type `OFPET_ROLE_REQUEST_FAILED` and the code as `OFPRRFC_STALE`.

The procedure to handle a role request message from the controller is as follows:

```
handle_role_request_message (struct ofp_role_request role_request) {
  struct ofp_role_request role_reply;
  /* pseudo-code to validate the generation_id. Here the
   * generation_is_defined and cached_generation_id are global
   * variables */
  if (generation_is_defined && (int64_t)
     (role_request.generation_id - cached_generation_id) < 0)
  {
     send_error_message(OFPET_ROLE_REQUEST_FAILED, OFPRRFC_STALE);
  }
  else
  {
     cached_generation_id = role_request.generation_id;
     generation_is_defined = true;
    /* Here connection is the connection data structure which is
   * maintained by the switch */
     connection.role = role_request.role;
     role_reply.role = role_request.role;
     role_reply.generation_id = cached_generation_id;
     send_openflow_message (connection, role_reply);
  }
}
```

The procedure to send error messages is explained in the *Setting the role of a controller's communication channel* recipe in *Chapter 1, OpenFlow Channel Connection Establishment (Part 2)*.

There's more...

If the requested role is `OFPCR_ROLE_MASTER`, then the switch should change the role of the existing master controller to `OFPCR_ROLE_EQUAL`.

If the requested role is `OFPCR_ROLE_SLAVE` and after successfully setting the role of this communication channel as a slave in the switch, the switch:

- Should not send asynchronous messages.

- Should not execute the controller-switch command. For example OFPT PACKET_OUT, OFPT_FLOW_MOD, OFPT_GROUP_MOD, OFPT_PORT_MOD, OFPT_TABLE_MOD requests, and OFPMP_TABLE_FEATURES multipart requests with a non-empty body must be rejected.
- If it receives any controller-switch command then the switch must send the OFPT_ERROR message of the type field and code as OFPET_BAD_REQUEST and OFPBRC_IS_SLAVE respectively. The procedure to send error messages is explained in the recipe, *Setting the role of a controller's communication channel* recipe in *Chapter 1, OpenFlow Channel Connection Establishment (Part 2)*.

See also

- For more information about sending the role request message from the controller, refer to the *Setting the role of a controller's communication channel* recipe in *Chapter 1, OpenFlow Channel Connection Establishment (Part 2)*

Establishing an auxiliary connection to the controller

Apart from the main connection, a switch can initiate one or more connections towards the controller to improve its processing performance and exploit the parallelism of most switch implementations. These connections are termed auxiliary connections. For auxiliary connections, the switch should assign the auxiliary ID value as a non-zero value and the Datapath ID the same as that of the main connection towards that controller.

The switch must not initiate an auxiliary connection to a controller until the main connection has been successfully established.

Getting started

To establish an auxiliary connection to the controller, the main connection between the switch and controller should have been successfully established.

How to do it...

The procedure to establish an auxiliary connection to a controller is similar to that of establishing a main connection to the controller which was explained in the first recipe of this chapter. The IP address of the controller used by the switch to establish an auxiliary connection should be the same as that of the main connection. However auxiliary connections are not restricted to use the same transport protocols as those of the main connection. Depending on the configuration, the switch can use TCP, TLS, UDP or DTLS to establish auxiliary connections. When a switch detects that the main connection to a controller is closed or broken, it must close all its auxiliary connections to that controller immediately.

There's more...

The switch must accept any OpenFlow message types and sub-types on any connections. The main connection or an auxiliary connection cannot be restricted to a specific message type or sub-type. However, the processing performance of different connections may be different. The switch may choose to process the different auxiliary connections with different priorities; for example, one auxiliary connection may be dedicated to high priority requests and another may be dedicated to lower priority requests.

The OpenFlow specification provides some guidelines for sending and receiving messages in main and auxiliary connections, as follows:

- All OpenFlow messages which are not Packet in should be sent over the main connection.
- A Mechanism should be provided in the switch to keep track of the packet of the same flow mapped to the same connection, when there are multiple auxiliary connections between the switch and controller.
- An OpenFlow switch which uses an unreliable auxiliary connection should follow recommendations specified in RFC 5405 wherever it is required. RFC 5405 provides guidelines on the usage of UDP protocol such as congestion control, message sizes, reliability, checksums, and middle box traversal, etc.
- If the auxiliary connection from the switch is established in unreliable transport protocols like UDP and DTLS, then only the following message type should be supported to send /receive in an auxiliary connection:

  ```
  OFPT_HELLO
  OFPT_ERROR
  OFPT_ECHO_REQUEST
  OFPT_ECHO_REPLY
  ```

OFPT_FEATURES_REQUEST
OFPT_FEATURES_REPLY
OFPT_PACKET_IN
OFPT_PACKET_OUT
OFPT_EXPERIMENTER

Support to send and receive other message types should not be provided

- After establishing the auxiliary connection over unreliable transport protocols, if the switch receives a first message other than OFPT_HELLO then the switch should either:
    - Assume the connection is set up properly and use the version number from that message or it must return an error message of the OFPET_BAD_REQUEST type with the code as OFPBRC_BAD_VERSION.
- If the OpenFlow switch receives an error message with the error type OFPET_BAD_REQUEST and the code OFPBRC_BAD_VERSION on an unreliable auxiliary connection, then it must either send a new Hello message or terminate the unreliable auxiliary connection.
- If the switch doesn't receive any message on an auxiliary connection after a chosen amount of time lower than 5 seconds, the switch must either send a new Hello message or terminate the unreliable auxiliary connection.

See also

- For more information about establishing the main connection to the controller, refer to the *Connection setup on TCP and TLS* recipe of *Chapter 1, OpenFlow Channel Connection Establishment (Part 2)*

Handling a handshake message from the controller

The handshake messages (OFPT_FEATURES_REQUEST / OFPT_FEATURES_REPLY) are used by the controller to fetch the basic capabilities and features supported by the switch. The switch should respond with supported features via an OFPT_FEATURES_REPLY message.

> The OFPT_FEATURES_REQUEST message should be sent from the controller once the connection setup is completed.

Getting started

To get the features supported by switch, the communication channel between the switch and controller should have been successfully established.

How to do it...

On reception of `OFPT_FEATURES_REQUEST`, the switch should prepare an `OFPT_FEATURES_REPLY` message and send the reply message to the controller.

The `OFPT_FEATURES_REQUEST` message sent from the controller doesn't contain any body other than the OpenFlow header which is defined in the *OpenFlow Header* section of the *Appendix*.

The format of `OFPT_FEATURES_REPLY` is as follows:

```
/* Switch features. */
struct ofp_switch_features {
struct ofp_header header;
uint64_t datapath_id; /* Datapath unique ID. The lower 48-bits are
                         for a MAC address, while the upper
                         16-bits are implementer-defined. */
uint32_t n_buffers;  /* Max packets buffered at once. */
uint8_t n_tables;    /* Number of tables supported by datapath. */
uint8_t auxiliary_id;/* Identify auxiliary connections */
uint8_t pad[2];      /* Align to 64-bits. */
        /* Features. */
uint32_t capabilities; /* Bitmap of support "ofp_capabilities". */
uint32_t reserved;
};
```

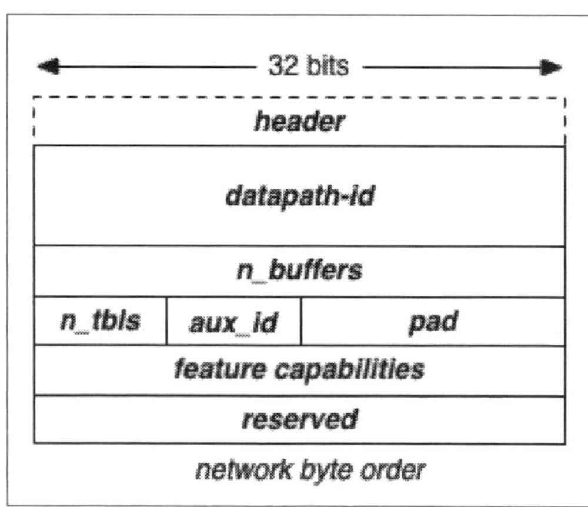

Let's see the brief description of the image:

- `datapath_id`: This field should be filled with `datapath_id` of the connection on which the switch receives this request message. Typically the `datapath_id` is a 64 bit variable wherein the lower 48 bits are assigned from the switch MAC address, while the top 16 bits are assigned based on the implementer's logic.
- `n_buffers`: This field should be set with the maximum number of packets that can be buffered by the switch while sending packets to the controller using packet-in messages.
- `n_tables`: This field should be set with the number of tables supported by the switch, each of which can have a different set of supported match fields, actions and number of entries.
- `auxiliary_id`: This should be set to the auxiliary ID of the connection. For the main connection, this field value is zero, while the auxiliary connection has this field value as a non-zero value.

Based on the capability of the switch, it should set the bitmap with the following flag values:

```
/* Capabilities supported by the datapath. */
enum ofp_capabilities {
OFPC_FLOW_STATS = 1 << 0,      /* Value 1. Flow statistics. */
OFPC_TABLE_STATS = 1 << 1,     /* Value 2. Table statistics. */
OFPC_PORT_STATS = 1 << 2,      /* Value 4. Port statistics. */
OFPC_GROUP_STATS = 1 << 3,     /* Value 8. Group statistics. */
OFPC_IP_REASM = 1 << 5,        /* Value 16. Can reassemble IP
  fragments. */
OFPC_QUEUE_STATS = 1 << 6,     /* Value 32. Queue statistics. */
OFPC_PORT_BLOCKED = 1 << 8     /* Value 64. Switch will block looping
ports. */
};
```

The procedure to handle the feature request message is as follows:

```
handle_features_request_message (struct ofp_header
  features_request)
{
  struct ofp_switch_features features_reply;
  features_reply.datapath_id = htonnl(datapath_id);
  features_reply.n_buffers = htonl(buffer_size);
  features_reply.n_tables = supported_no_of_flow_tables;
  features_reply.capabilities = htonl (OFPC_FLOW_STATS |
    OFPC_TABLE_STATS);
  features_reply.auxiliary_id = 0; /* Assuming main connection */
  send_openflow_message (connection, features_reply);
  /* The send_openflow_message function adds the OF header */
}
```

See also

- For more information about sending the feature request message from the controller, refer to the *Sending a handshake message to the switch* recipe in *Chapter 1, OpenFlow Channel Connection Establishment (Part 2)*

Handling a switch configuration message from the controller

Switch configuration messages are used by the controller to set and get switch configuration parameters.

The Switch should be able to handle `OFPT_SET_CONFIG` and `OFPT_GET_CONFIG` messages from the controller and should reply back with `OFPT_GET_CONFIG_REPLY` messages to the controller.

`OFPT_SET_CONFIG` and `OFPT_GET_CONFIG` messages are sent from the controller to the switch whereas the `OFPT_GET_CONFIG` message is sent from the switch to the controller.

How to do it...

On reception of an `OFPT_GET_CONFIG_REQUEST` message, the switch should prepare an `OFPT_GET_CONFIG_REPLY` message and send it to the controller.

The `OFPT_GET_CONFIG_REQUEST` message doesn't contain a body other than an OpenFlow header which is defined in the *OpenFlow Header* section of the *Appendix*.

The `OFPT_GET_CONFIG_REPLY` message uses the following message format:

```
/* Switch configuration. */
struct ofp_switch_config {
struct ofp_header header;
uint16_t flags;          /* Bitmap of OFPC_* flags. */
uint16_t miss_send_len;  /* Max bytes of packet that datapath
                            should send to the controller.*/
};
```

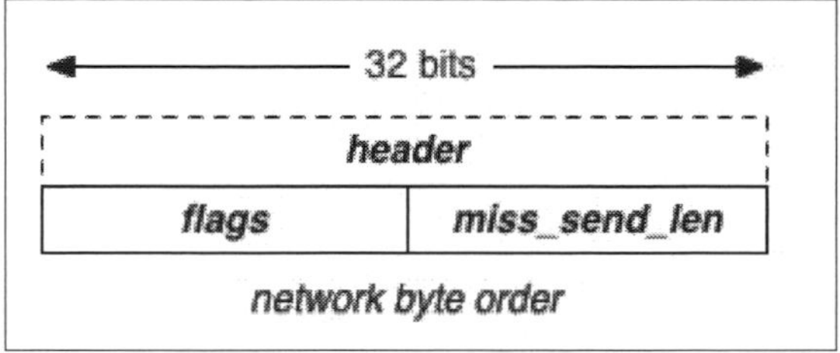

The flags take the value as:

```
enum ofp_config_flags {
/* Handling of IP fragments. */
OFPC_FRAG_NORMAL = 0,      /* No special handling for fragments. */
OFPC_FRAG_DROP = 1 << 0,   /* Drop fragments. */
OFPC_FRAG_REASM = 1 << 1,  /* Reassemble (only if
                              OFPC_IP_REASM set). */
OFPC_FRAG_MASK = 3,
};
```

The value in `miss_send_len` should be set to the switch's current maximum bytes of data that will be sent to the controller while sending buffered packets. By default this value is 128 bits.

The flag value should be set to the configured value of the IP fragment detail.

On reception of `OFPT_SET_CONFIG`, which has the same message format as that of `OFPT_GET_CONFIG_REPLY`, the switch should set the value of `miss_send_len` and IP fragment related details.

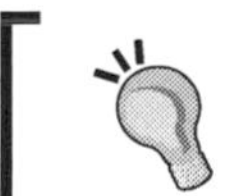

The switch need not send a reply message to the `OFPT_SET_CONFIG` message.

The procedure to handle `OFPT_GET_CONFIG_REQUEST` is as follows;

```
handle_get_config_message (struct ofp_header
  get_config_request)
{
  struct ofp_switch_config config_reply;
  features_reply.flags = htons(supported_flags);
  features_reply.miss_send_len = 128; /* default value */
  send_openflow_message (connection, config_reply);
  /* The send_openflow_message function adds the OF header */
}
```

See also

- For more information about sending the switch configuration message from the controller, refer to the *Sending a switch configuration message to the switch* recipe of *Chapter 1, OpenFlow Channel Connection Establishment (Part 2)*

Connection interruption procedures

The OpenFlow switch should maintain the connectivity to all controllers.If for any reason the switch loses the connection to all configured controllers, then the switch should follow the procedure defined in this section.

How to do it...

If a switch loses its connection with all the connected or configured controllers, then the switch should immediately enter either *fail secure mode* or *fail standalone mode* depending upon the switch configuration or implementation. The connection loss can be identified by either OpenFlow echo request timeouts or TLS session timeouts or other disconnection procedures such as TCP socket close, etc.

How it works...

When the switch is in fail secure mode, the switch should drop all the packets and messages destined to controllers. However, all the flow entries programmed by the controller should persist in the switch and expire based on the configured timeout value in fail secure mode.

The fail standalone mode is usually possible only on Hybrid switches. When a switch is in fail standalone mode, the switch should act as a legacy Ethernet switch or router and should process all the packets.

There's more...

Upon connecting to a controller again, the existing flow entries remain intact. The controller can delete all the existing flow entries, if desired. The switch can be configured to start up with the operational mode either as fail secure mode or fail standalone mode until it successfully connects to a controller.

1
OpenFlow Channel Connection Establishment (Part 2)

In this chapter we will cover the following topics:

- Connection setup on TCP and TLS
- Multiple controllers managing a switch with different roles
- Setting the role of a controller's communication channel
- Auxiliary connection establishment
- Sending a handshake message to the switch
- Sending switch configuration messages to the switch

Introduction

The OpenFlow channel is used to exchange OpenFlow messages between an OpenFlow switch and an OpenFlow controller. An OpenFlow controller must be able to accept connections from one or more switches over TCP/IP connectivity and manage these connections as OpenFlow channels. An OpenFlow controller typically runs in a remote node and manages a switch over a network. This network may be a separate network dedicated to controller-switch communication, or may use the existing network managed by the OpenFlow switch (in-band controller connection). If a switch is connected to multiple controllers, then one of the controllers will act as master and all the other controllers will act either as slave or equal. This chapter describes the steps and mechanisms involved in establishing an OpenFlow channel from controller to switch along with the handling of different messages related to the OpenFlow channels and controller roles:

Connection setup on TCP and TLS

The OpenFlow controller should be able to accept connections from one or more switches over TCP/IP using a default transport port or a user-specified port. The controller should support establishing a connection over TCP and optionally over TLS, and the default port for both these protocols is 6653. The previous versions of OpenFlow used the default port of either 6633 or 976. However, IANA has allocated port number 6653 to ONF for OpenFlow protocol.

Getting started

If the controller wants to use a user-configured port number to accept connections from the switch, then there should be a mechanism to specify the user-defined port number during controller initialization.

How to do it...

Based on the supported transport path protocol, the controller should follow either the TCP procedure or the TLS procedure explained in this section for establishing connectivity to the switch.

TCP Procedure

Standard TCP/IP socket procedures should be used to establish the OpenFlow communication channel between the controller and switch. The controller should create a TCP socket and bind the socket to a standard port, which is 6653, or a user-defined port. The controller should use the created socket for listening and accepting new connections from switches.

As the controller manages multiple channels from switches, the controller should be able to process requests concurrently from multiple switches. So the controller should employ mechanisms to read and process the message from multiple channels. This can be done either by having different threads or different processes each handling requests from multiple controllers or should use some of the constructs provided by the operating system such as the `select()` system call.

The controller procedure to establish the connection to the switch in C on Unix-based operating systems is as follows:

```
/* Create server socket for incoming connections */
if((sock = socket(PF_INET, SOCK_STREAM, IPPROTO_TCP)) < 0)
  {
    printf("\n Error : Could not create socket \n");
      return 1;
  }
/* Construct local address structure */memset(&OFServAddr, 0,
  sizeof(OFServAddr));
/* Internet address family */
OFServAddr.sin_family = AF_INET; /* Internet address family */
OFServAddr.sin_addr.s_addr = htonl(INADDR_ANY); /* Any incoming if
  */
OFServAddr.sin_port = htons(6653);      /* Local port */
/* Bind to local address */
if (bind(sock, (struct sockaddr *) & OFServAddr,
    sizeof(OFServAddr)) < 0)
    {
      printf("\n Error : Could not bind the socket\n");
        return 1;
    }
/* Listen for incoming connections */
if (listen(sock, 5) < 0)
    {
        printf("\n Error : Could not listen in socket\n");
          return 1;
    }
/* Wait for client to connect */
if ((clntSock = accept(servSock, (struct sockaddr *)
    &echoClntAddr, &clntLen)) < 0)
    {
      printf("\n Error : Accept failed\n");
      return 1;
    }
```

TLS Procedure

The switch and controller should mutually authenticate each other by exchanging certificates signed by a site-specific private key. Each switch must be configured with one certificate for authenticating the controller (the controller certificate) and the other for authenticating to the controller (the switch certificate) from the switch. The standard SSL socket procedures should be used to establish the secure communication channel between the switch and controller.

For establishing a secure communication channel across the controller and switch using TLS, OpenSSL library can be used. OpenSSL is an open-source implementation of the SSL and TLS protocols. The core library, written in the C programming language, implements the basic cryptographic functions and provides various utility functions.

As the OpenSSL connection requires a TCP connection between the client and server, the first step is to create TCP sockets, as mentioned in TCP procedure section of this recipe. Once the TCP connection is established, the procedure in C on Unix-based operating systems for accepting a secure communication channel from the switch using OpenSSL is as follows:

```
SSL_METHOD *method;
SSL_CTX *ctx;
OpenSSL_add_all_algorithms();    /* load & register cryptos */
SSL_load_error_strings();        /* load all SSL error messages */
method = SSLv2_server_method(); /* create SSL server instance */
ctx = SSL_CTX_new(method);          /* create SSL context */

/* set the local certificate from CertFile */
SSL_CTX_use_certificate_file(ctx, CertFile, SSL_FILETYPE_PEM);
 /* set the private key from KeyFile */
SSL_CTX_use_PrivateKey_file(ctx, KeyFile, SSL_FILETYPE_PEM);
 /* verify private key */
if ( !SSL_CTX_check_private_key(ctx) )
  abort();

SSL *ssl = SSL_new(ctx);  /* get new SSL context */
SSL_set_fd(ssl, sock);  /* set connection to SSL state */
SSL_accept(ssl);          /* start the handshaking */
```

There's more...

When a connection between the switch and controller is first established, either side of the connection must immediately send the hello (`OFPT_HELLO`) message. The procedure to send and receive the `OFPT_HELLO` message is explained in detail in the *Sending and processing hello message* recipe in *Chapter 2, Symmetric Messages and Asynchronous Messages*.

The OpenFlow specification doesn't mandate any failure handling while accepting a new connection from the switch.

See also

- For more information regarding the procedure to send and receive the `OFPT_HELLO` message, refer to the *Sending and processing hello message* recipe in *Chapter 2, Symmetric Messages and Asynchronous Messages*

Multiple controllers managing a switch with different roles

The controller should be able to accept multiple connections from the same switch or different switches. When a switch is connected to the controller, the controller can take any one of the following roles:

- **Role Equal** (`OFPCR_ROLE_EQUAL`): This role provides complete access to the switch for a controller. In this role, the controller gets equal priority and control over the other controllers in the same role. When a controller is in this role, the controller should receive all asynchronous messages from the switch by default. Also, the controller may be able to send controller-to-switch commands to modify the state of switch.
- **Role Slave** (`OFPCR_ROLE_SLAVE`): This role provides read-only access to the switch for a controller. When a controller is in this role, it won't receive any asynchronous messages from the switch, apart from Port-status message (by default). Also, the controller is denied the ability to execute all controller-switch commands by the switch.
- **Role Master** (`OFPCR_ROLE_MASTER`): This role provides complete access to the switch and is similar to `OFPCR_ROLE_EQUAL`. The difference between role equal and role master is that only one controller should be in `OFPCR_ROLE_MASTER`. The switch ensures that only one controller is in this state.

The default role of a controller is `OFPCR_ROLE_EQUAL`.

As the controller can manage multiple switches, the controller can take the MASTER role for some switches and SLAVE / EQUAL role for other switches. The controller's role is defined as the function of the communication channel between the controller and the switch.

How to do it...

The procedure to accept an OpenFlow communication channel from multiple switches is similar to that of accepting a connection from a single controller which is explained in the *Connection setup on TCP and TLS* recipe in *Chapter 1, OpenFlow Channel Connection Establishment (Part 2)*.

How it works...

The controller can instruct the switch to send what type of asynchronous message it is interested in. This can be done using the asynchronous configuration message which is described in the *Configuring a switch to send list of asynchronous events interested by this channel / controller* recipe in *Chapter 2, Symmetric Messages and Asynchronous Messages*. Using this message, a different controller can instruct a switch to send different messages or notifications to different controllers which will provide load balancing across controllers.

The next recipe explains in detail how to set the role of the controller. Refer to the recipe, *Setting the role of communication channel towards a controller* in *Chapter 1, OpenFlow Channel Connection Establishment (Part 1)* for how the switch handles the various role change messages from the controller.

See also

- For more information about establishing the connection to a controller, refer to the *Multiple controllers managing switch with different roles* recipe in *Chapter 1, OpenFlow Channel Connection Establishment (Part 2)*
- The next recipe describes how to set the role of the controller in detail

Setting the role of a controller's communication channel

The `OFPT_ROLE_REQUEST` messages are used to change the role of the communication channel. The different controller roles are described in the previous recipe of this chapter. The controller can change its role at any time. The role request message offers a lightweight mechanism to help the controller master election process. Usually, all the controllers in the system require coordination among themselves for the controller election process. Any slave controller or equal controller can elect itself as master.

> The switch cannot change the controller state. The controller state in a switch is always changed due to a request from one of the controllers.

How to do it...

The controller should send the role request in the following format. The switch uses the same message format for sending the reply message back to the controller:

```
/* Role request and reply message. */
struct ofp_role_request {
struct ofp_header header; /* Type OFPT_ROLE_REQUEST/OFPT_ROLE_REPLY.
*/
uint32_t role; /* One of OFPCR_ROLE_*. */
uint8_t pad[4]; /* Align to 64 bits. */
uint64_t generation_id; /* Master Election Generation Id */
};
```

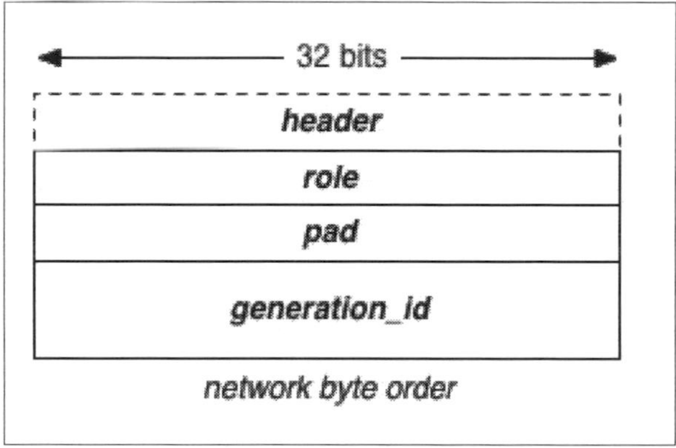

The roles of the controllers are defined in the following enumeration:

```
/* Controller roles. */
enum ofp_controller_role {
OFPCR_ROLE_NOCHANGE = 0, /* Don't change current role. */
OFPCR_ROLE_EQUAL = 1, /* Default role, full access. */
OFPCR_ROLE_MASTER = 2, /* Full access, at most one master. */ OFPCR_
ROLE_SLAVE = 3, /* Read-only access. */
};
```

When the controller wants to change its role, it should form a role request message and send the message to the switch via the channel that is connecting to the switch. Upon sending the role request message the controller should wait for the `OFPT_ROLE_REPLY` message from the switch. If the role value in the `OFPT_ROLE_REPLY` message is equal to the `OFPT_ROLE_REQUEST` message then the role of controller is changed successfully in the switch.

See also

- For more information on the handling of this role request message in the switch, refer to the recipe, *Setting the role of communication channel towards a controller* in *Chapter 1, OpenFlow Channel Connection Establishment (Part 1)*

Auxiliary connection establishment

Apart from the main connection, a switch can initiate one or more connections towards the controller to improve switch processing performance and exploit the parallelism of most switch implementations. These connections are termed auxiliary connections. The controller should recognize incoming connections with a non-zero Auxiliary ID as auxiliary connections and bind them to the main connection with the same Datapath ID. The Datapath ID of the main connection and the auxiliary connection is the same; this helps the controller to bind the auxiliary connection to the main connection.

The controller must not accept an auxiliary connection from the switch until the main connection is successfully established.

Getting started

The controller should not accept an auxiliary connection from the switch until the main connection is successfully established.

How to do it...

The procedure to establish an auxiliary connection from a switch is similar to that of establishing a main connection from the switch. The auxiliary connection can be established in unreliable communication protocols like UDP. the controller should be able to receive messages from switches via UDP. The controller must be able to accept/send any OpenFlow message types and sub-types on any connections.

There's more...

The main connection or an auxiliary connection cannot be restricted to a specific message type or sub-type. The OpenFlow specification provides some guidelines for sending and receiving messages in main and auxiliary connections to maximize the switch performance. These guidelines are common to both the switch and controller so refer to the recipe, *Establishing auxiliary connection to controller* in *Chapter 1, OpenFlow Channel Connection Establishment (Part 2)* for more information regarding these guidelines:

- All OpenFlow controller messages which are not Packet-out (flow-mod, statistic request and so on) should be sent over the main connection.
- All Packet-out messages containing a packet from a Packet-in message should be sent on the connection where the Packet-in came from.
- All other Packet-out messages should be spread across the various auxiliary connections. However, it is better to send packets of the same flow via the same OpenFlow connection.
- If the desired auxiliary connection is not available, the controller should use the main connection.
- An OpenFlow Controller which uses an unreliable auxiliary connection should follow recommendations specified in RFC 5405 wherever it is required.
- If the auxiliary connection is established in unreliable transport protocols like UDP and DTLS, then only the following message type should be supported to send /receive in an auxiliary connection.

```
OFPT_HELLO
OFPT_ERROR
OFPT_ECHO_REQUEST
OFPT_ECHO_REPLY
OFPT_FEATURES_REQUEST
OFPT_FEATURES_REPLY
OFPT_PACKET_IN
OFPT_PACKET_OUT
OFPT_EXPERIMENTER
```

Support to send and receive other message types should not be provided:

- After establishing the auxiliary connection over unreliable transport protocols, if the controller receives the first message other than `OFPT_HELLO`, then the controller should either:
    - Assume the connection is set up properly and use the version number from that message or It must return an error message with an `OFPET_BAD_REQUEST` type with the code `OFPBRC_BAD_VERSION`.
- If the OpenFlow controller receives an error message with an error type of `OFPET_BAD_REQUEST` and a code of `OFPBRC_BAD_VERSION` on an unreliable auxiliary connection, then it must either send a new Hello message or terminate the unreliable auxiliary connection.
- If the controller doesn't receive any message on an auxiliary connection after a chosen amount of time lower than 5 seconds, then the controller must either send a new `Hello` message or terminate the unreliable auxiliary connection.

See also

- For more information about establishing a main connection, refer to the *Connection setup on TCP and TLS* recipe in *Chapter 1, OpenFlow Channel Connection Establishment (Part 2)*

Sending a handshake message to the switch

The handshake messages (`OFPT_FEATURES_REQUEST/OFPT_FEATURES_REPLY`) are used by the controller to fetch basic capabilities and features supported by the switch. On receipt of this message, switch will respond with the `OFPT_FEATURES_REPLY` message. The `OFPT_FEATURE_REPLY` message informs the controller about the switch capabilities.

Getting started

On establishment of a successful connection, the controller should know the list of features and tables supported by the switch. This is required because, if the switch doesn't have support for some feature or functionalities, then the controller should provide those functionalities. For instance, if the switch sends a reply message with a capability field having `OFPC_PORT_BLOCKED` set, then the switch indicates to the controller that the switch has the capability to block the relevant port to prevent packet loops. If the bit is not set, then the controller should implement mechanisms to avoid packet loops.

How to do it...

The controller should form the `OFPT_FEATURES_REQUEST` and send the message to the switch. The message `OFPT_FEATURES_REQUEST` doesn't contain body other than the OpenFlow header which is defined in the *OpenFlow Header* section of the *Appendix*.

The switch responds back with the `OFPT_FEATURES_REPLY` message which provides switch capabilities that can be interpreted by the controller. Refer to the recipe, *Handling a handshake message from the controller* in *Chapter 1, OpenFlow Channel Connection Establishment (Part 1)*.

On receiving this `OFPT_FEATURES_REPLY` message from the switch, the controller should store these fields in the message for its future usage and also choose to intimate the controller application for the capability of the switch.

See also

- For more information on the handling of the feature request message in the switch, refer to the *Handling a handshake message from the controller* recipe in *Chapter 1, OpenFlow Channel Connection Establishment (Part 1)*

Sending a switch configuration message to the switch

The switch configuration messages are used by the controller to set and get switch configuration parameters.

The OpenFlow specification defines the following three switch configuration messages:

- `OFPT_SET_CONFIG`: This message is sent from the controller to configure the switch. Typically this message is sent from the controller upon a successful connection establishment and after identifying the switch's features using the `OFPT_FEATURES_REQUEST` message.
- `OFPT_GET_CONFIG_REQUEST`: This message is sent from the controller to get configuration information from the switch. This message can be sent from the controller at any time.
- `OFPT_GET_CONFIG_REPLY`: This message is the reply message sent from the switch for the `OFPT_GET_CONFIG_REQUEST` message.

The controller can configure the following parameters in the switch:

- The maximum bytes of data that the switch should send to the controller while sending the buffered packets.
- IP fragmentation related information which contains how the switch should treat IP fragmented packets. The switch can treat IP fragmented packet in either of the following ways, which can be configured from the controller.
    - Treat IP fragments in the same way as other packets (`OFPC_FRAG_NORMAL`). This is the default mode.
    - Drop all IP fragments without passing them through the flow table (`OFPC_FRAG_DROP`).
    - Reassemble the IP fragments before passing them through the flow table (`OFPC_FRAG_REASM`).

Getting started

Before sending the configuration get / set message to switch, the communication channel between the controller and the switch should have been established successfully.

How to do it...

When the controller wants to get switch configuration information, the controller should generate `OFPT_GET_CONFIG_REQUEST` toward the switch. The `OFPT_GET_CONFIG_REQUEST` message doesn't contain a body other than the OpenFlow header. Hence the message format of `OFPT_GET_CONFIG_REQUEST` is the same as that of the one defined in the *OpenFlow Header* section of the *Appendix*.

The switch responds back with the `OFPT_GET_CONFIG_REPLY` message. Refer to the recipe, *Handling a handshake message from the controller* in *Chapter 1, OpenFlow Channel Connection Establishment (Part 1)* for the format of this message.

When the controller wants to set the above mentioned configuration details then the controller should form the `OFPT_SET_CONFIG_REQUEST` message, which has the same message format as that of `OFPT_GET_CONFIG_REPLY`.

The switch will not send a reply message to the `OFPT_SET_CONFIG` message.

See also

- For more information on sending the switch configuration message from the controller, refer to the *Handling a handshake message from the controller* recipe in *Chapter 1, OpenFlow Channel Connection Establishment (Part 2)*

2
Symmetric Messages and Asynchronous Messages (Part 1)

This chapter describes the steps involved in sending and processing symmetric messages and asynchronous messages in the switch and contains the following recipes:

- Sending and processing a hello message
- Sending and processing an echo request and a reply message
- Sending and processing an error message
- Sending and processing an experimenter message
- Handling a Set Asynchronous Configuration message from the controller, which shows a list of asynchronous events of interest to the controller
- Handling a Get Asynchronous Configuration message from the controller, which is used to fetch a list of asynchronous events that will be sent from the switch
- Sending a Packet-In message to the controller
- Sending a Flow-removed message to the controller
- Sending a port-status message to the controller
- Sending a controller-role status message to the controller
- Sending a table-status message to the controller
- Sending a request-forward message to the controller
- Handling a packet-out message from the controller
- Handling a barrier-message from the controller

Symmetric messages can be sent from both the controller and the switch without any solicitation between them. The OpenFlow switch should be able to send and process the following symmetric messages to or from the controller, but error messages will not be processed by the switch:

- Hello message
- Echo request and echo reply message
- Error message
- Experimenter message

Asynchronous messages are sent by both the controller and the switch when there is any state change in the system. Like symmetric messages, asynchronous messages also should be sent without any solicitation between the switch and the controller. The switch should be able to send the following asynchronous messages to the controller:

- Packet-in message
- Flow-removed message
- Port-status message
- Table-status message
- Controller-role status message
- Request-forward message

Similarly, the switch should be able to receive, or process, the following controller-to-switch messages:

- Packet-out message
- Barrier message

The controller can program or instruct the switch to send a subset of interested asynchronous messages using an asynchronous configuration message. Based on this configuration, the switch should send the subset of asynchronous messages only via the communication channel.

> The switch should replicate and send asynchronous messages to all the controllers based on the information present in the asynchronous configuration message sent from each controller. The switch should maintain asynchronous configuration information on a per communication channel basis.

Sending and processing a hello message

The `OFPT_HELLO` message is used by both the switch and the controller to identify and negotiate the OpenFlow version supported by both the devices. Hello messages should be sent from the switch once the TCP/TLS connection is established and are considered part of the communication channel establishment procedure.

The switch should send a hello message to the controller immediately after establishing the TCP/TLS connection with the controller.

Getting started

To send a hello message, the switch should have established the TCP/TLS connection defined in the *Connection setup on TCP and TLS* recipe in *Chapter 1, OpenFlow Channel Connection Establishment (Part 1)*.

How to do it...

As hello messages are transmitted by both the switch and the controller, the switch should be able to send, receive, and process the hello message. The following section explains these procedures in detail.

Sending the OFPT_HELLO message

The message format to be used to send the hello message from the switch is as follows. This message includes the OpenFlow header along with zero or more elements that have variable size:

```
/* OFPT_HELLO. This message includes zero or more
   hello elements having variable size.  */
struct ofp_hello {
struct ofp_header header;
/* Hello element list */
struct ofp_hello_elem_header elements[0]; /* List of elements */
};
```

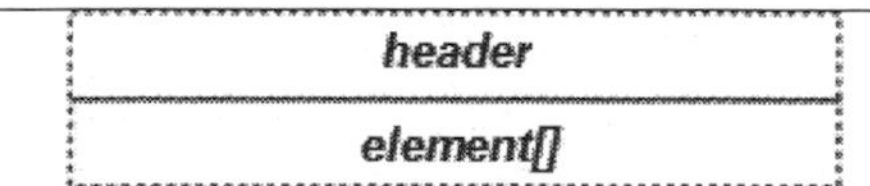

The `version` field in the `ofp_header` should be set with the highest OpenFlow protocol version supported by the switch. The `elements` field is an optional field and might contain the element definition, which takes the following TLV format:

```
/* Version bitmap Hello Element */
struct ofp_hello_elem_versionbitmap {
uint16_t type;           /* OFPHET_VERSIONBITMAP. */
uint16_t length;         /* Length in bytes of this element. */
        /* Followed by:
         * - Exactly (length - 4) bytes containing the bitmaps,
         * then Exactly (length + 7)/8*8 - (length) (between 0
         * and 7) bytes of all-zero bytes */
uint32_t bitmaps[0]; /* List of bitmaps - supported versions */
};
```

The `type` field should be set with `OFPHET_VERSIONBITMAP`. The `length` field should be set to the length of this element.

The `bitmaps` field should be set with the list of the OpenFlow versions the switch supports. The number of bitmaps included in the field should depend on the highest version number supported by the switch. The `ofp_versions` 0 to 31 should be encoded in the first bitmap, `ofp_versions` 32 to 63 should be encoded in the second bitmap, and so on. For example, if the switch supports only version 1.0 (`ofp_versions` = 0 x 01) and version 1.3 (`ofp_versions` = 0 x 04), then the first bitmap should be set to 0 x 00000012.

Refer to the `send_hello_message()` function in the `of/openflow.c` file for the procedure to build and send the `OFPT_Hello` message.

Receiving the OFPT_HELLO message

The switch should be able to receive and process the `OFPT_HELLO` messages that are sent from the controller. The controller also uses the same message format, structures, and enumerations as defined in the previous section of this recipe. Once the switch receives the hello message, it should calculate the protocol version to be used for messages exchanged with the controller. The procedure required to calculate the protocol version to be used is as follows:

- If the hello message received from the switch contains an optional `OFPHET_VERSIONBITMAP` element and the bitmap field contains a valid value, then the negotiated version should be the highest common version among the supported protocol versions in the controller, with the bitmap field in the `OFPHET_VERSIONBITMAP` element.
- If the hello message doesn't contain any `OFPHET_VERSIONBITMAP` element, then the negotiated version should be the smallest of the switch-supported protocol versions and the version field set in the OpenFlow header of the received hello message.

If the negotiated version is supported by the switch, then the OpenFlow connection between the controller and the switch continues. Otherwise, the switch should send an `OFPT_ERROR` message with the type field set as `OFPET_HELLO_FAILED`, the code field set as `OFPHFC_INCOMPATIBLE`, and an optional ASCII string explaining the situation in the data and terminate the connection. Refer to the *Sending and processing error messages* recipe in this chapter for the procedure for sending error messages.

There's more...

Once the switch and the controller negotiate the OpenFlow protocol version to be used, the connection setup procedure is complete. From then on, both the controller and the switch can send OpenFlow protocol messages to each other.

See also

- For more information regarding the procedure to establish the TCP/TLS connection, refer to the *Connection setup on TCP and TLS* recipe in *Chapter 1, OpenFlow Channel Connection Establishment (Part 1)*

Sending and processing an echo request and a reply message

Echo request and reply messages are used by both the controller and the switch to maintain and verify the liveliness of the controller-switch connection. Echo messages are also used to calculate the latency and bandwidth of the controller-switch connection.

On reception of an echo request message, the switch should respond with an echo reply message.

Getting started

To send echo request and reply messages, the TCP/TLS connection establishment procedure defined in the *Connection setup on TCP and TLS* recipe in *Chapter 1, OpenFlow Channel Connection Establishment (Part 1)*, should be used.

How to do it...

As echo messages are transmitted by both the switch and the controller, the switch should be able to send, receive, and process them. The following section explains these procedures in detail.

Sending the OFPT_ECHO_REQUEST message

The OpenFlow specification doesn't specify how frequently this echo message has to be sent from the switch. However, the switch might choose to send an echo request message periodically to the controller with the configured interval. Similarly, the OpenFlow specification doesn't mention what the timeout (the longest period of time the switch should wait) for receiving echo reply message from the controller should be.

After sending an echo request message to the controller, the switch should wait for the echo reply message for the configured timeout period. If the switch doesn't receive the echo reply message within this period, then it should initiate the connection interruption procedure as defined in the *Connection interruption procedure* recipe in *Chapter 1, OpenFlow Channel Connection Establishment (Part 1).*

The `OFPT_ECHO_REQUEST` message contains an OpenFlow header followed by an undefined data field of arbitrary length. The data field might be filled with the timestamp at which the echo request message was sent, various lengths or values to measure the bandwidth, or be zero-size for just checking the liveliness of the connection. In most open source implementations of OpenFlow, the echo request message only contains the header field and doesn't contain any body.

Refer to the `send_echo_request()` function in the `of/openflow.c` file for the procedure to build and send the `echo_request` message.

Receiving OFPT_ECHO_REQUEST

The switch should be able to receive and process `OFPT_ECHO_REQUEST` messages that are sent from the controller. The controller also uses the same message format, structures, and enumerations as defined in the previous section of this recipe. Once the switch receives the echo request message, it should build the `OFPT_ECHO_REPLY` message. This message consists of `ofp_header` and an arbitrary-length data field. While forming the echo reply message, the switch should copy the content present in the arbitrary-length field of the request message to the reply message.

Refer to the `process_echo_request()` function in the `of/openflow.c` file for the procedure to handle and process the echo request message and send the echo reply message.

Processing OFPT_ECHO_REPLY message

The switch should be able to receive the echo reply message from the controller. If the switch sends the echo request message to calculate the latency or bandwidth, on receiving the echo reply message, it should parse the arbitrary-length data field and can calculate the bandwidth, latency, and so on.

There's more...

If the OpenFlow switch implementation is divided into multiple layers, then the processing of the echo request and reply should be handled in the deepest possible layer. For example, if the OpenFlow switch implementation is divided into user-space processing and kernel-space processing, then the echo request and reply message handling should be in the kernel space.

Sending and processing an error message

Error messages are used by both the controller and the switch to notify the other end of the connection about any problem. Error messages are typically used by the switch to inform the controller about failure of execution of the request sent from the controller.

How to do it...

Whenever the switch wants to send the error message to the controller, it should build the `OFPT_ERROR` message, which takes the following message format:

```
/* OFPT_ERROR: Error message (datapath -> the controller). */
struct ofp_error_msg {
struct ofp_header header;
uint16_t type;
uint16_t code;
uint8_t data[0]; /* Variable-length data. Interpreted based
on the type and code. No padding. */
};
```

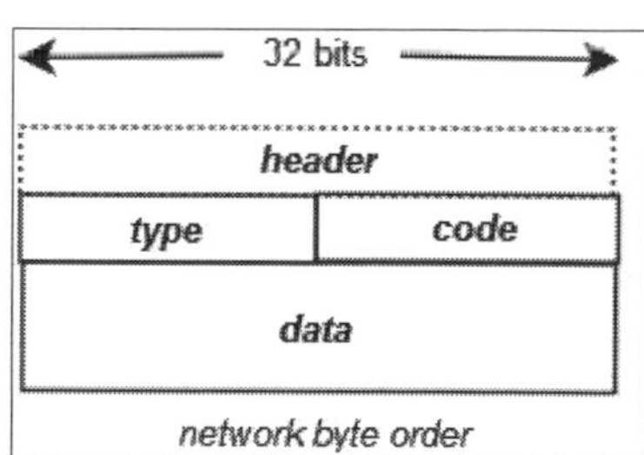

The `type` field indicates a high-level type of error. The `code` value is interpreted based on the type. The `data` value is a piece of variable-length data that is interpreted based on both the type and the value. The `data` field should contain an ASCII text string that adds details about why the error occurred.

Unless specified otherwise, the data field should contain at least 64 bytes of the failed message that caused this error. If the failed message is shorter 64 bytes, then the data field should contain the full message without any padding.

If the switch needs to send an error message in response to a specific message from the controller (say, `OFPET_BAD_REQUEST`, `OFPET_BAD_ACTION`, `OFPET_BAD_INSTRUCTION`, `OFPET_BAD_MATCH`, or `OFPET_FLOW_MOD_FAILED`), then the `xid` field of the OpenFlow header in the error message should be set with the offending request message.

Refer to the `send_error_message()` function in the `of/openflow.c` file for the procedure to build and send an error message.

If the switch needs to send an error message for a request message sent from the controller (because of an error condition), then the switch need not send the reply message to that request.

See also

- For more information regarding the possible values that the type, code, and data fields can take, refer to the *Common OpenFlow error codes* recipe in *Appendix, Common OpenFlow Headers, Structures, and Error Codes*

Sending and processing an experimenter message

Experimenter messages provide a way for the switch to offer additional vendor-defined functionalities.

How to do it...

The controller sends the experimenter message with the format as defined in the *Sending and processing experimenter messages* recipe of *Chapter 2, Symmetric Messages and Asynchronous Messages (Part 2)*. Once the switch receives this message, it should invoke the appropriate vendor-specific functions.

Handling a "Set Asynchronous Configuration message"

The OpenFlow specification provides a mechanism in the controller to inform the switch about the list of asynchronous events that the controller or controller channel is interested in. This is achieved by sending the Set Asynchronous Configuration message (`OFPT_SET_ASYNC`) to the switch. The switch should maintain a per-controller asynchronous configuration in its database, which will be used as a filter before sending the asynchronous configuration message to the controller.

The switch need not send any reply message to the controller for the `OFPT_SET_ASYNC` message.

How to do it...

The message format that will be used by the controller to send the `OFPT_SET_ASYNC` is defined in the *Configuring the switch to send a list of asynchronous events the controller channel is interested in* recipe of *Chapter 2, Symmetric Messages and Asynchronous Messages (Part 2)*.

How it works...

When the controller sends the `OFPT_SET_ASYNC` message to the switch, the switch should save this information in its database or data structure where it maintains the controller connection. Later on, whenever the switch wants to send an asynchronous message to the controller, the switch should use this database data structure, and based on the configuration, it can either send the asynchronous message to the controller or just avoid sending the event.

There are two kinds of asynchronous messages generated from the switch, as follows:

- Global asynchronous messages, such as port-status change messages, packet-in messages, and so on.
- Table-entry-based asynchronous messages, such as `OFPT_FLOW_REMOVED`. These messages are generated from the switch when there is a change in the table entry state based on a per-entry flag.

In both the cases, the `OFPT_SET_ASYNC` message can be used to control the sending of the previously mentioned events from the switch to the controller. For per-table-entry-based asynchronous messages, `OFPT_SET_ASYNC` acts as an additional per-controller filter along with the per-entry flag.

See also

- For more information about the procedure to send the switch configuration message from the controller, refer to the *Configuring the switch to send a list of asynchronous events the controller channel is interested in* recipe of *Chapter 2, Symmetric Messages and Asynchronous Messages (Part 2)*

Handling a "Get Asynchronous Configuration message" from the controller

The OpenFlow specification provides a mechanism in the controller to fetch the list of asynchronous events that can be sent from the switch to the controller channel. This is achieved by sending the "Get Asynchronous Configuration message" (`OFPT_GET_ASYNC_REQUEST`) to the switch.

How to do it...

The message format to be used to get the asynchronous configuration message (`OFPT_GET_ASYNC_REQUEST`) doesn't have any body other than `ofp_header`. On receiving this `OFPT_GET_ASYNC_REQUEST` message, the switch should respond with the `OFPT_GET_ASYNC_REPLY` message. The message format of `OFPT_GET_ASYNC_REPLY` is the same as that of the `OFPT_SET_ASYNC` message as described in the *Handling the set asynchronous configuration message* recipe of this chapter. The switch should fill the `property` list with the list of asynchronous configuration events / property types that the relevant controller channel is preconfigured to receive. The switch should get this information from its internal data structures.

Refer to the `process_async_config_request()` function in the `of/openflow.c` file for the procedure to process the get asynchronous configuration request message from the controller.

See also

- For more information about the procedure to fetch the switch configuration message from the controller, refer to the *Fetching the list of possible asynchronous events that can be sent from the switch to the controller channel* recipe in *Chapter 2, Symmetric Messages and Asynchronous Messages (Part 2)*
- For more information on how to process the `OFPT_SET_ASYNC` message in the switch, refer to the previous recipe

Sending a packet-in message to the controller

Packet-in messages (`OFP_PACKET_IN`) are sent from the switch to the controller to transfer a packet received from one of the switch-ports to the controller for further processing.

By default, a packet-in message should be sent to all the controllers that are in equal (`OFPCR_ROLE_EQUAL`) and master (`OFPCR_ROLE_MASTER`) roles. This message should not be sent to controllers that are in the slave state.

There are three ways by which the switch can send a packet-in event to the controller:

1. Table-miss entry: When there is no matching flow entry for the incoming packet, the switch can send the packet to the controller. Refer to the *Handling switch configuration messages from the controller* recipe in *Chapter 1, OpenFlow Channel Connection Establishment (Part 1)*, for the switch configuration required to send a table-miss packet to the controller.
2. TTL checking: When the TTL value in a packet reaches zero, the switch can send the packet to the controller. Refer to the *Handling switch configuration messages from the controller* recipe of *Chapter 1, OpenFlow Channel Connection Establishment (Part 1)*, for the switch configuration required to send a TTL check failure packet to the controller.
3. The "send to the controller" action in the matching entry (either the flow table entry or the group table entry) of the packet: Refer to the *Adding a new flow entry to the flow table* recipe of *Chapter 3, Flow Table and Flow Entry Modification Messages (Part 1)*, to know how to set a flow entry with the action as send to the controller.

How to do it...

When the switch wants to send a packet received in its data path to the controller, the following message format should be used:

```
/* Packet received on port (datapath -> the controller). */
struct ofp_packet_in {
struct ofp_header header;
uint32_t buffer_id; /* ID assigned by datapath. */
uint16_t total_len; /* Full length of frame. */
uint8_t reason;     /* Reason packet is being sent
                     * (one of OFPR_*) */
```

```
uint8_t table_id;     /* ID of the table that was looked up */
uint64_t cookie;      /* Cookie of the flow entry that was
                       * looked up. */
struct ofp_match match; /* Packet metadata. Variable size. */
/* The variable size and padded match is always followed by:
* - Exactly 2 all-zero padding bytes, then
* - An Ethernet frame whose length is inferred from header.length.
* The padding bytes preceding the Ethernet frame ensure that IP
* header (if any) following the Ethernet header is 32-bit aligned.
*/
uint8_t pad[2]; /* Align to 64 bit + 16 bit */
uint8_t data[0]; /* Ethernet frame */
};
```

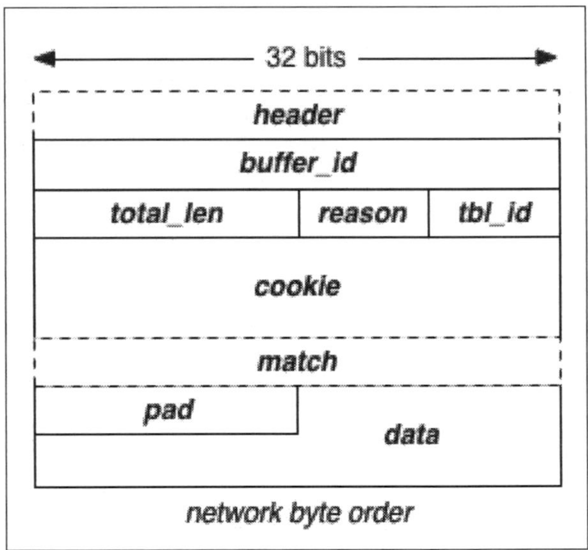

The `buffer-id` field should be set to the opaque value generated by the switch. When the packet is buffered, the data portion of the packet-in message should contain some bytes of data from the incoming packet. If the packet is sent to the controller because of the "send to the controller" action of a table entry, then the `max_len` field of `ofp_action_output` should be used as the size of the packet to be included in the packet-in message. If the packet is sent to the controller for any other reason, then the `miss_send_len` field of the `OFPT_SET_CONFIG` message should be used to determine the size of the packet. If the packet is not buffered, either because of unavailability of buffers or an explicit configuration via `OFPCML_NO_BUFFER`, then the entire packet should be included in the data portion of the packet-in message with the `buffer-id` value as `OFP_NO_BUFFER`.

The date field should be set to the complete packet or a fraction of the packet.
The total_length field should be set to the length of the packet included in the data field.

The reason field should be set with any one of the following values defined in the enumeration, based on the context that triggers the packet-in event:

```
/* Why is this packet being sent to the controller? */
enum ofp_packet_in_reason {
OFPR_TABLE_MISS = 0,     /* No matching flow (table-miss
                          * flow entry). */
OFPR_APPLY_ACTION = 1, /* Output to the controller in
                          * apply-actions. */
OFPR_INVALID_TTL = 2,    /* Packet has invalid TTL */
OFPR_ACTION_SET = 3,     /* Output to the controller in action set.
*/
OFPR_GROUP = 4,          /* Output to the controller in group
bucket. */
OFPR_PACKET_OUT = 5,     /* Output to the controller in packet-out.
*/
};
```

If the packet-in message was triggered by the flow-entry "send to the controller" action, then the cookie field should be set with the cookie of the flow entry that caused the packet to be sent to the controller. This field should be set to -1 if the cookie cannot be associated with a particular flow.

When the packet-in message is triggered by the "send to the controller" action of a table entry, there is a possibility that some changes have already been applied over the packet in previous stages of the pipeline. This information needs to be carried along with the packet-in message, and it can be carried in the match field of the packet-in message with a set of **OXM** (short for **OpenFlow Extensible Match**) TLVs. If the switch includes an OXM TLV in the packet-in message, then the match field should contain a set of OXM TLVs that include context fields. The standard context fields that can be added into the OXL TLVs are OFPXMT_OFB_IN_PORT, OFPXMT_OFB_IN_PHY_PORT, OFPXMT_OFB_METADATA, and OFPXMT_OFB_TUNNEL_ID.

When the switch receives the packet in the physical port, and this packet information needs to be carried in the packet-in message, then OFPXMT_OFB_IN_PORT and OFPXMT_OFB_IN_PHY_PORT should have the same value, which is the OpenFlow port number of that physical port. When the switch receives the packet in the logical port and this packet information needs to be carried in the packet-in message, then the switch should set the logical port's port number in OFPXMT_OFB_IN_PORT and the physical port's port number in OFPXMT_OFB_IN_PHY_PORT. For example, consider a packet received on a tunnel interface defined over a **Link Aggregation Group** (**LAG**) with two member ports. Then the packet-in message should carry the tunnel interface's port_no to the OFPXMT_OFB_IN_PORT field and the physical interface's port_no to the OFPXMT_OFB_IN_PHY_PORT field.

Refer to the send_packet_in_message() function in the of/openflow.c file for the procedure to send a packet-in message event to the controller.

How it works...

The switch can send either the entire packet it receives from the switch port to the controller, or a fraction of the packet to the controller. When the switch is configured to send only a fraction of the packet, it should buffer the packet in its memory and send a portion of packet data. This is controlled by the switch configuration. Refer to the *Handling switch configuration messages from the controller* recipe in *Chapter 1, OpenFlow Channel Connection Establishment (Part 1)*, for the procedure to set this configuration.

If the switch is configured to buffer the packet, and it has sufficient memory to buffer the packet, then the packet-in message should contain the following:

1. A fraction of the packet. This is the size of the packet to be included in the packet-in message, configured via the switch configuration message. By default, it is 128 bytes. When the packet-in message is resulted by a table-entry action, then the output action itself can specify the size of the packet to be sent to the controller. For all other packet-in messages, it is defined in the switch configuration. Refer to the *Handling switch configuration messages from the controller* recipe of *Chapter 1, OpenFlow Channel Connection Establishment (Part 1)*, to set this parameter.
2. The buffer ID to be used by the controller when the controller wants to forward the message at a later point in time.

There's more...

The switch that implements buffering should be expected to expose some details, such as the amount of available buffers, the period of time the buffered data will be available, and so on, through documentation. The switch should implement the procedure to release the buffered packet when there is no response from the controller to the packet-in event.

See also

- For more information regarding how the controller processes this packet-in message, refer to the *Processing packet-in asynchronous messages from the switch* recipe in *Chapter 2, Symmetric Messages and Asynchronous Messages (Part 2)*

Sending a flow-removed message to the controller

A flow-removed message (`OFPT_FLOW_REMOVED`) is sent from the switch to the controller when a flow entry is removed from the flow table. This message should be sent to the controller only when the `OFPFF_SEND_FLOW_REM` flag in the flow entry is set. Refer to the *Adding a new flow entry to the flow table* recipe in *Chapter 3, Flow Table and Flow Entry Modification Messages*, requesting the switch to send a flow removed message when the flow entry is getting expired/deleted for setting this `OFPFF_SEND_FLOW_REM` flag.

The switch should send this message only to the controller channel wherein the controller requested the switch to send this event. The controller can express its interest in receiving this event by sending the switch configuration message to the switch. Refer to the *Sending a switch configuration message to the switch* recipe in *Chapter 1, OpenFlow Channel Connection Establishment (Part 2)*, of this book for the procedure to send this switch configuration message from the controller.

By default, `OFPT_FLOW_REMOVED` should be sent to all the controllers that are in equal (`OFPCR_ROLE_EQUAL`) and master (`OFPCR_ROLE_MASTER`) roles. This message should not be sent to a controller that is in the slave state.

How to do it...

When the switch removes an entry from the flow table, it should build an `OFPT_FLOW_REMOVED` message with the following format and send this message to the controllers that have already shown interest in this event:

```
 /* Flow removed (datapath -> the controller). */
struct ofp_flow_removed {
struct ofp_header header;
uint64_t cookie;         /* Opaque the controller-issued identifier. */
uint16_t priority;       /* Priority level of flow entry. */
uint8_t reason;          /* One of OFPRR_*. */
uint8_t table_id;        /* ID of the table */
uint32_t duration_sec;   /* Time flow was alive in seconds. */
uint32_t duration_nsec;  /* Time flow was alive in nanoseconds
                          * beyond duration_sec. */
uint16_t idle_timeout;   /* Idle timeout from original flow mod. */
uint16_t hard_timeout;   /* Hard timeout from original flow mod. */
```

```
uint64_t packet_count;
uint64_t byte_count;
struct ofp_match match; /* Description of fields.Variable size. */
};
```

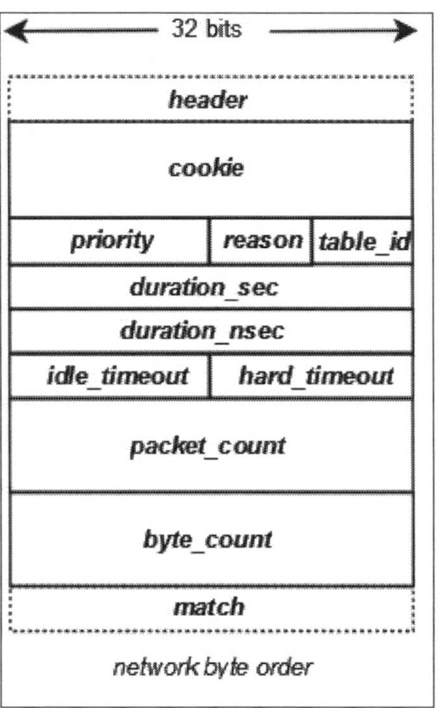

The `cookie` field should be set with the cookie of the flow entry, the `priority` field should be set with the priority of the flow entry, and the `reason` field should be set with one of the following values defined in the enumeration:

```
/* Why was this flow removed? */
enum ofp_flow_removed_reason {
OFPRR_IDLE_TIMEOUT = 0,/* Flow idle time exceeded idle_timeout. */
OFPRR_HARD_TIMEOUT = 1, /* Time exceeded hard_timeout. */
OFPRR_DELETE = 2,       /* Evicted by a DELETE flow mod. */
OFPRR_GROUP_DELETE = 3, /* Group was removed. */
OFPRR_METER_DELETE = 4, /* Meter was removed. */
OFPRR_EVICTION = 5,     /* the switch eviction to free resources.
*/
};
```

The `duration_sec` and `duration_nsec` should be set with the elapsed time of the flow entry in the switch. The total duration in nanoseconds can be computed as `duration_sec*109 + duration_nsec`.

All the other fields, such as `idle_timeout`, `hard_timeoutm`, and so on, should be set with the appropriate value from the flow entry, that is, these values can be directly copied from the flow mode that created this entry.

The `packet_count` and `byte_count` should be set with the number of packet count and the byte count associated with the flow entry, respectively. If the values are not available, then these fields should be set with the maximum possible value.

Refer to the `send_flow_removed_message()` function in the `of/openflow.c` file for the procedure to send a flow removed event message to the controller.

See also

- For more information regarding how the controller processes this flow-removed message, refer to the *Processing an asynchronous flow removed message from the switch* recipe in *Chapter 2, Symmetric Messages and Asynchronous Messages (Part 2)*

Sending a port-status message to the controller

Port-status messages (`OFPT_PORT_STATUS`) are sent from the switch to the controller when there is any change in the port status or when a new port is added, removed, or modified in the switch's data path. The switch should send this message only to the controller channel that the controller requested the switch to send it. The controller can express its interest to receive this event by sending an asynchronous configuration message to the switch. Refer to the *Configuring the switch to send a list of asynchronous events the controller channel is interested in* recipe in *Chapter 2, Symmetric Messages and Asynchronous Messages (Part 2)*, for the procedure to configure the switch to send a port-status message to the controller.

By default, the port-status message should be sent to all configured controllers in the switch, including the controller in the slave role (`OFPCR_ROLE_SLAVE`).

How to do it...

The switch should construct an `OFPT_PORT_STATUS` message with the following format and send this message to the controllers that have already shown interest in this event:

```
 /* A physical port has changed in the datapath */
struct ofp_port_status {
struct ofp_header header;
uint8_t reason; /* One of OFPPR_*. */
uint8_t pad[7]; /* Align to 64-bits. */
struct ofp_port desc;
};
```

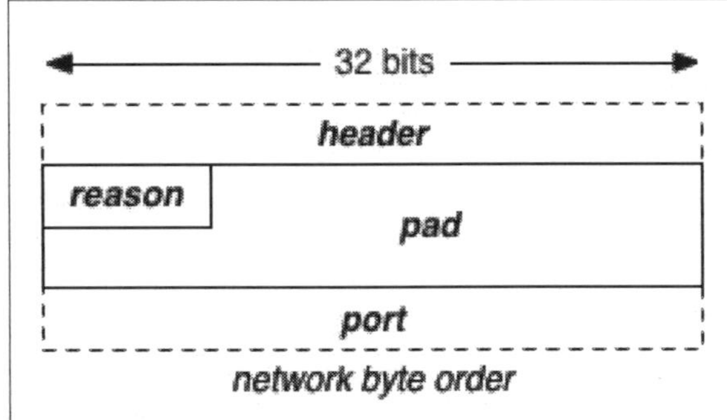

The `reason` field should be set to one of the following values as defined in the enumeration:

```
/* What changed about the physical port */
enum ofp_port_reason {
OFPPR_ADD = 0,     /* The port was added. */
OFPPR_DELETE = 1, /* The port was removed. */
OFPPR_MODIFY = 2, /* Some attribute of the port has changed. */
};
```

The `desc` field should be set to the port description. Refer to the *Port structures* section of *Appendix, Common OpenFlow Headers, Structures, and Error Codes*, for detailed information regarding the port description's structure. In the port description, all properties need not be filled by the switch. The switch should fill the properties that have changed, whereas the unchanged properties can be included optionally.

Refer to the `send_port_status_message()` function in the `of/openflow.c` file for the procedure to send `port_status_message` to the controller.

See also

- For more information regarding how the controller processes this port status message, refer to *Processing a port-status asynchronous message from the switch* recipe in *Chapter 2, Symmetric Messages and Asynchronous Messages (Part 2)*

Sending a controller role-status message to the controller

Controller role-status messages (`OFPT_ROLE_STATUS`) are sent from the switch to the set of controllers when the role of a controller is changed as a result of an `OFPT_ROLE_REQUEST` message. For example, if there are three the controllers connected to a switch (say `controller1`, `controller2`, and `controller3`) and `controller1` sends an `OFPT_ROLE_REQUEST` message to the switch, then the switch should send an `OFPT_ROLE_STATUS` message to `controller2` and `controller3`.

How to do it...

The switch should build the `OFPT_ROLE_STATUS` message with the following format and send it to all the other controllers:

```
/* Role status event message. */
struct ofp_role_status {
struct ofp_header header; /* Type OFPT_ROLE_REQUEST /
                           * OFPT_ROLE_REPLY. */
uint32_t role;             /* One of OFPCR_ROLE_*. */
uint8_t reason;            /* One of OFPCRR_*. */
uint8_t pad[3];            /* Align to 64 bits. */
uint64_t generation_id;    /* Master Election Generation Id */
/* Role Property list */
struct ofp_role_prop_header properties[0];
};
```

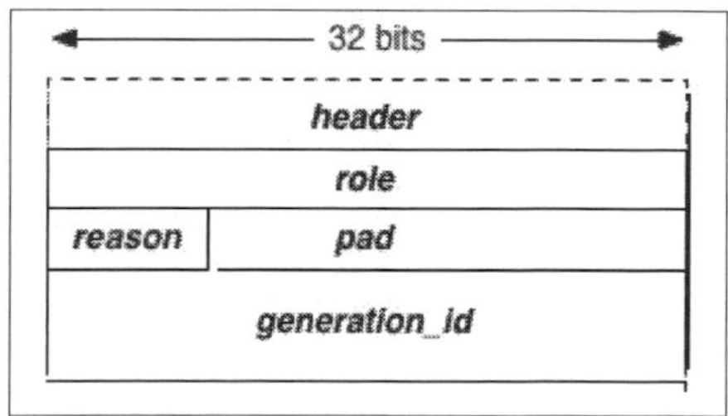

The `reason` field should be set with one of the following values as defined in the enumeration:

```
/* What changed about the controller role */
enum ofp_controller_role_reason {
OFPCRR_MASTER_REQUEST = 0, /* Another the controller asked
                            * to be master. */
OFPCRR_CONFIG = 1,         /* Configuration changed on the
                            * the switch. */
OFPCRR_EXPERIMENTER = 2,   /* Experimenter data changed. */
};
```

The `role` should be set to the new role of the controller. The `generation_id` should be set with the generation ID of the `OFPT_ROLE_REQUEST` message that triggered the `OFPT_ROLE_STATUS` message.

If the reason code is `OFPCRR_EXPERIMENTER`, then the role property list should be set in the following format:

```
/* Role property types.
*/
enum ofp_role_prop_type {
OFPRPT_EXPERIMENTER = 0xFFFF, /* Experimenter property. */
};

/* Experimenter role property */
struct ofp_role_prop_experimenter {
uint16_t type;          /* One of OFPRPT_EXPERIMENTER. */
uint16_t length;        /* Length in bytes of this property. */
uint32_t experimenter; /* Experimenter ID which takes the same
                         * form as struct
                         * ofp_experimenter_header. */
uint32_t exp_type;      /* Experimenter defined. */
/* Followed by:
 * - Exactly (length - 12) bytes containing the experimenter data,
 * - Exactly (length + 7)/8*8 - (length) (between 0 and 7)
 * bytes of all-zero bytes */
uint32_t experimenter_data[0];
};
```

The `experimenter` field in the experimenter ID should take the same format as the experimenter structure, which is described in the *Sending and processing an experimenter message* recipe in this chapter.

Refer to the `send_role_status_message()` function in the `of/openflow.c` file for the procedure to send a role status message to the controller.

See also

- For more information regarding how the controller processes this role status message, refer to the *Processing the controller role status message from the switch* recipe in *Chapter 2, Symmetric Messages and Asynchronous Messages (Part 2)*

Sending a table-status message to the controller

Table-status messages (`OFPT_TABLE_STATUS`) are sent from the switch to the controller when there is any change in the table status; for example, the number of entries in the table crosses the threshold value, called the vacancy threshold. The switch should send this message only to the controller channel in which the controller requested the switch to send it. The controller can express its interest to receive this event by sending the asynchronous configuration message to the switch. Refer to the *Configuring the switch to send a list of asynchronous events the controller channel is interested in* recipe in *Chapter 2, Symmetric Messages and Asynchronous Messages (Part 2)*, for the procedure to configure the switch to send a table status message to the controller.

How to do it...

The switch should build an `OFPT_TABLE_STATUS` message with the following format and send this message to the controllers that have already shown interest in this event:

```
/* A table config has changed in the datapath */
struct ofp_table_status {
struct ofp_header header;
uint8_t reason;              /* One of OFPTR_*. */
uint8_t pad[7];              /* Pad to 64 bits */
struct ofp_table_desc table; /* New table config. */
};
```

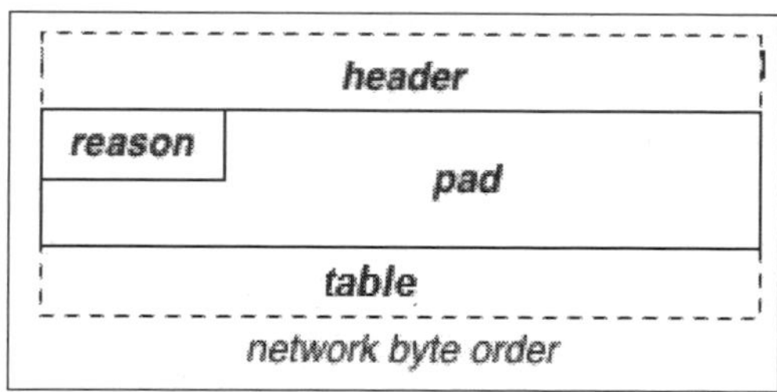

The `reason` field should be set with one of the following values defined in the enumeration:

```
/* What changed about the table */
enum ofp_table_reason {
OFPTR_VACANCY_DOWN = 3, /* Vacancy down threshold event. */
OFPTR_VACANCY_UP = 4,   /* Vacancy up threshold event. */
};
```

When the number of free entries in the table crosses the `vacancy_down` threshold, the switch should set the reason code as `OFPTR_VACANCY_DOWN`. Once the `vacancy_down` event is generated by the switch, the switch should not generate any further vacancy down event until a vacancy up event is generated. When the number of free entries in the table crosses the `vacancy_up` threshold value, the switch should set the reason code as `OFPTR_VACANCY_UP`. Again, once the vacancy up event is generated by the switch, the switch should not generate any further vacancy up event until a vacancy down event is generated. For more information regarding setting up these vacancy threshold values, refer to the *Modifying a flow table with vacancy enabled* recipe in *Chapter 3, Flow Table and Flow Entry Modification Messages (Part 1)*.

The table field should be set with the table description. Refer to the *Table structures* section in *Appendix, Common OpenFlow Headers, Structures, and Error Codes*, for detailed information regarding the table description's structure. Refer to the `send_table_status_message()` function in the `of/openflow.c` file for the procedure to send a table status message to the controller.

See also

- For more information regarding how the controller processes table status messages, refer to the *Processing a table-status asynchronous message from the switch* recipe in *Chapter 2, Symmetric Messages and Asynchronous Messages (Part 2)*

Sending a request-forward message to the controller

When a the switch receives a modify request message from the controller to modify the state of a group or meter entries, after successful modification of the state, the switch should forward this request message to all other controllers as a request forward message (`OFPT_REQUESTFORWAD`). The switch should send this message only to the controller channel in which the controller requested the switch to send this event. The controller can express its interest to receive this event by sending an asynchronous configuration message to the switch. Refer to the *Configuring the switch to send a list of asynchronous events the controller channel is interested in* recipe in *Chapter 2, Symmetric Messages and Asynchronous Messages (Part 2)*, for the procedure to configure the switch to send a request forward message to the controller.

How to do it...

The switch should build the OFPT_REQUESTFORWAD message with the following format, and send this message to the controllers that have already shown interest in this event:

```
/* Group/Meter request forwarding. */
struct ofp_requestforward_header {
struct ofp_header header;  /* Type OFPT_REQUESTFORWARD. */
struct ofp_header request; /* Request being forwarded. */
};
```

The `request` field should be set with the request that received from the controller. Refer to the `send_request_forward_message()` function in the `of/openflow.c` file for the procedure to send `request_forward_message` to the controller.

See also

- For more information regarding how the controller processes these request forward messages, refer to the *Processing a request forward message from the switch* recipe in *Chapter 2, Symmetric Messages and Asynchronous Messages (Part 2)*

Handling a packet-out message from the controller

Packet-out (`OFPT_PACKET_OUT`) messages are sent from the controller to the switch when the controller wishes to send a packet out through the switch's data path via a switch port.

How to do it...

There are two ways in which the controller can send a packet-out message to the switch:

1. Construct the full packet: In this case, the controller generates the complete packet and adds the action list field to the packet-out message. The action field contains a list of actions defining how the packet should be processed by the switch. If the switch receives a `packet_out` message with `buffer_id` set as `OFP_NO_BUFFER`, then the switch should look into the action list, and based on the action to be performed, it can do one of the following:
    1. Modify the packet and send it via the switch port mentioned in the action list
    2. Hand over the packet to OpenFlow's pipeline processing, based on the `OFPP_TABLE` specified in the action list

2. Use a packet buffer in the switch: In this mechanism, the switch should use the buffer that was created at the time of sending the `packet-in` message to the controller. While sending the `packet_in` message to the controller, the switch adds the `buffer_id` to the `packet_in` message. When the controller wants to send a `packet_out` message that uses this buffer, the controller includes this `buffer_id` in the `packet_out` message. On receiving the `packet_out` message with a valid `buffer_id`, the switch should fetch the packet from the buffer and send it via the switch port. Once the packet is sent out, the switch should free the memory allocated to the buffer, which was cached.

See also

- For more information regarding how the controller sends this packet-out message, refer to the *Sending a packet-out message to the switch* recipe in *Chapter 2, Symmetric Messages and Asynchronous Messages (Part 2)*

Handling a barrier message from the controller

The switch implementation could arbitrarily reorder the message sent from the controller to maximize its performance. So, if the controller wants to enforce the processing of the messages in order, then barrier messages are used. Barrier messages (`OFPT_TABLE_STATUS`) are sent from the controller to the switch to ensure message ordering.

The switch should not reorder any messages across the barrier message. For example, if the controller is sending a group add message, followed by a flow add message referencing the group, then the message order should be preserved in the barrier message.

How to do it...

When the controller wants to send messages that are related to each other, it sends a barrier message between these messages. The switch should process these messages as follows:

1. Messages before a barrier request should be processed fully before the barrier, including sending any resulting replies or errors.
2. The barrier request message should then be processed and a barrier reply should be sent. While sending the barrier reply message, the switch should copy the `xid` value from the barrier request message.
3. The switch should process the remaining messages.

Both the barrier request and barrier reply messages don't have any body. They only have the `ofp_header`.

See also

- For more information regarding how the controller sends this packet-out message, refer to the *Sending a barrier message to the switch* recipe in *Chapter 2, Symmetric Messages and Asynchronous Messages (Part 2)*

2

Symmetric Messages and Asynchronous Messages (Part 2)

This chapter describes the steps involved in sending and processing symmetric messages and asynchronous messages from the controller:

- Sending and processing a hello message
- Sending and processing an echo request and a reply messages
- Sending and processing an error message
- Experimenter message sending and processing
- Configuring the switch to send a list of asynchronous events the channel controller is interested in
- Fetching the list of possible asynchronous events that can come from the switch to the controller channel
- Processing a packet-in asynchronous message from the switch
- Processing a flow-removed asynchronous message from the switch
- Processing a port-status asynchronous message from the switch
- Processing a controller role-status message from the switch
- Processing a table-status asynchronous message from the switch
- Processing a request-forward message from the switch
- Sending a packet-out message to the switch
- Sending a barrier-message to the switch

For more information regarding symmetric messages and asynchronous messages, refer to the *Introduction* of *Chapter 2, Symmetric Messages and Asynchronous Messages (Part 1).*

Sending and processing a hello message

The `OFPT_HELLO` message is used by both the switch and the controller to identify and negotiate the OpenFlow version supported by both the devices. Hello messages should be sent from the controller once the TCP/TLS connection is established and is considered to be part of the communication channel establishment procedure.

> The controller should send a hello message to the switch immediately after establishing the TCP/TLS connection with the switch.

Getting started

To send a hello message, the controller should have established the TCP/TLS connection as defined in the *Connection setup on TCP and TLS* recipe of *Chapter 1, OpenFlow Channel Connection Establishment (Part 1).*

How to do it...

As the hello messages are transmitted by both the switch and the controller, the controller should be able to send, receive, and process the hello message. The following section explains these procedures in detail.

Sending the OFPT_HELLO message

The procedure to send a `OPPT_HELLO` message from the controller is similar to that of the switch. Refer to the *Sending and processing a hello message* recipe of *Chapter 2, Symmetric Messages and Asynchronous Messages (Part 1)*, for detailed information regarding the hello message format and the procedure used to send it.

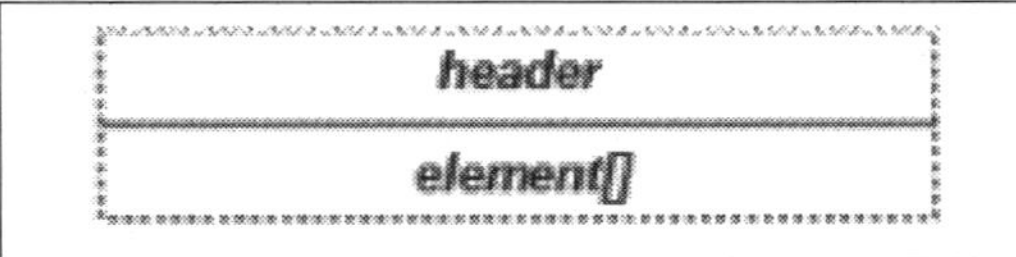

Receiving the OFPT_HELLO message

The controller should be able to receive and process `OFPT_HELLO` messages that are sent from the switch. The switch also uses the same message format, structures, and enumerations as defined in the previous section of this recipe. Once the controller receives the hello message, it should calculate the protocol version to be used for message exchange towards the switch. The procedure required to calculate the protocol version to be used is as follows:

- If the received hello message from the controller contains the optional `OFPHET_VERSIONBITMAP` element and the bitmap field contains a valid value, then the negotiated version should be the highest common version between the supported protocol versions in the switch, with the bitmap field in `OFPHET_VERSIONBITMAP` element.
- If the hello message doesn't contain any `OFPHET_VERSIONBITMAP` element, then the negotiated version should be the smallest of the controller-supported protocol version and the version field set in the OpenFlow header of the received hello message.

If the negotiated version is supported by the controller, then the OpenFlow connection between the controller and the switch continues. Otherwise, the controller should send an `OFPT_ERROR` message with the type field set `as OFPET_HELLO_FAILED`, the code field set as `OFPHFC_INCOMPATIBLE`, and an optional ASCII string explaining the situation in the data, and terminate the connection. Refer to the *Sending and processing error messages* recipe in this chapter for the procedure to send error messages.

There's more...

Once the controller and the switch negotiate the OpenFlow protocol version to be used, the connection establishment procedure is complete. From this instance, both the controller and the switch can send OpenFlow protocol messages among themselves. The controller should send a `OFPT_FEATURES_REQUEST` message to get the data path ID of the switch after successfully establishing the connection and negotiating the protocol version. Refer to the *Sending the switch configuration message to the switch* recipe in *Chapter 1, OpenFlow Channel Connection Establishment (Part 2)*, for the procedure to send the switch configuration message to the switch.

See also

- For more information regarding the procedure to establish the TCP/TLS connection, refer to the *Connection setup on TCP and TLS* recipe of *Chapter 1, OpenFlow Channel Connection Establishment (Part 1)*

Sending and processing an echo request and a reply message

Echo request and reply messages are used by both the controller and the switch to maintain and verify the liveliness of the controller-switch connection. Echo messages are also used to calculate the latency and bandwidth of the controller-switch connection.

On reception of the echo request message, the controller should respond an with echo reply message.

Getting started

To send echo request and reply messages, the TCP/TLS connection establishment procedure defined in the *Connection setup on TCP and TLS* recipe of *Chapter 1, OpenFlow Channel Connection Establishment (Part 1)* should be used.

How to do it...

As echo messages are transmitted by both the switch and the controller, the controller should be able to send, receive, and process these messages. The following sections explain these procedures in detail.

Sending the OFPT_ECHO_REQUEST message

The OpenFlow specification doesn't mention how frequently this echo message is to be sent from the controller. Similarly, it doesn't mention what the timeout (the longest period of time the switch should wait) for receiving the echo reply message from the switch should be. The controller may choose to send the echo request message at any time.

After sending the echo request message to the switch, the controller should wait for the echo reply message for the configured timeout period. If the controller doesn't receive the reply message from the switch, then it can terminate the TCP/TLS connection to the switch and wait for the switch to re-establish the connection.

The `OFPT_ECHO_REQUEST` message contains an OpenFlow header, followed by an undefined data field of arbitrary length. The data field might be filled with timestamp stating the time the echo request message was sent, or various lengths or values to measure the bandwidth, or zero-size to just check the liveliness of the connection.

Receiving OFPT_ECHO_REQUEST message

The controller should be able to receive and process `OFPT_ECHO_REQUEST` messages that are sent from the switch. The switch also uses the same message format, structures, and enumerations as defined in the previous section of this recipe. Once the controller receives the echo request message, it should create the `OFPT_ECHO_REPLY` message. The `OFPT_ECHO_REPLY` message consists of `ofp_header` and an optional arbitrary-length data field. While forming the echo reply message, the controller should copy the content present in arbitrary-length field of the request message to the reply message.

Processing OFPT_ECHO_REPLY message

The controller should be able to receive the echo reply message from the switch. If the controller sends the echo request message to calculate the latency or bandwidth, on receiving the echo reply message, the controller should parse the arbitrary-length data field. Then it can calculate the bandwidth, latency, and so on.

There's more...

If the OpenFlow controller implementation is divided into multiple layers, then echo request and reply processing should be handled in the deepest possible layer. For example, if the OpenFlow controller implementation is divided into user-space processing and kernel-space processing, then echo request and reply message handling should be present in the kernel space.

Sending and processing error message

Error messages are used by both the controller and the switch to notify the problem to other end of the connection. Error messages are typically used by the switch to inform the controller about failure of execution of the request sent from the controller.

How to do it...

Whenever the controller wants to send an error message to the switch, it should create the `OFPT_ERROR` message, which takes the following message format:

```
/* OFPT_ERROR: Error message (datapath -> the controller). */
struct ofp_error_msg {
struct ofp_header header;
uint16_t type;
uint16_t code;
```

```
uint8_t data[0]; /* Variable-length data. Interpreted based
on the type and code. No padding. */
};
```

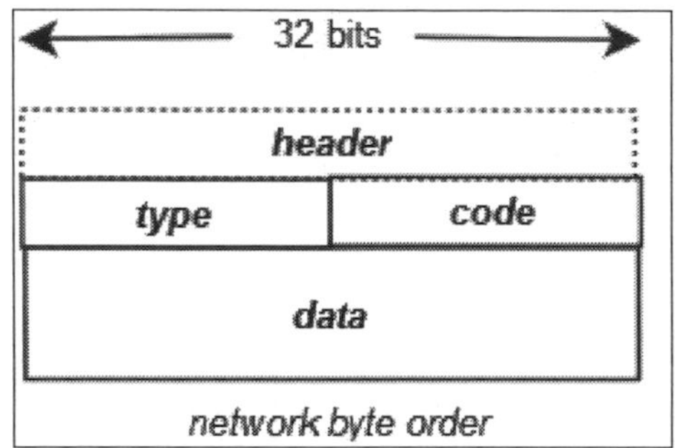

The `type` indicates the high-level type of the error. The `code` value is interpreted based on the type. The `data` value is a piece of variable-length data that is interpreted based on both type and value. The `data` field should contain an ASCII text string that adds details on why the error occurred. Refer to the *Common OpenFlow error codes* recipe in *Appendix, Common OpenFlow Headers, Structures, and Error Codes* for the possible values that the `type`, `code`, and `data` fields can take.

Unless otherwise specified, the `data` field should contain at least 64 bytes of the failed message that caused the error. If the failed message is shorter than 64 bytes, then the data field should contain the full message without any padding.

See also

- For more information regarding the possible values that the type, code, and data fields of the error message can take, refer to the *Common OpenFlow error codes* recipe in *Appendix, Common OpenFlow Headers, Structures, and Error Codes*

Sending and processing experimenter message

The experimenter messages are used by the vendor to define any additional functionality that is not covered as part of the OpenFlow specification. It is possible for a vendor to define their own functionality in the switch, which can be configured by the OpenFlow message.

How to do it...

The controller should create the experimenter message with the following format and send it to the switch:

```
/* Experimenter extension message. */
struct ofp_experimenter_msg {
struct ofp_header header; /* Type OFPT_EXPERIMENTER. */
uint32_t experimenter;     /* Experimenter ID:
* - MSB 0: low-order bytes are IEEE OUI.
* - MSB != 0: defined by ONF. */
uint32_t exp_type;         /* Experimenter defined. */
/* Experimenter-defined arbitrary additional data. */
uint8_t experimenter_data[0];
};
```

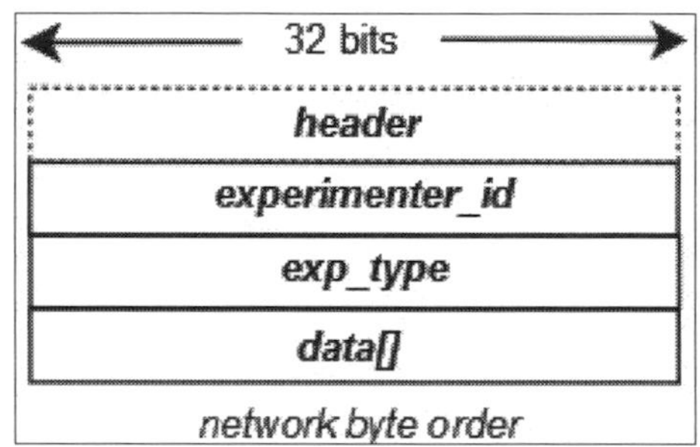

The `experimenter` field should be set with the identifier value that uniquely identifies the experimenter. The `experimenter` identifier could be allocated either by IEEE OUI or by the **Open Networking Foundation** (**ONF**). If the `experimenter` identifier is allocated by IEEE OUI, then the controller should set `MSB` as `0`. The next 3 bytes represent the experimenter ID. If the `experimenter` identifier is allocated by ONF, then the MSB should be set as a nonzero value.

If the experimenter doesn't have an identifier, they should contact the ONF for a unique experimenter ID.

The `exp_type` should be set with the `experimenter` type. The `experimenter` type is managed by the `experimenter` and can have any 32-bit value.

The `experimenter_data` field should be set with the value arbitrarily defined by `experimenter` and is uninterpreted by standard OpenFlow processing.

Configuring the switch to send a list of asynchronous events the controller channel is interested in

The OpenFlow specification provides a mechanism for the controller to inform a switch about the list of asynchronous events that the controller/controller channel is interested in. This is achieved by sending a "Set Asynchronous Configuration message" (`OFPT_SET_ASYNC`) to the switch. This is mostly useful when a switch is managed by multiple controllers and every controller wants to process only a subset of events. Using this feature, different controllers can subscribe to receive different notification messages from switches, resulting in the controller load balancing.

How to do it...

The message format to be used to send the `OFPT_SET_ASYNC` message is as follows:

```
/* Asynchronous message configuration. */
struct ofp_async_config {
struct ofp_header header; /* OFPT_GET_ASYNC_REPLY or
                           * OFPT_SET_ASYNC. */
/* Async config Property list - 0 or more */
struct ofp_async_config_prop_header properties[0];
};
```

The `property` list should be set with the list of asynchronous configuration events or property types that this controller channel is interested in. The `property` definition contains the property type, length, and associated data. The common header that will be used to send asynchronous configuration message is as follows:

```
/* Common header for all async config Properties */
struct ofp_async_config_prop_header {
uint16_t type;   /* One of OFPACPT_*. */
uint16_t length; /* Length in bytes of this property. */
};
```

The `type` field in the preceding structure will take any one of the values in the following enumeration:

```
/* Async Config property types.
* Low order bit cleared indicates a property for the slave role.
* Low order bit set indicates a property for the
* master/equal role.
*/
```

```
enum ofp_async_config_prop_type {
OFPACPT_PACKET_IN_SLAVE = 0,     /* Packet-in mask for slave. */
OFPACPT_PACKET_IN_MASTER = 1,    /* Packet-in mask for master. */
OFPACPT_PORT_STATUS_SLAVE = 2,   /* Port-status mask for slave. */
OFPACPT_PORT_STATUS_MASTER = 3,  /* Port-status mask for master. */
OFPACPT_FLOW_REMOVED_SLAVE = 4,  /* Flow removed mask for slave. */
OFPACPT_FLOW_REMOVED_MASTER = 5,/* Flow removed mask for master. */
OFPACPT_ROLE_STATUS_SLAVE = 6,   /* Role status mask for slave. */
OFPACPT_ROLE_STATUS_MASTER = 7,  /* Role status mask for master. */
OFPACPT_TABLE_STATUS_SLAVE = 8,  /* Table status mask for slave. */
OFPACPT_TABLE_STATUS_MASTER = 9,/* Table status mask for master. */
OFPACPT_REQUESTFORWARD_SLAVE = 10, /* RequestForward mask for
                                    * slave. */
OFPACPT_REQUESTFORWARD_MASTER = 11, /* RequestForward mask for
                                     * master. */
OFPTFPT_EXPERIMENTER_SLAVE = 0xFFFE, /* Experimenter for slave. */
OFPTFPT_EXPERIMENTER_MASTER = 0xFFFF,/* Experimenter for master. */
};
```

The controller in the OFPCR_ROLE_EQUAL or OFPCR_ROLE_MASTER role should use the property field in the OFPT_SET_ASYNC message, with the suffix as _MASTER. Similarly, the controller in the OFPCR_ROLE _SLAVE role should use the property field in the OFPT_SET_ASYNC message, with the suffix as _SLAVE. For instance, if a controller in OFPCR_ROLE_EQUAL wants to receive the packet-in event from the switch, then it should send an OFPT_SET_ASYNC message with the property type set as OFPACPT_PACKET_IN_MASTER.

The OFPACPT_PACKET_IN_SLAVE, OFPACPT_PACKET_IN_MASTER, OFPACPT_PORT_STATUS_SLAVE, OFPACPT_PORT_STATUS_MASTER, OFPACPT_FLOW_REMOVED_SLAVE, OFPACPT_FLOW_REMOVED_MASTER, OFPACPT_ROLE_STATUS_SLAVE and OFPACPT_ROLE_STATUS_MASTER, OFPACPT_TABLE_STATUS_SLAVE, OFPACPT_TABLE_STATUS_MASTER, and OFPACPT_REQUESTFORWARD_SLAVE and OFPACPT_REQUESTFORWARD_MASTER properties use the following structure and fields:

```
/* Various reason based properties */
struct ofp_async_config_prop_reasons {
uint16_t type;    /* One of OFPACPT_PACKET_IN_*,
                   * OFPACPT_PORT_STATUS_*,
                   * OFPACPT_FLOW_REMOVED_*,
                   * OFPACPT_ROLE_STATUS_*,
                   * OFPACPT_TABLE_STATUS_*,
                   * OFPACPT_REQUESTFORWARD_*. */
uint16_t length; /* Length in bytes of this property. */
uint32_t mask;    /* Bitmasks of reason values. */
};
```

If the controller wants to receive the asynchronous messages that you just saw, then it should send an asynchronous configuration message with the mask bit in `ofp_async_config_prop_reasons` set as `1`; `0` will disable the controller receiving the message of interest. For example, if a controller in the slave role wants to receive a port status change event with the reason as `OFPPR_MODIFY` (its value is 2; refer to the *Sending a port-status message to the controller* recipe in this chapter for the port status message's reason code), then it should send a message with the second bit set in the mask.

The `OFPTFPT_EXPERIMENTER_SLAVE` and `OFPTFPT_EXPERIMENTER_MASTER` properties use the following structure and fields:

```
/* Experimenter async config property */
struct ofp_async_config_prop_experimenter {
uint16_t type;    /* One of OFPTFPT_EXPERIMENTER_SLAVE,
                   * OFPTFPT_EXPERIMENTER_MASTER. */
uint16_t length; /* Length in bytes of this property. */
uint32_t experimenter; /* Experimenter ID which takes the
                        * same form as in struct
                        * ofp_experimenter_header. */
uint32_t exp_type;     /* Experimenter defined. */
/* Followed by:
* - Exactly (len - 12) bytes containing the experimenter data,then
* - Exactly (length + 7)/8*8 - (length) (between 0 and 7)
* bytes of all-zero bytes */
uint32_t experimenter_data[0];
};
```

The `experimenter` field in the experimenter ID should take the same format as the experimenter structure, which was described in the previous recipe.

How it works...

When the controller sends an `OFPT_SET_ASYNC` message to the switch, the switch saves this information and uses it as a filter to either send or drop asynchronous events to the controller.

Sending an asynchronous message on one channel does not affect any other channel (currently established or established in the future) to the same switch.

See also

- For more information regarding, how a switch processes an asynchronous configuration message, refer to the *Handling a Set Asynchronous Configuration message from the controller, which depicts the list of asynchronous events interested by the controller* recipe in *Chapter 2, Symmetric Messages & Asynchronous Messages (Part 1)*

Fetching the list of possible asynchronous events that can come from the switch to the controller channel

The OpenFlow specification provides a mechanism in the controller to fetch the list of asynchronous events that can be sent from the switch to the controller channel. This is achieved by sending the "Get Asynchronous Configuration message" (`OFPT GET_ASYNC_REQUEST`) to the switch.

How to do it...

The message format to be used to get the asynchronous configuration message (`OFPT_GET_ASYNC_REQUEST`) doesn't have any body other than `ofp_header`.

On receiving this `OFPT_GET_ASYNC_REQUEST` message, the switch responds with an `OFPT_GET_ASYNC_REPLY` message. The message format of `OFPT_GET_ASYNC_REPLY` is the same as that of the `OFPT_SET_ASYNC` message as described in the *Configuring the switch to send a list of asynchronous events the controller channel is interested in* recipe in this chapter.

The `property` list in the reply message contains the list of asynchronous configuration events or property types that the controller channel is interested in.

See also

- For more information on the switch procedure for handling the `OFPT_GET_ASYNC_REQUEST` message, refer to the *Handling a Get Asynchronous Configuration message from the controller, which is used to fetch the list of asynchronous events that will be sent from the switch* recipe in *Chapter 2, Symmetric Messages and Asynchronous Messages (Part 1)*
- For more information on how to send the `OFPT_SET_ASYNC` message from the controller, refer to the previous recipe

Processing a packet-in asynchronous message from the switch

Packet-in messages are sent from the switch to the controller to transfer a packet received from one of the switch ports to the controller for further processing.

Getting started

There are three ways in which the switch can send a packet-in event to the controller:

1. Table-miss entry. When there is no matching flow entry for the incoming packet, the switch can send the packet to the controller. Refer to the *Sending a switch configuration message to the switch* recipe in *Chapter 1, OpenFlow Channel Connection Establishment (Part 2)*, for the switch configuration required to send a table-miss packet to the controller.
2. TTL checking. After decrementing the TTL value in the packet, and if the TTL value reaches zero, the switch can send the packet to the controller. Refer to the *Sending a switch configuration message to the switch* recipe in *Chapter 1, OpenFlow Channel Connection Establishment (Part 2)*, for the switch configuration required to send a TTL check failure packet to the controller.
3. The "send to the controller" action in the matching entry (either the flow table entry or the group table entry) of the packet. Refer to the *Adding a new flow entry to the flow table* recipe in *Chapter 3, Flow Table and Flow Entry Modification Messages (Part 1)*, to know how to set a flow entry with action as send to the controller.

If the controller wants to receive the entire packet from the switch in the packet-in message, then the controller should configure the switch accordingly. Refer to the *Sending a switch configuration message to the switch* recipe in *Chapter 1, OpenFlow Channel Connection Establishment (Part 2)*, for the procedure to configure the switch to send a complete packet inside the packet-in message.

How to do it...

The message format that will be used by the switch to send a packet-in message is defined in the *Sending a packet-in message to the controller* recipe of *Chapter 2, Symmetric Messages and Asynchronous Messages (Part 1)*.

When the controller receives this message, it can process payload content of the packet-in message, and based on its control logic, it should take necessary action. The action could be either programming a flow entry or rewriting the packet content. Then it can do any one of the following: send it to the switch as a packet out message, send it to any controller application, or simply ignore this event.

See also

- For more information regarding how the switch sends packet-in message, refer to the *Sending a packet-in message to the controller* recipe of *Chapter 2, Symmetric Messages and Asynchronous Messages (Part 1)*

Processing a flow removed asynchronous message from the switch

Flow removed messages (`OFPT_FLOW_REMOVED`) are sent from the switch to the controller when a flow entry is removed from the flow table. The switch sends this message only to the controller channel wherein the controller requested the switch to send it.

Getting started

If the controller wants to receive flow removed events from a switch, then the controller should configure the switch accordingly. Refer to the *Sending a switch configuration message to the switch* recipe of *Chapter 1, OpenFlow Channel Connection Establishment (Part 2)* for the procedure to configure the switch to send flow removed messages.

How to do it...

The message format that will be used by the switch to send a `OFPT_FLOW_REMOVED` message is defined in the *Sending a flow-removed message to the controller* recipe in *Chapter 2, Symmetric Messages and Asynchronous Messages (Part 1)*.

When the controller receives this message, based on its control logic, it should take the necessary action. The action could be one of the following: reprogram the flow entry, send this event or notification to any controller application, or simply ignore this event.

See also

- For more information on how the switch sends this flow removed message, refer to the *Sending a flow-removed message to the controller* recipe of *Chapter 2, Symmetric Messages and Asynchronous Messages (Part 1)*

Processing a port-status asynchronous message from the switch

Port-status messages (`OFPT_PORT_STATUS`) are sent from the switch to the controller when there is any change in the port status or when a new port is added, removed, or modified in the switch's data path.

Getting started

If the controller wants to receive a port-status event from the switch, then it should configure the switch accordingly. Refer to the *Sending a switch configuration message to the switch* recipe of *Chapter 1, OpenFlow Channel Connection Establishment (Part 2)*, for the procedure to configure the switch to send a port status message.

How to do it...

The message format that will be used by the switch to send an `OFPT_PORT_STATUS` message is defined in the *Sending a port-status message to the controller* recipe in *Chapter 2, Symmetric Messages and Asynchronous Messages (Part 1)*.

When the controller receives this message, based on its control logic, it should take the necessary action. The action could be one of these: remove/modify some flow entries, send this event/notification to any controller application, or simply ignore this event.

See also

- For more information regarding how the switch sends this port status message, refer to the *Sending a port-status message to the controller* recipe in *Chapter 2, Symmetric Messages and Asynchronous Messages (Part 1)*

Processing the controller role-status message from the switch

Controller role-status messages (`OFPT_ROLE_STATUS`) are sent from a switch to a set of controllers when the role of a controller is changed as a result of the `OFPT_ROLE_REQUEST` message. For example, suppose there are three controllers connected to a switch (say `controller1`, `controller2`, and `controller3`) and `controller1` sends an `OFPT_ROLE_REQUEST` message to the switch. Then the switch sends `OFPT_ROLE_STATUS` to `controller2` and `controller3`.

Getting started

If the controller wants to receive a port-status event from the switch, then it should configure the switch accordingly. Refer to the *Sending a switch configuration message to the switch* recipe of *Chapter 1, OpenFlow Channel Connection Establishment (Part 2)*, for the procedure to configure the switch to send a port status message.

How to do it...

The message format that will be used by the switch to send an `OFPT_ROLE_STATUS` message is defined in the *Sending a controller role-status message to the controller* recipe in *Chapter 2, Symmetric Messages and Asynchronous Messages (Part 1)*.

The controller role-status message helps the controller in the master election process, as controller co-ordination is minimized by this asynchronous message. On reception of this message, the controller could reinitiate the master election within the set of controllers that are connected to the switch.

See also

- For more information on how the switch sends this controller role status message, refer to the *Sending a controller role-status message to the controller* recipe in *Chapter 2, Symmetric Messages and Asynchronous Messages (Part 1)*

Processing a table status asynchronous message from the switch

Table-status messages (`OFPT_TABLE_STATUS`) are sent from the switch to the controller when there is any change in the table status; for example, the number of entries in the table crosses the threshold value called the vacancy threshold.

Getting started

If the controller wants to receive a table status event from the switch, then it should configure the switch accordingly. Refer to the *Sending a switch configuration message to the switch* recipe in *Chapter 1, OpenFlow Channel Connection Establishment (Part 2)*, for the procedure to configure the switch to send a table status message.

How to do it...

The message format that will be used by the switch to send a `OFPT_TABLE_STATUS` message is defined in the *Sending a table-status message to the controller* recipe in *Chapter 2, Symmetric Messages and Asynchronous Messages (Part 1)*.

When the controller receives the table status message with the reason code as `vacancy_down`, it can choose to delete some entries from the table until it receives the `vacancy_up` event from the switch.

The table field represents the table description. Refer to the *Table structures* section of *Appendix, Common OpenFlow Headers, Structures, and Error Codes*, for detailed information on the table description's structure.

See also

- For more information on how the switch sends this table status message, refer to the *Sending a table-status message to the controller* recipe in *Chapter 2, Symmetric Messages and Asynchronous Messages (Part 1)*

Processing a request forward message from the switch

When a switch receives a modify request message from the controller to modify the state of a group or meter entries, after successful modification of the state, the switch should forward this request message to all other controllers as request forward messages (`OFPT_REQUESTFORWAD`). The switch sends this message only to the controller channel wherein the controller requested the switch to send it.

Getting started

If the controller wants to receive request forward messages from the switch, then it should configure the switch accordingly. Refer to the *Sending a switch configuration message to the switch* of *Chapter 1, OpenFlow Channel Connection Establishment (Part 2)*, for the procedure to configure the switch to send a request forward message.

How to do it...

The message format that will be used by the switch to send the `OFPT_REQUESTFORWAD` message is defined in the *Sending a request-forward message to the controller* recipe of *Chapter 2, Symmetric Messages and Asynchronous Messages (Part 1)*.

When the controller receives this message, based on its control logic, it should take the necessary action. The action could be to update the switch's copy of the flow table / meter table for high-availability purposes, send this event/notification to any controller application, or simply ignore this event.

Sending a packet-out message to the switch

Packet-out (`OFPT_PACKET_OUT`) messages are sent from the controller to the switch when the controller wishes to send a packet through the switch data path via a switch port.

There are two ways by which the controller can send packet-out message to the switch:

1. Construct the full packet. In this case, the controller generates the complete packet and adds an action list field in the `packet-out` message. The `action` field contains a list of actions defining how the packet should be processed by the switch. It may include packet modification, group processing, and an output port. It can also specify the `OFPP_TABLE` reserved port as an output action to process the packet through the OpenFlow pipeline.
2. Use a packet buffer in the switch. In this mechanism, the controller uses the buffer that was created at the time of sending the `packet-in` message to the controller by the switch. While sending the `packet_in` message to the controller, the switch adds the `buffer_id` in the `packet_in` message. When the controller wants to send a `packet_out` message that uses this buffer, it should include this `buffer_id` in the `packet_out` message.

How to do it...

The controller should form an `OFPT_PACKET_OUT` message with the following format and send it to the switch:

```
/* Send packet (controller -> datapath). */
struct ofp_packet_out {
struct ofp_header header;
uint32_t buffer_id;  /* ID assigned by datapath
                      * (OFP_NO_BUFFER if none). */
uint32_t in_port;    /* Packet's input port or OFPP_CONTROLLER. */
uint16_t actions_len;/* Size of action array in bytes. */
uint8_t pad[6];
struct ofp_action_header actions[0]; /*Action list - 0 or more. */
/* The variable size action list is optionally followed by
 * packet data. This data is only present and meaningful if
 * buffer_id == -1. */
```

```
uint8_t data[0]; /* Packet data. The length is inferred
                  * from the length field in the header. */
};
```

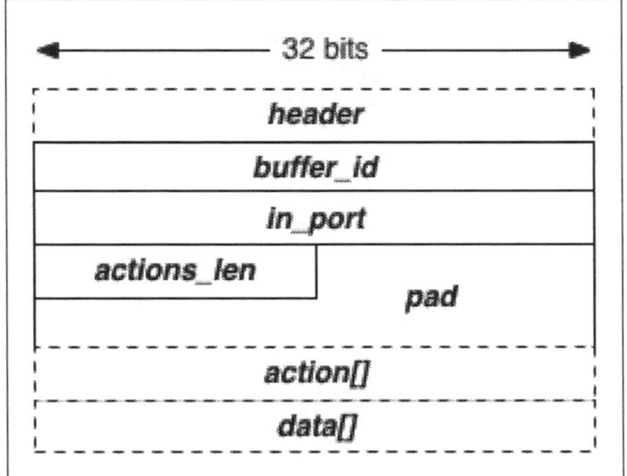

The `buffer_id` represents the ID of the packet buffer which switch should be used while forwarding the packet outside. If the controller doesn't want to use the packet buffer, then this field should be set as `OFP_NO_BUFFER`, whose value is `0 x ffffffff`.

The `in_port` field should be set with the ingress port that must be associated with the packet for OpenFlow processing. It should be either a valid standard switch or controller port (`OFPP_CONTROLLER`).

The `action` field should be set with the list of actions defining how the packet should be processed by the switch. It might include packet modification, group processing, and an output port. It could also specify the `OFPP_TABLE` reserved port as an output action to process the packet through the OpenFlow pipeline. If `OFPP_TABLE` is specified, the `in_port` field is used as the ingress port in the flow table lookup. There is a possibility that the `OFPP_TABLE` lookup in the switch results in forwarding the packet once again to the controller.

The controller should have a mechanism to detect and take action of these kinds of loops.

The `data` should be set with the packet that is constructed from the controller. Depending on the way, the fields in the packet-out message should be constructed in the controller.

Construct the packet and sending it for further pipeline processing in the switch

The `buffer_id` should be set to `OFP_NO_BUFFER`, whose value is `0 x ffffffff`.

The `in_port` field should be set with `OFPP_CONTROLLER`, and the `actions_len` should be set with the size of the action list.

The `actions` arrays should be set with a list of actions to be performed on the packet. The `actions` could be filled with `OFPP_TABLE` in order to send the packet via pipeline processing in the switch, starting from the first flow table. The `data` should be set with the packet that is constructed from the controller.

Using packet buffer in the switch

The `buffer_id` should be set with the valid buffer ID value, which was sent in the packet-in message from the switch to the controller. The `in_port` field should be set with a valid standard port, and the `actions_len` should be set with the size of the action list.

The `actions` arrays should be set with a list of actions to be performed on the packet. The `data` should be set with the packet that is constructed from the controller.

See also

- For more information regarding how the switch processes this packet-out message, refer to the *Handling a packet-out message from the controller* recipe in *Chapter 2, Symmetric Messages and Asynchronous Messages (Part 1)*

Sending a barrier message to the switch

Barrier messages (`OFPT_BARRIER_REQUEST`) are sent from a controller to a switch to ensure message ordering. If two controller messages are related to each other and need to be processed in the order, then a barrier message should be sent separating these messages. This is because the switch may arbitrarily reorder the message sent from the controller to maximize its performance. The switch won't reorder messages across a barrier message. For example, if the controller is sending a group add message, followed by a flow add message referencing the group, then the message order should be preserved in a barrier message.

How to do it...

When the controller wants to send a barrier request message, it should create a `OFPT_BARRIER_REQUEST` message. `OFPT_BARRIER_REQUEST` doesn't have any body, and so it takes the format of `ofp_header`.

After sending `OFPT_BARRIER_REQUEST`, the controller should wait for the `OFPT_BARRIER_REPLY` message from the switch.

See also

- For more information on how the switch processes this barrier message, refer to the *Handling a barrier message from the controller* recipe in *Chapter 2, Symmetric Messages and Asynchronous Messages (Part 1)* of this book

3
Flow Table and Flow Entry Modification Messages (Part 1)

This chapter describes in detail the flow table, flow table entries, flow table operations, and so on. It contains the following recipes:

- Modifying a flow table with eviction enabled
- Modifying a flow table with vacancy enabled
- Adding a new flow entry to a flow table
- Deleting a flow entry from a flow table
- Modifying a flow entry in a flow table
- Flow table synchronizations

Introduction

The OpenFlow flow table is one of the main components in the OpenFlow switch in packet processing. The OpenFlow switch should consist of one or more flow tables, which are part of the OpenFlow pipeline processing. The OpenFlow pipeline processing determines how the packets are processed and forwarded by the switch. The flow table acts as a datapath forwarding table of the traditional switch. When the OpenFlow switch contains more than one flow table, these tables should be numbered sequentially from zero to *n-1*, and the pipeline processing should start from the zeroth table.

The OpenFlow switch should have either a software-based or a hardware-based pipeline processing mechanism. The number of flow tables supported by the switch depends on the capability of the switch. The switch should initiate this capability to the controller at the time of initialization of the controller communication channel using a handshake message. Refer to the *Handling handshake message from the controller* recipe in *Chapter 1, OpenFlow Channel Connection Establishment (Part 1)* for more details on this.

Typically in hardware-based pipeline processing, one stage of the pipeline processing can process particular packet headers. That is, the first flow table will be able to process only the L2 header in the packet, the second flow table will be able to process only the L3 header, and so on. The controller has to know the capability of these pipeline stages before the flow programming starts. The `OFPMP_TABLE_FEATURES` multipart message will be used by the controller to fetch the capability of the flow table. Refer to the *Getting information about the switch using multipart messages* recipe in *Chapter 6, Handling Multipart State Information Messages (Part 1)* for more details about the `OFPMP_TABLE_FEATURES` message.

The components of the flow table entry are described in detail in the following diagram:

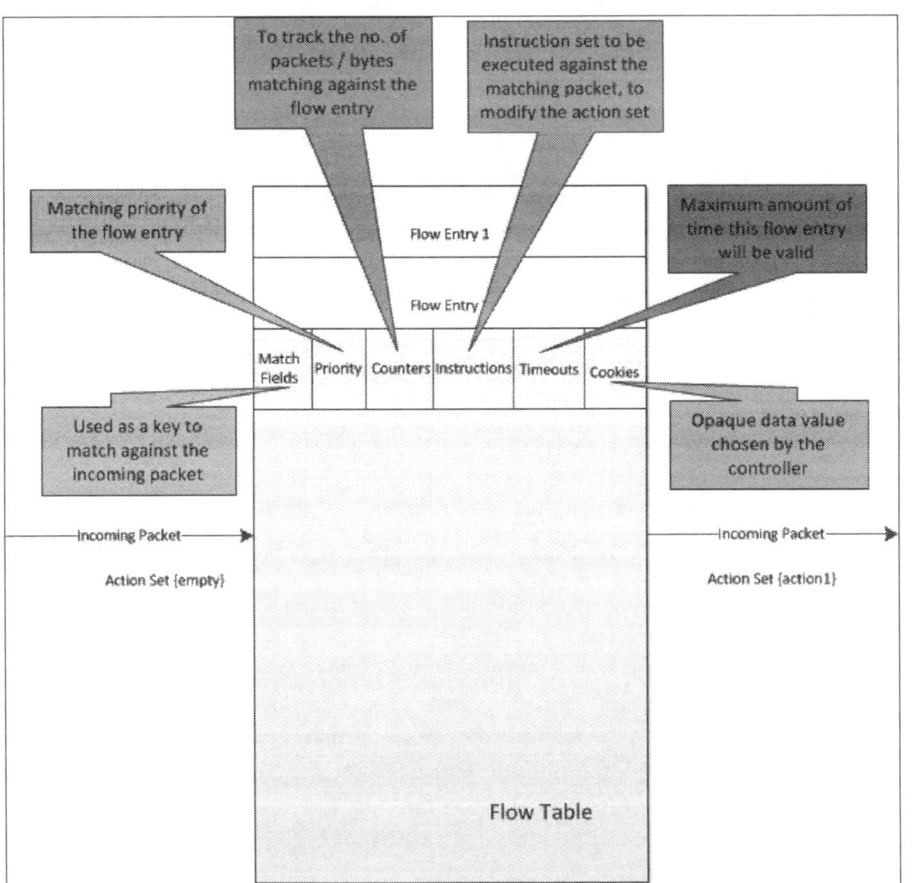

The flow table describes the following components:

- **Match Fields**: This is used as a key to match against the incoming packet
- **Priority**: This is the matching priority of the flow entries when there are two or more flow entries matched against the incoming packet
- **Counter**: This is used to track the number of packets matching against a particular flow entry
- **Instructions**: This is the instruction set to be executed against the matching packet
- **Timeout**: This specifies the maximum amount of time for which the flow entry is valid
- **Cookie**: This is an opaque value chosen by the controller

Refer to the subsequent recipes of this chapter for a detailed explanation of the flow table's entry fields.

The incoming packet should first be matched against the flow entries in the first flow table, and should then be matched to the subsequent flow tables based on the instruction set associated with the flow entry. The following diagram represents OpenFlow switch pipeline processing in detail:

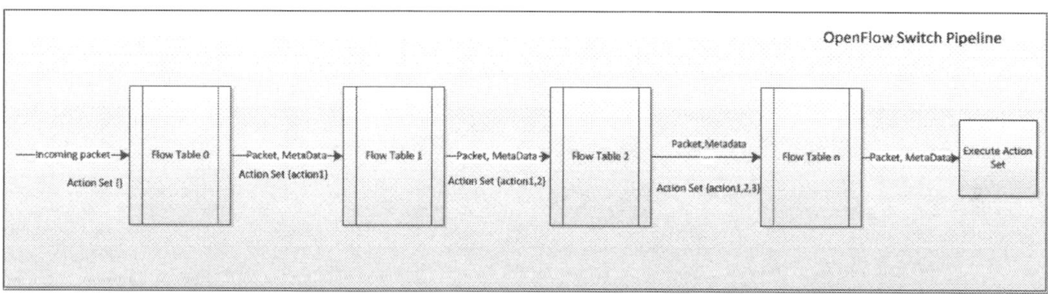

Here, **Flow Table 0**, **Flow Table 1**, and so on, represent the flow tables, which consist of flow entries. The input to each table consists of the incoming packet, metadata, and ingress port, along with the action set associated with the packet. The pipeline processing should start from **Flow Table 0**, with the incoming packets and a null/empty action set as the input. The packet headers, along with the metadata, incoming port, and so on, should be matched against the flow entries in the flow table, and the matching entry with the highest priority should be selected for further processing of the packet. Each flow entry is associated with the instruction set that should be executed before moving to the next stage of the pipeline. The instruction set may forward the packet to the next stage of the pipeline, add some metadata, update the action set, or forward the packet to subsequent pipeline stage.

Pipeline processing of the switch is described in detail in the following flowchart:

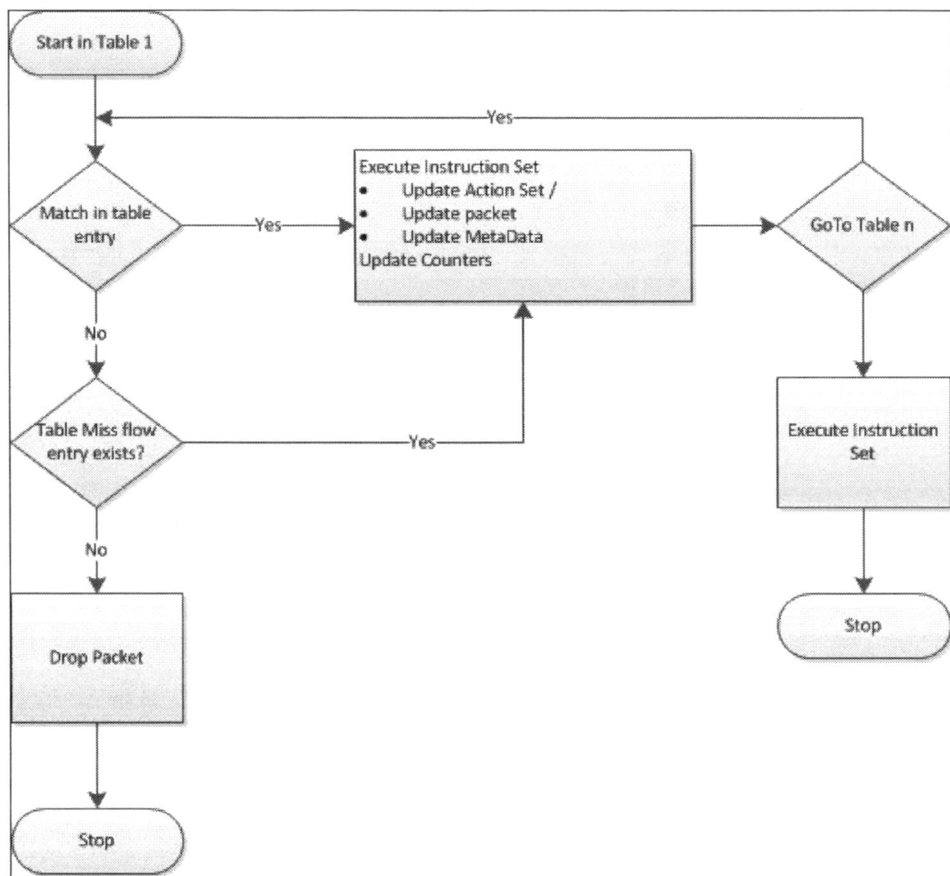

Every flow table in the OpenFlow switch should support a special entry called **table-miss flow entry**, which should be executed when there is no matching flow entry while performing the pipeline processing. Like other flow entries, the table-miss entry should also be added explicitly from the controller, and it has its configured value of expiry time.

> If a table-miss entry is not present in a flow table and the incoming packet is not matched against any of the flow entries, the packet should be dropped by default. However, this behavior can be changed by the switch configuration message, as explained in the *Handling the switch configuration message from the controller* recipe of *Chapter 1, OpenFlow Channel Connection Establishment (Part 1)*.

The switch should be able to create a flow table entry with the following constructs.

Flow table entry

The OpenFlow specification defines the flow table entry with constructs. This section describes these flow table entry constructs in detail:

- Match Fields
- Priority
- Counter
- Instructions
- Timeout
- Cookie

Match Fields

The OpenFlow match should consist of a match header and zero or more flow match fields. The flow match fields are described in the **OpenFlow Extensible Match** (**OXM**) format, which is a compact **type-length-value** (**TLV**) format of size ranging from 5 to 259 bytes. The flow match with a single OXM match field will look like this:

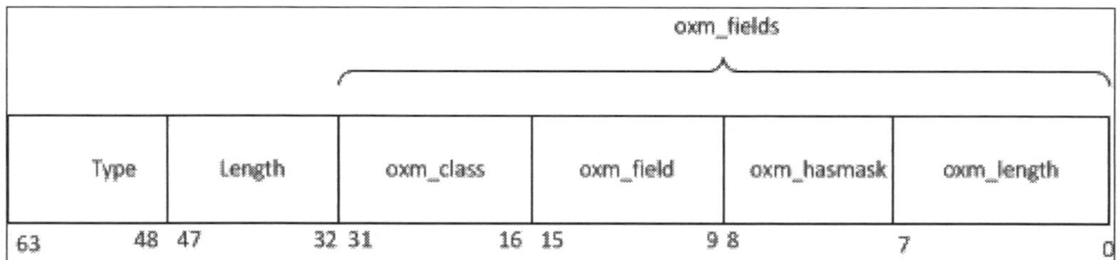

The type field should be set with the value as `OFPMT_OXM (1)`, which is defined in the `ofp_match_type` enumeration. The `length` field should be set with the actual length of the `ofp_match` structure, including all the match fields.

The `payload` field should be set with the set of OXM flow match fields. The OXM flow match field consists of a 4-byte header, followed by the entry's body. The OXM TLV header is described in *OpenFlow Switch Specification Version 1.4.0* as follows, which is in the network byte order:

Field	Width	Usage
`oxm_class`	16	Match a class, which can either be a member class or a reserved class
`oxm_field`	7	Match a field within a class
`oxm_hasmask`	1	Represent bitmask is included in the payload
`oxm_length`	8	Length of the OXM payload

The `oxm_class` and `oxm_field` (the most significant 23 bits of the header) are collectively known as `oxm_type`.

Oxm_class

The OXM match class (`oxm_class`) consists of match types. The OpenFlow specification defines two types of match classes, as follows:

- **ONF reserved classes**: These classes are allocated by ONF on a need basis, which uniquely identifies an ONF member and can be used by that ONF member. In this class, the higher order bit is set with a value of `0`.
- **ONF member classes**: These classes are used by the OpenFlow specification itself. In them, the higher order bit is set with a value of `1` (that is, `0x8***`).

The `oxm_class` are defined as follows:

```
/* OXM Class IDs.
 * The high order bit differentiate reserved classes from member
 * classes.
 * Classes 0x0000 to 0x7FFF are member classes, allocated by ONF.
 * Classes 0x8000 to 0xFFFE are reserved classes, reserved for
 * standardisation.
 */
enum ofp_oxm_class {
OFPXMC_NXM_0 = 0x0000, /* Backward compatibility with NXM */
OFPXMC_NXM_1 = 0x0001, /* Backward compatibility with NXM */
OFPXMC_OPENFLOW_BASIC = 0x8000, /* Basic class for OpenFlow */
OFPXMC_EXPERIMENTER = 0xFFFF,   /* Experimenter class */
};
```

The first two match classes are reserved for the **Nicira Extensible Match** (**NXM**) specification. `OFPXMC_OPENFLOW_BASIC` should be used for this OpenFlow specification, and `OFPXMC_EXPERIMENTER` should be used for experimenter matches.

Oxm_field

The `oxm_field` will be used by pipeline processing of the switch to match against the packets that hit a particular flow table. The OpenFlow specification defines the set of match fields for the `OFPXMC_OPENFLOW_BASIC` class which are defined in *Table 3.3*.

Oxm_haskmask

The `oxm_hasmask` field indicates that the bitmask is included in the payload. When `oxm_hasmask` is not set, the OXM TLV's body contains the value of the field, called `oxm_value`, to be matched against the packet.

When `oxm_hasmask` is set, the OXM TLV's body contains the value of the field to be matched along with the bitmask, which should be used while performing the match. The `length` value of the bitmask is the same as the length of the value to be matched. The bit value of `1` in bitmask with position *x* means the packet should be matched against `oxm_value` on position *x*. A `0` value on `oxm_mask` doesn't add any constraint on the corresponding bit in the field. Similarly, 0 in `oxm_mask`, and 1 in `oxm_value` on the same position, result in an error, and the switch should send an error message of the `OFPET_BAD_MATCH` type and the `OFPBMC_BAD_WILDCARDS` code in such a case.

When the `oxm_hasmask` value is 1, the OXM TLV's body contains the bitmask, along with the actual value. Hence, the effective length of the OXM TLV's body is doubled, and it is always even.

The following table explains the constraints that the `oxm_mask` and `oxm_value` bits place on the corresponding field bits in the packet when using masking:

	oxm_value	
oxm_mask	0	1
0	no constraint	error
1	must be 0	must be 1

Table 3.2

All match fields are in different sizes. They have different prerequisites and masking capabilities as follows, which is also described in OpenFlow Switch Specification Version 1.4.0. All fields mentioned in the following table refer to outermost header unless explicitly mentioned:

Field	Bits	Mask	Prerequisite	Description
`OXM_OF_IN_PORT*`	32	No	None	Ingress port. Numerical representation of the incoming port, starting from 1. This may be a physical or switch-defined logical port.

Field	Bits	Mask	Prerequisite	Description
OXM_OF_IN_PHY_PORT	32	No	IN_PORT present	Physical port. In ofp_packet_in messages, underlying physical port when packet received on a logical port.
OXM_OF_METADATA	64	Yes	None	Table metadata. This field is used to pass information between tables.
OXM_OF_ETH_DST*	48	Yes	None	The Ethernet destination MAC address.
OXM_OF_ETH_SRC*	48	Yes	None	The Ethernet source MAC address.
OXM_OF_ETH_TYPE*	16	No	None	The Ethernet type of the OpenFlow packet payload, after VLAN tags.
OXM_OF_VLAN_VID	12 + 1	Yes	None	This is the VLAN-ID from the 802.1Q header. The CFI bit indicates the presence of a valid VLAN-ID.
OXM_OF_VLAN_PCP	3	No	VLAN_VID!=NONE	VLAN-PCP from the 802.1Q header.
OXM_OF_IP_DSCP	6	No	ETH_TYPE=0x0800/ ETH_TYPE=0x86dd	DiffServ Code Point (DSCP). Part of the IPv4 ToS field or the IPv6 Traffic Class field.
OXM_OF_IP_ECN	2	No	ETH_TYPE=0x0800/ ETH_TYPE=0x86dd	ECN bits of the IP header. Part of the IPv4 ToS field or the IPv6 Traffic Class field.
OXM_OF_IP_PROTO*	8	No	ETH_TYPE=0x0800/ ETH_TYPE=0x86dd	IPv4 or IPv6 protocol number.

Field	Bits	Mask	Prerequisite	Description
OXM_OF_IPV4_SRC*	32	Yes	ETH TYPE=0x0800	This is the IPv4 source address. It can use a subnet mask or arbitrary bitmask.
OXM_OF_IPV4_DST*	32	Yes	ETH TYPE=0x0800	This is the IPv4 destination address. It can use a subnet mask or arbitrary bitmask.
OXM_OF_TCP_SRC*	16	No	IP PROTO=6	The TCP source port.
OXM_OF_TCP_DST*	16	No	IP PROTO=6	The TCP destination port.
OXM_OF_UDP_SRC*	16	No	IP PROTO=17	The UDP source port.
OXM_OF_UDP_DST*	16	No	IP PROTO=17	The UDP destination port.
OXM_OF_SCTP_SRC	16	No	IP PROTO=132	The SCTP source port.
OXM_OF_SCTP_DST	16	No	IP PROTO=132	The SCTP destination port.
OXM_OF_ICMPV4_TYPE	8	No	IP PROTO=1	The ICMP type.
OXM_OF_ICMPV4_CODE	8	No	IP PROTO=1	The ICMP code.
OXM_OF_ARP_OP	16	No	ETH TYPE=0x0806	The ARP opcode.
OXM_OF_ARP_SPA	32	Yes	ETH TYPE=0x0806	This is the source IPv4 address in the ARP payload. Can use a subnet mask or arbitrary bitmask
OXM_OF_ARP_TPA	32	Yes	ETH TYPE=0x0806	Target IPv4 address in the ARP payload. Can use subnet mask or arbitrary bitmask.
OXM_OF_ARP_SHA	48	Yes	ETH TYPE=0x0806	Source Ethernet address in the ARP payload.
OXM_OF_ARP_THA	48	Yes	ETH TYPE=0x0806	Target Ethernet address in the ARP payload.

Field	**Bits**	**Mask**	**Prerequisite**	**Description**
OXM_OF_IPV6_SRC*	128	Yes	ETH TYPE=0x86dd	IPv6 source address. Can use a subnet mask or arbitrary bitmask
OXM_OF_IPV6_DST*	128	Yes	ETH TYPE=0x86dd	IPv6 destination address. Can use a subnet mask or arbitrary bitmask
OXM_OF_IPV6_FLABEL	20	Yes	ETH TYPE=0x86dd	IPv6 flow label.
OXM_OF_ICMPV6_TYPE	8	No	IP PROTO=58	ICMPv6 type.
OXM_OF_ICMPV6_CODE	8	No	IP PROTO=58	ICMPv6 code.
OXM_OF_IPV6_ND_TARGET	128	No	ICMPV6 TYPE=135 or ICMPV6 TYPE=136	The target address in an IPv6 Neighbor Discovery message.
OXM_OF_IPV6_ND_SLL	48	No	ICMPV6 TYPE=135	The source link-layer address option in an IPv6 Neighbor Discovery message.
OXM_OF_IPV6_ND_TLL	48	No	ICMPV6 TYPE=136	The target link-layer address option in an IPv6 Neighbor Discovery message.
OXM_OF_MPLS_LABEL	20	No	ETH TYPE=0x8847 or ETH TYPE=0x8848	The `LABEL` in the first MPLS shim header.
OXM_OF_MPLS_TC	3	No	ETH TYPE=0x8847 or ETH TYPE=0x8848	The TC in the first MPLS shim header.
OXM_OF_MPLS_BOS	1	No	ETH TYPE=0x8847 or ETH TYPE=0x8848	The BoS bit (Bottom-of-Stack bit) in the first MPLS shim header.
OXM_OF_PBB_ISID	24	Yes	ETH TYPE=0x88E7	The `I-SID` field in the first PBB service instance tag.
OXM_OF_TUNNEL_ID	64	Yes	None	The Metadata associated with a logical port*.

Field	Bits	Mask	Prerequisite	Description
OXM_OF_IPV6_EXTHDR	9	Yes	ETH TYPE=0x86dd	IPv6 Extension Header pseudo-field.
OXM_OF_PBB_UCA	1	No	ETH TYPE=0x88E7	The UCA field in the first PBB service instance tag.

Table 3.3

When there are multiple OXM TLVs, the packet field should be matched against all the matching fields and constraints of all the OXM TLVs.

Priority

The `priority` field specifies the matching precedence of this flow entry. When an incoming packet is matched against two or more entries in a flow table, then the `priority` field will be used to break the tie.

Counter

The `counter` field is used for statistical purposes; it will be updated when the packet is matched against this entry. The following table specifies the list of counters related to the flow table and flow entries defined in OpenFlow Switch Specification Version 1.4.0:

Counter	Bits	Required?
Per flow table		
Reference count (active entries)	32	Yes
Packet lookups	64	No
Packet matches	64	No
Per flow entry		
Received packets	64	No
Received bytes	64	No
Duration (seconds)	32	Yes
Duration (nanoseconds)	32	No

Table 3.4

Instructions

The instruction set contains a set of instructions that should be executed when the packet is matched against the flow entry. This instruction set may change the packet header or action set associated with the packet or stage in the pipeline processing. The OpenFlow specification has imposed some constraints on instructions related to the order in which the instruction should be executed by the switch. All instructions defined in the specifications are not mandatory instructions.

The following table describes the instructions in detail, which is defined in OpenFlow Switch Specification Version 1.4.0:

Instruction	**Required instruction**	**Constraint**	**Description**
Meter **meter-id**	No	Should be executed before the Apply-Actions instruction	This instructs the packets to be directed to a meter table with id as meter-id.
Apply-actions **action(s)**	No	None	This specifies that the actions should be applied immediately over the packet, without any change to the action set. This instruction is used to change the packet headers before forwarding the packet to the next table. The actions are specified as an action list, which is described in detail in the next recipe.
Clear-Actions	No	Should be executed before Write-Actions	This clears all the existing actions in the action list associated with the packet.
Write-Actions **action(s)**	Yes	None	This inserts a new action into the existing action list. If the specified action with the type is already present in the action list, the switch should overwrite the existing action with this new action.
Write-Metadata **metadata / mask**	No	None	This instruction is used to insert a masked metadata value into the metadata field.
Goto-Table **next-table-id**	Yes	Should be executed after applying all the instructions	This specifies the next table to be used by the switch for its pipeline processing. Here, the table-id should be greater that the current table-id.

Table 3.5

The instruction set associated with a flow entry should not contain more than one entry of the same type and the order of execution of instructions in the instruction set should be the same as the order you just saw.

If the OpenFlow switch can't execute the instruction set, the switch should reject the flow table entry and send an unsupported flow error message to the controller. The structures used to define the various flow instructions are described in detail in the `of/openflow.c` file.

Action set

Unlike all the fields in the flow entry that are associated with the flow-entry, the action set is associated with the packet, and not the flow-entry. The action set will be empty when the pipeline processing starts. Then, entries get added or removed from it, either by the Write-Action instruction or by the Clear-Action instruction. Among the tables, the action set will be carried over. When executing the instruction set, if the instruction set doesn't contain the Goto-Table instruction, the pipeline processing will stop and the actions present in the action set will be executed.

Action list

When the switch wants to change or update the packet header before forwarding it to the next stage of pipeline processing, the action list can be used. The action list is also used to execute multiple actions of the same type. It is associated with the Apply-Action instruction and the Packet-Out message. The switch should execute the actions in the actions list in the order.

After the execution of all the actions in the action list in the Apply-Action instruction, the modified packet should be forwarded to the pipeline execution. The action set of the packet should remain unchanged because of the execution action list.

Action

The set of actions specified in OpenFlow Switch Specification Version 1.4.0 are as follows:

Action	Required action	Description
Output	Yes	This action is used to forward a packet to an OpenFlow port. The ports can either be physical, logical, or reserved ports.
Set-queue	No	This action is used in conjunction with the Output action. It specifies on which queue attached to a port should be used to queue and forward the packet.
Drop	Yes	The OpenFlow specification doesn't specify an explicit drop action. When there is no action set associated with the packet after the pipeline processing, the packet should be dropped.
Group	Yes	When a packet has to be processed by the group table, the action should be set to group action.

Action	Required action	Description
Push-tag/ pop-tag	No	This action is used to push/pop a tag from the packet. The tag can be any one of a MPLS header, VLAN header or PBB header. The tags should be pushed as outermost tag in the outermost valid location for that tag. Refer to *Table 1.1* for more details.
Set-field	No	When a packet header value has to be set, this action should be used. The various set field actions are identified by the field type, and each field represents a particular header field to be set or modified. The Set-field action type is always associated with the outermost headers unless it is mentioned explicitly in the set-field.
Change-TTL	No	When the TTL value in the packet header needs to be changed, the Change-TTL action should be used. This action should be used to change the TTL of an IP header, MPLS header or the IPv6 hop limit. Similar to other actions, the Change-TTL action is associated with the outermost header. *Table 1.2* covers the various TTL actions, the associated data, and descriptions.

Table 3.6

The following table illustrates the VLAN header with its actions and associated data :

Action	Associated data	Description
Push VLAN header	Ethertype	Push a new VLAN header onto the packet
Pop VLAN header		Pop the outer-most VLAN header from the packet
Push MPLS header	Ethertype	Push a new MPLS shim header onto the packet
Pop MPLS header	Ethertype	Pop the outermost MPLS tag or shim header from the packet
Push PBB header	Ethertype	Push a new PBB service instance header (I-TAG TCI) onto the packet
Pop PBB header		Pop the outermost PBB service instance header (I-TAG TCI) from the packet

Table 1.1

The following table covers the TTL actions and its associated data:

Action	Associated Data	Description
Set MPLS TTL	New MPLS TTL (8 bits)	Replace the existing MPLS TTL. This applies only to packets with an existing MPLS shim header.
Decrement MPLS TTL		Decrement the MPLS TTL. This applies only to packets with an existing MPLS shim header.
Set IP TTL	New IP TTL (8 bits)	Replace the existing Ipv4 TTL or Ipv6 Hop Limit and update the IP checksum. This applies only to Ipv4 and Ipv6 packets.
Decrement IP TTL		Decrement the Ipv4 TTL or Ipv6 Hop Limit field, and update the IP checksum. This applies only to Ipv4 and Ipv6 packets.
Copy TTL outwards		Copy the TTL from the next-to-outermost header to the outermost header with TTL. The copy can be IP-to-IP, MPLS-to-MPLS, or IP-to-MPLS.
Copy TTL inwards		Copy the TTL from the outermost header to the next-to-outermost header with TTL. The copy can be IP-to-IP, MPLS-to-MPLS, or MPLS-to-IP.

Table 1.2

The actions inside the action set should be executed in the following order, irrespective of the order in which they are added to the action set:

- Copy TTL inwards
- Pop
- Push-MPLS
- Push-PBB
- Push-VLAN
- Copy TTL outwards
- Decrement TTL
- Set

- Qos
- Group
- Output

Timeout

The OpenFlow specification has defined two different timeouts for each flow entry as `idle_timeout` and `hard_timeout`. These values are set by the controller to tell the switch the timeout, or expiry time, of a flow entry. On expiration of any of these timeout values, the switch should remove the flow entry from the flow table.

`Idle_timeout` is the timeout period that a switch should use to remove a flow entry when there is no matching packet for that flow entry. If a switch doesn't receive a packet during a period of `idle_timeout`, the switch should remove that entry from the flow table.

`Hard_timeout` is the timeout period that a switch should use to remove the flow entry from the time of its installation. If the `hard_timeout` period lapses in a switch for a particular flow entry, the switch should remove that entry from the flow table.

Cookie

The `cookie` field is filled with an opaque number generated by the controller. This `cookie` field will be used for any subsequent operation on the flow entry, such as removing the flow entry or querying the flow entry for statistics.

Modifying a flow table with eviction enabled

Eviction is one of the mechanisms provided by the OpenFlow specification to remove flow entries from the flow table to avoid overflow in the flow table entries. When the flow table in the switch is full, new flow entries can't be added to the flow table, which results in the switch returning an error message to the controller. This leads to a problematic situation for the controller, and the controller should take the necessary steps to remove some flow entries from the switch while it is in this adverse condition. To avoid this situation and come out of this problematic scenario, the OpenFlow Specification defines two mechanisms, as follows:

- **Eviction**: This mechanism is described in detail in this recipe
- **Vacancy**: This mechanism is described in detail in the next recipe

With eviction enabled on a particular flow table, the switch itself should remove the flow entry from the flow table, based on some specific criteria of the flow entry. The `OFP_TABLE_MOD` message is used to enable or disable eviction in a flow table.

Eviction is an optional feature that can be supported in the switch.

How to do it...

The controller sends a `OFP_TABLE_MOD` message to the switch to enable flow entry eviction for a particular flow table. The switch should be able to process this message, and based on the eviction scheme to be used, it should create appropriate functions to perform eviction.

`OFP_TABLE_MOD` is also used to enable vacancy on the flow table. Refer to the next recipe for more information regarding vacancy.

The message format that will be used by the controller to send the table modification message is defined in the *Modifying a flow table with eviction enabled* recipe in *Chapter 3, Flow Table and Flow Entry Modification Messages (Part 2)*. If a particular flow table is configured with flow eviction, then the switch could evict flow entries from the flow table when it wants to reclaim or reuse some of the flow entries. The entries to be evicted from the flow table are implementation-specific. However, the OpenFlow specification defines three mechanisms for choosing the flow entry to be evicted, as follows:

- **Eviction based on the importance field**: In this scheme, the switch's eviction mechanism should use the importance field in the flow entry. The flow entry with less importance should be evicted before the flow entries with higher importance.
- **Eviction based on the remaining lifetime**: In this scheme, the switch's eviction mechanism should use the remaining lifetime field of the flow entry to choose the entry to be evicted. The entries with the shortest remaining lifetime should be evicted first.
- **Eviction based on other switch criteria**: In this scheme, the switch can implement its own constraint to choose the flow entry to be evicted first.

See also

- For more information regarding how the controller sends the `OFP_TABLE_MOD` message, refer to the *Modifying a flow table with eviction enabled* recipe in *Chapter 3, Flow Table and Flow Entry Modification Messages (Part 2)*
- Refer to the `process_table_modify_message()` function in the `of/openflow.c` file for the procedure to handle the table modification message from the controller

Modifying a flow table with vacancy enabled

The OpenFlow specification defines a mechanism in the switch to intimate the controller whenever the switch's resources (especially the number of flow table entries) are reaching a threshold value, called vacancy threshold. Unlike the eviction mechanism—wherein the switch itself removes the flow entry from the flow table—when the vacancy is enabled, the switch intimates the controller about this. This mechanism takes care of the controller to gracefully delete or modify the existing flow entries in the system whenever the switch is reaching its threshold point.

How to do it...

The controller sends an `OFP_TABLE_MOD` message to the switch, with the `config` field set as `OFPTC_VACANCY_EVENTS` to enable vacancy for a particular flow table. The switch should process this message and generate the `OFPT_TABLE_STATUS` event or message for the controller whenever the number of flow entries in the flow tables crosses the vacancy threshold value.

`OFP_TABLE_MOD` is also used to enable the eviction mechanism for the flow table. Refer to the previous recipe for more information regarding the eviction mechanism.

The message format that will be used by the controller to send the table modification message is defined in the *Modifying a flow table with vacancy enabled* recipe in *Chapter 3, Flow Table and Flow Entry Modification Messages (Part 2)*.

When the vacancy is enabled in a switch, it can generate two types of vacancy events, as follows:

- `Vacancy_down`: This event should be generated by the switch when the remaining space in a flow table is less than the configured value of the `vacancy_down` threshold
- `Vacancy_up`: This event is generated by the switch when the remaining space in the flow table is more than the configured value of the `vacancy_up` threshold

Both the `Vacancy_down` and `Vacancy_up` events are intimated to the controller using `OFPT_TABLE_STATUS`, with the reason type as either `OFPTR_VACANCY_DOWN` or `OFPTR_VACANCY_UP`, based on the event. Refer to the *Sending a table-status message to the controller* recipe in *Chapter 2, Symmetric Messages and Asynchronous Messages (Part 1)* for the procedure to generate vacancy events from the switch.

In the `OFP_TABLE_MOD` message, if the value of `vacancy_down` is greater than `vacancy_up`, an error message should be sent to the controller with the type as `OFPET_BAD_PROPERTY` and code as `OFPBPC_BAD_VALUE`. To generate the error message, refer to the *Sending and processing error messages* section of *Chapter 2, Symmetric Messages & Asynchronous Messages (Part 1)*.

There's more...

When enabling the vacancy event, if the current vacancy is less than the `vacancy_up` event value, then the `vacancy_up` event should be enabled and the `vacancy_down` event should be disabled. The current vacancy refers to the number of empty/unconfigured flow entries present in the flow table as a percentage. If the current vacancy is greater than or equal to `vacancy_up`, the `vacancy_down` event should be enabled and the `vacancy_up` event should be disabled.

See also

- For more information regarding how the controller sends the `OFP_TABLE_MOD` message, refer to the *Modifying a flow table with eviction enabled* recipe in *Chapter 3, Flow Table and Flow Entry Modification Messages (Part 2)*
- Refer to the `process_table_modify_message()` function in the `of/openflow.c` file for the procedure to handle the table modification message from the controller

Adding a new flow entry to a flow table

When the controller wants to program the flow table entry, it sends a flow entry modification message (`OFPT_FLOW_MOD`) to the switch. This message contains the information required to program the flow table, which includes the flow match field, priority, instruction set, timeout, and so on.

The `OFPT_FLOW_MOD` message is used for flow entry operations such as adding a new flow entry, deleting an existing flow entry, and modifying a flow entry in a flow table.

How to do it...

The message format that will be used by the controller to send the `OFPT_FLOW_MOD` message is defined in the *Modifying a flow table with eviction enabled* recipe in *Chapter 3, Flow Table and Flow Entry Modification Messages (Part 2)*.

When OFPFF_SEND_FLOW_REM is set in the OFPFC_ADD message, the switch should send a flow removed message to the controller whenever a flow is deleted from the switch, either by timeout or by the eviction mechanism.

When OFPFF_CHECK_OVERLAP is set in the OFPFC_ADD message, the switch should check whether there is any conflicting entry present in the flow table with the same priority. If so, the switch should send an error message to the controller, with the type as OFPET_FLOW_MOD_FAILED and code as OFPFMFC_OVERLAP.

Two entries in a table are said to be a conflicting when a packet can be matched against two entries in the table that have the same match fields and priority.

OFPFF_RESET_COUNTS doesn't have any significance in the OFPFC_ADD message, and so the switch should ignore this flag.

If OFPFF_NO_PKT_COUNTS is set in the OFPFC_ADD message, the switch need not keep track of the packet count associated with that flow entry. Hence, the switch pipeline processing entity need not update the statistical counts for that entry.

If OFPFF_NO_PKT_COUNTS is set in the OFPFC_ADD message, the switch need not keep track of the byte count associated with that flow entry. Hence, the switch pipeline processing entity need not update the statistical counts for that entry.

The importance field is set with the importance of the flow entry. The switch should use this field value during the eviction processing. Refer to the previous recipe for more information about the switch eviction mechanism.

The instruction field is set with the instruction set associated with the flow entry.
If the instruction set is not valid, the switch should send an error message with the type as OFPET_BAD_INSTRUCTION and code as OFPBIC_UNKNOWN_INST.

See also

- For more information regarding how the controller sends the OFPT_FLOW_MOD message, refer to the *Adding a new flow entry to a flow table* recipe of *Chapter3, Flow Table and Flow Entry Modification Messages (Part 2)*
- Refer to the process_flow_modify_message() function in the of/openflow.c file for the procedure to handle flow add messages from the controller

Deleting a flow entry in a flow table

When the controller wants to delete a flow table entry, it sends a flow entry modification message (`OFPT_FLOW_MOD`) to the switch, with the command value set as `OFPFC_DELETE` / `OFPFC_DELETE_STRICT`. This flow table modification message contains the information required to identify and delete the entry from the flow table.

How to do it...

The message format that will be used by the controller to send the `OFPT_FLOW_MOD` message is defined in the *Adding a new flow entry to the flow table* recipe in *Chapter3, Flow Table and Flow Entry Modification Messages (Part 2)*. The OpenFlow specification defines two different variants for deleting the flow entry as strict and non-strict versions.

When the switch receives the `OFPT_FLOW_MOD` message with the command field set as `OFPFC_DELETE_STRICT`, all the fields in the flow modification message should be matched strictly against the flow table entry, and should be deleted from the flow table.

When the switch receives the `OFPT_FLOW_MOD` message with the command field set as `OFPFC_DELETE`, the switch should select the flow entry to be deleted, which either exactly matches or has more match fields present in it than the flow modification message. Once these messages are selected, these flow entries should be deleted. For example, suppose there are two flow entries in the flow table with match fields, as follows:

- TCP port 80 and Incoming port as 1
- TCP port 80 and Incoming port as 2

Also, the switch receives the flow delete message from the controller with the match as TCP port 80. Then the strict version of the delete message shouldn't delete any entry, as the match specifies that only the match field with port 80 should be deleted. However, the non-strict version should delete both of these entries.

See also

- For more information regarding how the controller sends the `OFPT_FLOW_MOD` message, refer to the *Deleting a flow entry from the flow table* recipe of *Chapter 3, Flow Table and Flow Entry Modification Messages (Part 2)*
- Refer to the `process_flow_modify_message()` function in the `of/openflow.c` file for the procedure to handle flow delete messages from the controller

Modifying a flow entry in a flow table

When the controller wants to modify a flow table entry, it sends a flow entry modification message (`OFPT_FLOW_MOD`) to the switch, with the command value set as `OFPFC_MODIFY` or `OFPFC_MODIFY_STRICT`. This flow table modification message contains the information required to identify and modify the entry from the flow table.

The OpenFlow specification defines two different variants for modifying a flow entry: strict and non-strict versions.

How to do it...

When the switch receives the `OFPT_FLOW_MOD` message with the command field set as `OFPFC_MODIFY_STRICT`, all the fields in the flow modification message should be matched strictly against the flow table entry, and should be modified from the flow table.

When the switch receives the `OFPT_FLOW_MOD` message with the command field set as `OFPFC_MODIFY`, then the switch should select the flow entry to be modified, which either exactly matches or has more match fields present in it than the flow modification message. Once these messages are selected, these flow entries should be modified. As an example, suppose there are two flow entries in the flow table with match fields, as follows.

- TCP port 80 and Incoming port as 1
- TCP port 80 and Incoming port as 2

The switch receives the flow modify message from the controller with the match as TCP port 80; the strict version of the modify message shouldn't modify any entry, as the match specifies that the match field is port 80 only. However, the non-strict version should modify both of these entries.

See also

- For more information regarding how the controller sends `OFPT_FLOW_MOD` message refer to recipe *Modifying a flow entry in flow table* in *Chapter3, Flow Table & Flow Entry Modification Messages (part 2)* in this book
- Refer to the function `process_flow_modify_message()` in `of/openflow.c` file for the procedure to handle flow modification messages from controller

Flow table synchronizations

The OpenFlow specification provides a mechanism to synchronize one flow table with another flow table.

How to do it...

The OpenFlow specification doesn't define any explicit message to enable flow table synchronization. The switch might implement the flow table synchronization. When two tables (say, a source table and a synchronized table) are synchronized, then the addition, or deletion, or modification of any flow entry in the source table should result in updating the same flow entry in the synchronized table of the switch.

The flow tables could be synchronized unidirectionally or bidirectionally. The flow entries that are added automatically to the synchronized table can be deleted or modified by the controller using the `OFPT_FLOW_MOD` message. This provides a mechanism for the controller to customize or post-program the flow entries after been synchronized by the switch.

The most common use of flow table synchronization is for mapping the traditional layer 2 ethernet learning/forwarding functions onto a different flow table. The first flow table provides the layer 2 learning functionality by adding a flow entry with the source address and source port. The second table provides the forwarding functionality, wherein the destination address will be matched against the flow entries. In this case, the synchronization of table 1 and table 2 provides a mechanism of the learning and forwarding functionality in two different flow tables.

3

Flow Table and Flow Entry Modification Messages (Part 2)

This chapter describes, in detail, controller procedure programs, flow tables, and flow entries. It contains the following recipes:

- Modifying a flow table with eviction enabled
- Modifying a flow table with vacancy enabled
- Adding a new flow entry to the flow table
- Deleting an entry from the flow table
- Modifying an entry in the flow table

Introduction

The OpenFlow flow table is one of the main components of the OpenFlow switch during packet processing. It acts as a datapath forwarding table of the traditional switch. For a detailed introduction to the flow table, flow table entries, and various components of a flow table, refer to the *Introduction to flow tables and flow entries* recipe of *Chapter 3, Flow Table and Flow Entry Modification Messages (Part 1)*.

Modifying a flow table with eviction enabled

Eviction is one of the mechanisms provided by the OpenFlow specifications to remove entries from the flow table to avoid overflow. When the flow table in the switch is full, new flow entries can't be added to the flow table, which results in the switch returning an error message to the controller. This results in a problematic situation for the controller, and the controller should take the necessary steps to remove some flow entries from the switch while the switch is in this adverse condition. To avoid this situation and come out of this problematic scenario, the OpenFlow specification defines two mechanisms, as follows:

- **Eviction**: This mechanism is described in detail in this recipe
- **Vacancy**: This mechanism is described in detail in the next recipe

With eviction enabled on a particular flow table, the switch itself removes a flow entry from the flow table based on some specific criteria of the flow entry. An `OFP_TABLE_MOD` message is used to enable or disable eviction in a flow table.

Eviction is an optional feature that can be supported in the switch.

How to do it...

The controller should create and send an `OFP_TABLE_MOD` message to the switch to enable flow entry eviction for a particular flow table. On receiving this message, and based on the eviction scheme to be used, the switch will create the appropriate functions to perform the eviction.

`OFP_TABLE_MOD` is also used to enable vacancy on the flow table. Refer to next recipe, *Modifying a flow table with vacancy enabled*, for more information regarding vacancy.

The `OFP_TABLE_MOD` message takes the following format:

```
  /* Configure/Modify behavior of a flow table */
struct ofp_table_mod {
struct ofp_header header;
uint8_t table_id; /* ID of the table, OFPTT_ALL indicates
                   * all tables */
uint8_t pad[3];    /* Pad to 32 bits */
```

```
uint32_t config;  /* Bitmap of OFPTC_* flags */
/* Table Mod Property list */
struct ofp_table_mod_prop_header properties[0];
};
```

Here is a figure that shows this format:

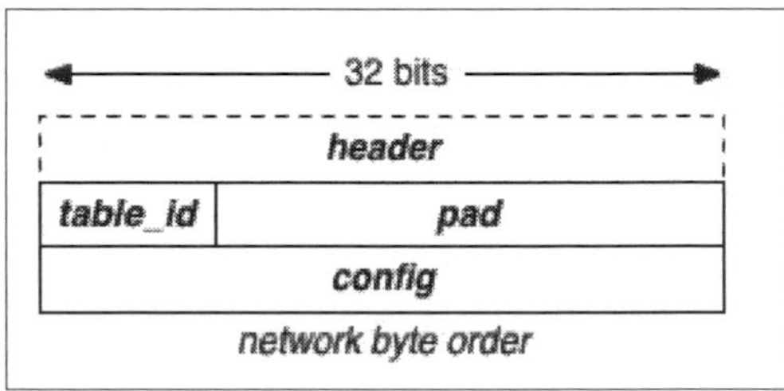

The `table_id` value should be filled with the ID of the table on which `eviction` has to be enabled. The `config` field should be filled with the configuration to be enabled on the flow table. This is described in the following enumeration:

```
/* Flags to configure the table. */
enum ofp_table_config {
OFPTC_DEPRECATED_MASK = 3, /* Deprecated bits */
OFPTC_EVICTION = 1 << 2,    /* Authorise table to evict flows. */
OFPTC_VACANCY_EVENTS = 1 << 3, /* Enable vacancy events. */
};
```

The `config` field should be set with a value of `0x04`, which represents the eviction to be enabled in a flow table. To disable eviction, this bitmask should not be set.

The `ofp_table_mod_prop_header` field represents the configuration values, such as the eviction scheme to be used, and takes the following format:

```
/* Eviction table mod Property. Mostly used in
 * OFPMP_TABLE_DESC replies. */
struct ofp_table_mod_prop_eviction {
uint16_t type;    /* OFPTMPT_EVICTION. */
uint16_t length; /* Length in bytes of this property. */
uint32_t flags;   /* Bitmap of OFPTMPEF_* flags */
};
```

For setting eviction, the controller should set the `type` field as `OFPTMPT_EVICTION`. The `flag` value is a bitmap that should be set with the type or scheme of eviction the switch has to employ. This is defined in the following enumeration:

```
/* Eviction flags. */
enum ofp_table_mod_prop_eviction_flag {
OFPTMPEF_OTHER = 1 << 0,       /* Using other factors. */
OFPTMPEF_IMPORTANCE = 1 << 1, /* Using flow entry importance. */
OFPTMPEF_LIFETIME = 1 << 2,    /* Using flow entry lifetime. */
};
```

See also

- For more information regarding how the switch evicts an entry from the flow table, refer to the *Modifying a flow table with eviction enabled* recipe of *Chapter 3, Flow Table and Flow Entry Modification Messages (Part 1)*, of this book

Modifying a flow table with vacancy enabled

When the controller does not want the switch to make its own decision in removing the flow entries, then the controller can use the vacancy mechanism. In this mechanism, the switch informs the controller whenever the switch's resources (especially the number of flow table entries) are reaching some threshold value, called the **vacancy threshold**. Unlike the eviction mechanism, wherein the switch itself removes the flow entry from the flow table, when the vacancy is enabled, the switch informs the controller about this. This mechanism enables of the controller to delete or modify the existing flow entries in the system whenever the switch reaches its threshold point.

How to do it...

The controller should send the `OFP_TABLE_MOD` message to the switch to enable vacancy for a particular flow table. The switch processes this message and generates an `OFPT_TABLE_STATUS` event or message for the controller whenever the number of flow table entries in the a flow table crosses the vacancy threshold value.

`OFP_TABLE_MOD` is also used to enable eviction on the flow table. Refer to the previous recipe for more information regarding eviction.

The OFP_TABLE_MOD message takes the following format:

```
  /* Configure/Modify behavior of a flow table */
struct ofp_table_mod {
struct ofp_header header;
uint8_t table_id; /* ID of the table, OFPTT_ALL indicates
                   * all tables */
uint8_t pad[3];   /* Pad to 32 bits */
uint32_t config;  /* Bitmap of OFPTC_* flags */
/* Table Mod Property list */
struct ofp_table_mod_prop_header properties[0];
};
```

Here is a figure that shows this format:

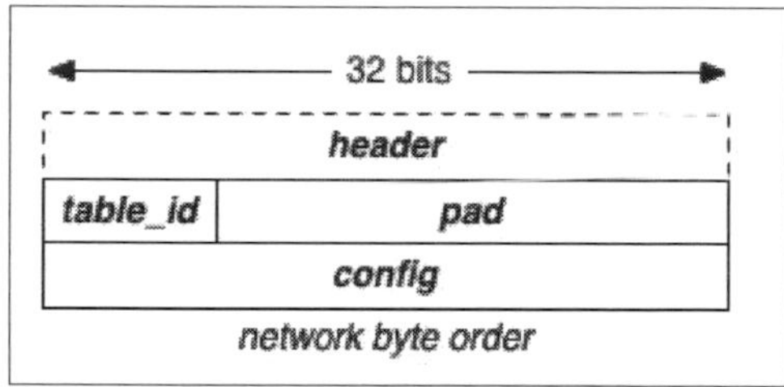

The table_id value should be filled with the ID of the table on which vacancy has to be enabled. The config field should be filled with the configuration to be enabled on the flow table. This is described in the following enumeration:

```
/* Flags to configure the table. */
enum ofp_table_config {
OFPTC_DEPRECATED_MASK = 3, /* Deprecated bits */
OFPTC_EVICTION = 1 << 2,   /* Authorise table to evict flows. */
OFPTC_VACANCY_EVENTS = 1 << 3, /* Enable vacancy events. */
};
```

The config field should be set to a value of 0x08, which represents the vacancy to be enabled on a flow table. To disable the vacancy, this bitmask should not be set. The ofp_table_mod_prop_header field represents the configuration values, such as vacancy_up and vacancy_down thresholds, and takes the following format:

```
/* Vacancy table mod property */
struct ofp_table_mod_prop_vacancy {
uint16_t type;          /* OFPTMPT_VACANCY. */
uint16_t length;        /* Length in bytes of this property. */
```

```
uint8_t vacancy_down; /* Vacancy threshold when space
                       * decreases (%). */
uint8_t vacancy_up;   /* Vacancy threshold when space
                       * increases (%). */
uint8_t vacancy;      /* Current vacancy (%) - only in
                       * ofp_table_desc. */
uint8_t pad[1];       /* Align to 64 bits. */
};
```

The `vacancy_down` and `vacancy_up` fields represent the threshold value for generating the vacancy event by the switch.

The `vacancy_down` and `vacancy_up` fields should be in percent values, and so should not be more than 100.

See also

- For more information regarding how the switch handles the vacancy event, refer to the *Modifying a flow table with vacancy enabled* recipe in *Chapter 3, Flow Table and Flow Entry Modification Messages (Part 2)*

Adding a new flow entry to the flow table

When the controller wants to program the flow table entry, then they should send a flow entry modification message (`OFPT_FLOW_MOD`) to the switch. This flow table modification message contains the necessary information required to program the flow table, which includes flow match field, priority, instruction set, timeout, and so on.

The `OFPT_FLOW_MOD` message is used for all flow entry operations, such as adding a new flow entry, deleting an existing flow entry, and modifying a flow entry in a flow table.

How to do it...

The message format that should be used by the controller to send the `OFPT_FLOW_MOD` message is as follows:

```
/* Flow setup and teardown (controller -> datapath). */
struct ofp_flow_mod {
struct ofp_header header;
uint64_t cookie;         /* Opaque controller-issued identifier. */
uint64_t cookie_mask;    /* Mask used to restrict the cookie bits
                          * that must match when the command is
                          * OFPFC_MODIFY* or OFPFC_DELETE*. A value
                          * of 0 indicates no restriction. */
/* Flow actions. */
uint8_t table_id;       /* ID of the table to put the flow in.
                         * For OFPFC_DELETE_* commands, OFPTT_ALL
                         * can also be used to delete matching
                         * flows from all tables. */
uint8_t command;        /* One of OFPFC_*. */
uint16_t idle_timeout; /* Idle time before discarding
                         * (seconds). */
uint16_t hard_timeout; /* Max time before discarding (seconds). */
uint16_t priority;      /* Priority level of flow entry. */
uint32_t buffer_id;     /* Buffered packet to apply to, or
                         * OFP_NO_BUFFER. Not meaningful for
                         * OFPFC_DELETE*. */
uint32_t out_port;      /* For OFPFC_DELETE* commands, require
                         * matching entries to include this as an
                         * output port. A value of OFPP_ANY
                        * indicates no restriction. */
uint32_t out_group;    /* For OFPFC_DELETE* commands, require
                        * matching entries to include this as an
                        * output group. A value of OFPG_ANY
                        * indicates no restriction. */
uint16_t flags;        /* Bitmap of OFPFF_* flags. */
uint16_t importance;   /* Eviction precedence (optional). */
struct ofp_match match; /* Fields to match. Variable size. */
```

```
                                /* The variable size and padded match is
                                 * always followed by instructions. */
   struct ofp_instruction_header instructions[0];
   /* Instruction set - 0 or more. The length
    * of the instruction set is inferred from
    * the length field in the header. */
   };
```

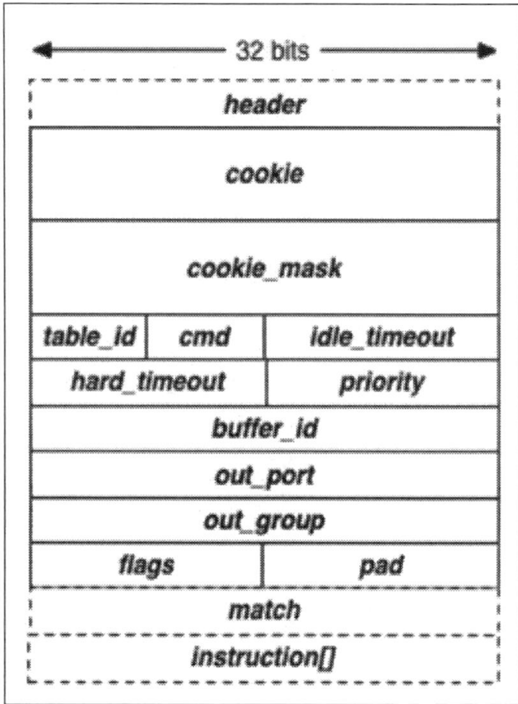

The `cookie` field should be filled with an opaque number generated by the controller. This field will be used for any subsequent operation on the flow entry, such as removing the flow entry or querying the flow entry for statistics.

The `cookie mask` field will be used along with the `cookie` field to select the flow entry while performing operations such as flow modification or deletion. This field doesn't have any significance for flow add messages.

The table-id field should be filled with the table ID of the flow table where this flow entry should be added. The command field represents the operation to be performed, which is represented by the following enumeration:

```
enum ofp_flow_mod_command {
OFPFC_ADD = 0,              /* New flow. */
OFPFC_MODIFY = 1,           /* Modify all matching flows. */
OFPFC_MODIFY_STRICT = 2, /* Modify entry strictly matching
                           * wildcards and priority. */
OFPFC_DELETE = 3,           /* Delete all matching flows. */
OFPFC_DELETE_STRICT = 4, /* Delete entry strictly matching
                           * wildcards and priority. */
};
```

For flow entry addition, the controller should set this value as OFPFC_ADD. The idle_timeout and hard_timeout values should be set with the timeout, or expiry time, of the flow entry to the switch.

idle_timeout is the timeout period that a switch uses to remove a flow entry when there is no matching packet for that flow entry. If a switch doesn't receive a packet during the period of idle_timeout, then the switch removes that entry from the flow table.

hard_timeout is the timeout period that a switch uses to remove a flow entry from the time of its installation. If the hard_timeout period lapses in a switch for a particular flow entry, then the switch removes that entry from the flow table.

On expiry of any of these timeout values, the switch removes the flow entry from the flow table.

The priority field should be set with the priority of the specified flow entry. While forwarding the packet via OpenFlow pipeline processing, the switch will match the flow entry with the maximum priority value when the packet is matched against multiple flow entries.

After adding the flow table, if the controller wants to send the packet that is already buffered in the switch via the OpenFlow pipeline, then this field should be set with the buffer_id value of the packet.

The out_port and out_group fields are used only for the IFPFC_DELETE message, and should be ignored by the switch for the OFPFC_ADD message.

When the controller sends a flow add message to the switch, it can instruct the switch to send some asynchronous event or perform some sanity check (for example, check whether there is any overlapping entry). This information will be present in the `flag` field of the `OFPFC_ADD` message. The `flag` field is filled with any one of the following values defined in the enumeration:

```
enum ofp_flow_mod_flags {
OFPFF_SEND_FLOW_REM = 1 << 0, /* Send flow removed message
                               * when flow expires or is deleted
OFPFF_CHECK_OVERLAP = 1 << 1, /* Check for overlapping entries
                               * first. */
OFPFF_RESET_COUNTS = 1 << 2,  /* Reset flow packet and byte
                               * counts. */
OFPFF_NO_PKT_COUNTS = 1 << 3, /* Don't keep track of packet count.
                               */
OFPFF_NO_BYT_COUNTS = 1 << 4, /* Don't keep track of byte count.
                               */
};
```

`OFPFF_SEND_FLOW_REM` should be set when the controller wants to receive an asynchronous flow removed event from the switch.

The `OFPFF_CHECK_OVERLAP` flag should be set if the controller wants the switch to perform a check of any conflicting flow table entry with the same priority. The switch returns an error message with the type as `OFPET_FLOW_MOD_FAILED` and code as `OFPFMFC_OVERLAP` when there is a conflicting flow entry.

Two entries in a table are said to be a overlapping when a packet can be matched against two entries in the table with the same priority.

`OFPFF_RESET_COUNTS` doesn't have any significance with the `OFPFC_ADD` message, so the controller can ignore this flag. If the controller doesn't want the switch to keep track of the packet counts associated with a particular flow entry, then `OFPFF_NO_PKT_COUNTS` should be set in the `OFPFC_ADD` message.

The `importance` field should be set as per the importance of the flow entry. The switch will use this field value during eviction processing. Refer to the previous recipe for more about the switch eviction mechanism.

The `instruction` field should be set with the instruction set associated with the flow entry.

See also

- For more information regarding how the switch handles the flow entry add message, refer to the *Adding a new flow entry to the flow table* recipe of *Chapter 3, Flow Table and Flow Entry Modification Messages (Part 1)*

Deleting an entry from a flow table

When the controller wants to delete a flow table entry, then they should send a flow entry modification message (`OFPT_FLOW_MOD`) with the command value set as `OFPFC_DELETE` / `OFPFC_DELETE_STRICT` to the switch. This flow table modification messages contains the necessary information required to identify and delete the entry from the flow table.

The `OFPT_FLOW_MOD` message is used for all the flow entry operations like adding a new flow entry, deleting an existing flow entry and modifying a flow entry in a flow table.

How to do it...

The message format that should be used by controller to send the `OFPT_FLOW_MOD` message is defined in the *Adding a new flow entry to the flow table* section in this chapter.

To delete a flow entry, the command field should be set to either `OFPFC_DELETE` or `OFPFC_DELETE_STRICT`. The OpenFlow specification defines two different variants for deleting the flow entry as strict and non-strict versions.

When the controller wants the switch to match all the fields in the flow modification message and delete flow entries, then they should set the command field as `OFPFC_DELETE_STRICT`. When they want the switch to match a set of matching fields with the matching field present in the flow delete message, then they should set the command field as `OFPFC_DELETE`. To illustrate with an example, let's suppose there are two flow entries in the flow table with the `match` fields, as follows:

- TCP port 80 and incoming port as 1
- TCP port 80 and incoming port as 2

Also, the controller sends a flow delete message with the match as TCP port 80. Then, with the strict version of the delete message, the switch won't delete any entry because the match specifies that the match field with only port 80 should be deleted. However, with the non-strict version, the switch will delete both of these entries.

While deleting the flow entry, if the controller wants to filter the flow entries from the flow table based on the `cookie` field and `mask`, then it should fill the `cookie` field and `mask`. The `cookie` field should be filled with the value that was generated at the time of adding the flow entry to the flow table. Using the `cookie` field and `cookie mask` filled, the switch will fetch the flow entry from the flow and delete it from the flow table.

The `table-id` value should be filled with the table ID of the flow table where this flow entry should be added.

The `idle_timeout` and `hard_timeout` values don't have any significance in the delete message, so the controller can ignore these fields. The `priority` field should be set with the priority of the specified flow entry. The `buffer_id` field doesn't have any significance in the delete message, and so the controller can ignore this field.

The `out_port` and `out_group` fields are used to add more constraints on the flow entry while matching. The constraint is that apart from the flow match, the flow entry action should direct the packets to the output port or group. This constraint will be applied along with the existing flow match field present in the message. So, if the controller wants to apply these constraints while deleting a flow entry, these fields should be set. To disable output filtering or apply this constraint, these values should be set as `OFPP_ANY` and `OFPG_ANY`.

The `flag` field and the `importance` field don't have any significance in the delete message, so the controller can ignore them. The `match` field consists of the variable length match criteria, which will be used to match the flow entry in the flow table for deletion. The `instruction` field should be set with the instruction set associated with the flow entry.

See also

- For more information regarding how the switch handles the flow entry delete message, refer to the *Deleting an entry from the flow table* recipe of *Chapter 3, Flow Table and Flow Entry Modification Messages (Part 1)*

Modifying an entry in the flow table

When the controller wants to modify a flow table entry, they send a flow entry modification message (`OFPT_FLOW_MOD`) with the command value set as `OFPFC_MODIFY` or `OFPFC_MODIFY_STRICT` to the switch. This flow table modification message contains the information required to identify and modify the entry from the flow table.

How to do it...

The message format that should be used by the controller to send the `OFPT_FLOW_MOD` is defined in the *Adding a new flow entry to flow table* recipe in this chapter.

To modify a flow entry, the command field should be set to either `OFPFC_MODIFY` or `OFPFC_MODIFY_STRICT`. The OpenFlow specification defines two different variants for modifying flow entries as strict and non-strict versions.

When the controller wants the switch to match all the fields in the flow modification message and modify the entries, the controller should set the command field as `OFPFC_MODIFY_STRICT`. When it wants the switch to match a set of matching fields against the matching field present in the flow modify message, it should set the command field as `OFPFC_MODIFY`. To illustrate with an example, let's suppose there are two flow entries in the flow table with the match field, as follows:

- TCP port 80 and Incoming port as 1
- TCP port 80 and Incoming port as 2

Also, the controller sends a flow modify message with the match as TCP port 80. Then, with the strict version of the modify message, the switch won't modify any entry because the match specifies that the match field with only port 80 will be modified. However, with the non-strict version, the switch will delete both of these entries.

If the controller wants to filter the flow entries from the flow table and then modify them based on this filter, then it should fill this field along with the `cookie mask` field. The cookie field should be filled with the value that was generated at the time of adding the flow entry to the flow table. Using the `cookie` field and the `cookie mask` field, the switch will fetch the flow entry from the flow, and it should modify the entry from the flow table.

The `table-id` value should be used by the switch to identify the flow table where this flow entry for modification resides. The `command` field should be filled with either `OFPFC_MODIFY` or `OFPFC_MODIFY_STRICT`. The `idle_timeout` and `hard_timeout` values don't have any significance in the modify message, so the controller can ignore them.

The `priority` field is set with the priority of the specified flow entry to be modified. The `buffer_id` field doesn't have any significance in the modify message, and so the switch can ignore this field.

The `out_port` and `out_group` fields are used only for the `OFPFC_DELETE` message, and the controller can ignore these fields. The `flag` field doesn't have any significance in the modify message, so the controller can ignore this field.

The `match` field consists of the variable length match criteria, which will be used to match the flow entry in the flow table for deletion. The `importance` field doesn't have any significance in the delete message, so the controller can ignore this field. The `instruction` field is set with the instruction set associated with the flow entry.

See also

- For more information regarding how the switch handles the flow entry modification message, refer to the *Modifying an entry in the flow table* recipe of *Chapter 3, Flow Table and Flow Entry Modification Messages (Part 1)*

4

Group Table and Meter Table Modification Messages (Part 1)

This chapter describes in detail about the group table entries and meter entries along with the operations that can be performed over these tables, and contains the following recipes:

- Adding a new group entry in a group table
- Deleting a group entry in a group table
- Modifying a group entry in a group table
- Adding a new meter in a meter table
- Deleting a meter entry
- Modifying a meter entry in a meter table

Introduction

The OpenFlow group table and meter table are two of the main components in the OpenFlow switch. They are used in conjunction with the flow table entry for performing some special operations. The OpenFlow meters are used to implement simple QoS operations such as rate-limiting to complex QoS frameworks such as **differentiated services** (**DiffServ**).

Group table

The group table is used to perform special operations such as multicast forwarding, multipath forwarding, switch port abstraction, fast failover support, and so on. The group table provides the following abstraction:

- Abstraction for multicast forwarding and multipath/**ECMP** (**Equal Cost Multi Path**) forwarding
- Abstraction to represent set of ports as a single entity for forwarding packets
- Abstraction for providing fast failover

When the incoming packet needs to be forwarded to a group table to perform special operations such as replicating the packet to multiple ports for multicast / broadcast forwarding, or forward the packet using multipath and so on, then the instruction in the flow entry should be programmed to write an action in the action list (using a Write-Actions action(s) instruction) with an action type as a group.

The OpenFlow switch should either have a software-based group table processing mechanism or a hardware-based group table processing mechanism-based on its capability. As described in the recipe, *Introduction to the flow table and flow entry* in *Chapter 3, Flow Table and Flow Entry Modification Messages (Part 1)*, all the incoming packets are be first matched against the flow entries and, if the action set of the packet contains a group action, then the switch should forward this packet to the group table with a group ID. The group entry in the group table contains a list of action buckets which defines how the packet should be forwarded along with its group type. The procedure to forward the packet based on the action type is explained in table.

The components of the group table entry and their association with the flow table is explained in detail in the following diagram:

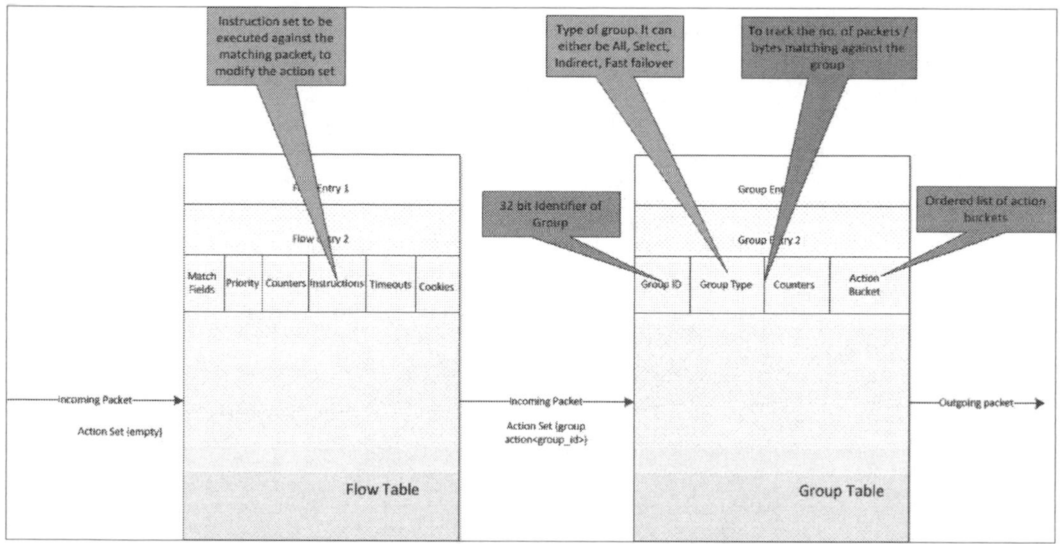

The group table entry should have the following components:

- **Group Identifier**: This is a 32-bit identifier, which is used as a key to identify an entry in the group table.
- **Group Type**: This field should represent the type of the group. Each group type has its own semantics and is explained in detail in the following section.

Group Type	Required	Descriptions	Constraints / Restrictions
all	Yes	This group type should be used for broadcast and multicast forwarding wherein an incoming packet needs to be replicated and forwarded to multiple outgoing ports. The incoming packets should be cloned as many as the number of buckets in the action bucket of this group table entry. Once the incoming packet is replicated / cloned, each cloned packet should be processed by each bucket of the group.	If a bucket directs the incoming packet to the ingress port, then the switch shouldn't replicate / clone the packet for that bucket.

Group Type	Required	Descriptions	Constraints / Restrictions
Select	No	This group type should be used for multipath / ECMP forwarding. In this group type, each group table entry could have multiple action buckets. However, each packet should be processed by one of the action buckets in the group. The buckets to be chosen depend on switch specific implementation. The selection algorithm should take care of equal load sharing of packets hitting the buckets.	
Indirect	Yes	This group type should be used for providing an indirection object wherein multiple entries use the same output action. For example, when large numbers of route entries are pointing to the same next hop route, this group entry could be used. Multiple flow entries having the same action to be performed can point to this group.	This group supports only a single bucket
Fast failover	No	This group type should be used for providing fast failover support for the flow entries. In this case, each group entry is associated with two or more action buckets. The incoming packet should be forwarded based on the first bucket which is associated with the live port/group. Each action bucket should be associated with a specific port and/or group that controls its liveliness.	

- **Counter**: Used to track the number of packets matching this group entry.
- **Action buckets**: Represents a list of action buckets wherein each bucket contains a set of actions to be executed along with the parameter. Refer to the *Introduction to the flow table and flow entry* recipe in *Chapter 3, Flow Table and Flow Entry Modification Messages (Part 1)*,for more information regarding the action and action set.

The OpenFlow switch might support chaining of groups wherein one group can forward the packet to another group for further processing. The switch may support a mechanism to verify that no loops are formed due to this group chaining.

Meter table

The OpenFlow meter table is one of the main components in the OpenFlow switch. The meter can be pointed by flow entry for performing various simple QoS operations such as rate-limiting, to complex QoS framework such as DiffServ.

The Meter table consists of per-flow meter entries which measure the rate of packets and enables the control of the rate of those packets. The meters are directly attached to the flow entries using the meter instruction set. For more information regarding the instruction set, refer to the *Introduction to the flow table and flow entry* recipe in *Chapter 3, Flow Table and Flow Entry Modification Messages (Part 1)*.

The OpenFlow switch should either have a software-based metering mechanism or a hardware-based metering mechanism, based on its capability. As described in the recipe, *Introduction to the flow table and flow entry* recipe in *Chapter 3, Flow Table and Flow Entry Modification Messages (Part 1)*, all the incoming packets are first matched against the flow entries and, if the instruction set of this flow entry contains a meter instruction, then the switch should forward this packet to the meter with its meter ID.

The meter entry contains a list of meter bands which define how the packet should be forwarded along with the meter type.

The components of the meter table entry and its association with the flow table are explained in detail in the following diagram:

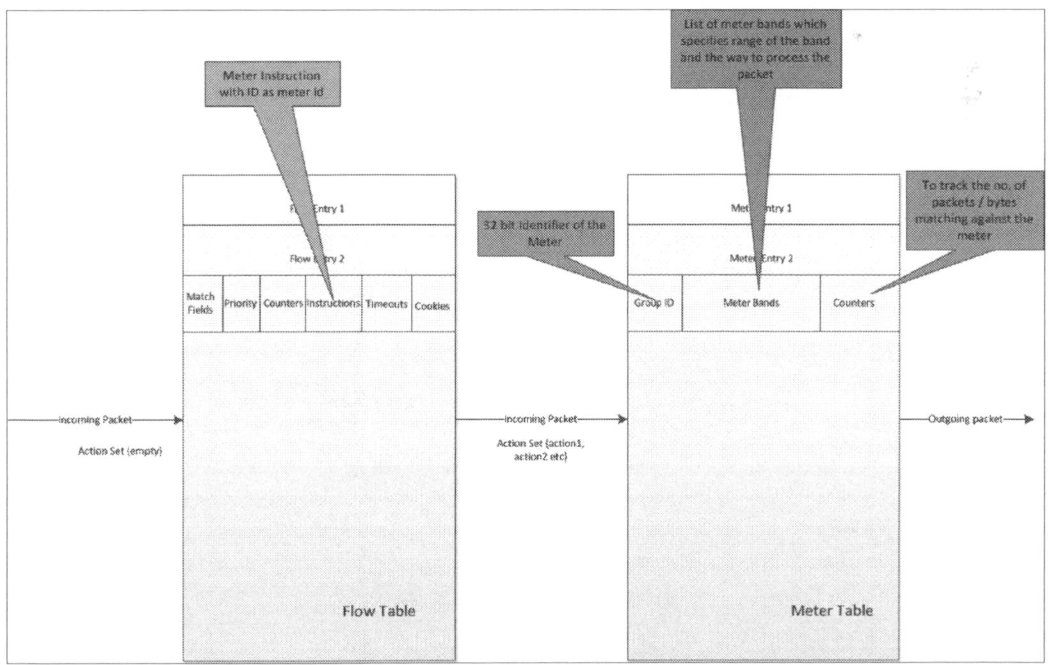

The meter entry has the following components.

- **Meter Identifier**: This is a 32-bit identifier used to identify an entry in the meter table.
- **Meter Bands**: In this, each meter entry has one or more meter bands. Each band specifies the rate at which the band applies and the way packets should be processed. Packets should be processed by a single meter among the set of meter bands based on the rate at which the packet is hitting the flow entry. Among the set of meter bands, the meter should process the packets with the meter band whose configured rate is the highest configured rate that is lower than the current measured rate.

  The meter band has the following components:

  - **Band Type**: Defines how the packets are processed. The band type can either be:
  - **Drop**: Drop the packet
  - **Dscp remark**: Increase the drop precedence of the DSCP field in the IP header of the packet
  - **Counters**: Meter band specific counters. Used to track the number of the packets processed by this meter band.
  - **Type-specific arguments**: These are optional arguments which are specific to a band type.
- **Counters**: Meter-specific counters. Used to track the number of packets processed by this meter.

Adding a new group entry in a group table

When the controller wants to program a group table entry, the controller sends a group table modification message (`OFPT_GROUP_MOD`) to the switch. This group table modification message contains the necessary information required to program the group table which includes the group identifier, bucket list, and so on.

> The `OFPT_GROUP_MOD` message is used for all the group table entry operations such as adding a new group entry, deleting an existing group entry, and modifying a group entry in the group table.

How to do it...

The message format that is used by the controller to send the OFPT_GROUP_MOD is defined in the *Adding a new group entry in a group table* recipe in *Chapter 4, Group Table and Meter Table modification Messages (Part 2).*

When the switch receives an OFPT_GROUP_MOD message to add a group entry, then the action set of each bucket should be validated using the same procedure as that of the flow modification message defined in the recipe, *Adding a new flow entry in the flow table* in *Chapter 3, Flow Table and Flow Entry Modification Messages (Part 1)*, along with additional group-specific checks as follows:

- If the action in any one of the buckets in the OFPT_GROUP_MOD message is not a valid action or is not supported by the switch, then the switch should respond to the controller with an error message with the type OFPET_BAD_ACTION and the code corresponding to the error as defined in the recipe, *Adding a new flow entry in the flow table* in *Chapter 3, Flow Table and Flow Entry Modification Messages (Part 1).*
- If the switch already has a matching group entry in the group table then the switch must ignore this add message and respond back with an error message with the type OFPET_GROUP_MOD_FAILED and the code OFPGMFC_GROUP_EXISTS.
- If the specified group type and the parameters of the OFPT_GROUP_MOD message are invalid, then the switch must respond to the controller with an error message with the type OFPET_GROUP_MOD_FAILED and the code OFPGMFC_INVALID_GROUP.
- If the switch cannot add the group entry due to lack of space, then the switch must respond to the controller with an error message with the type OFPET_GROUP_MOD_FAILED and the code OFPGMFC_OUT_OF_GROUPS.
- If the switch cannot add the group entry due to restrictions (hardware or otherwise) limiting the number of group buckets, then the switch must ignore the add message from the controller and must respond with an error message with the type OFPET_GROUP_MOD_FAILED and the code OFPGMFC_OUT_OF_BUCKETS.
- If the switch cannot add the group because it does not support the proposed liveliness configuration, then the switch must ignore the add message and must respond with an error message with the type OFPET_GROUP_MOD_FAILED and the code OFPGMFC_WATCH_UNSUPPORTED.
- If the switch doesn't support unequal load sharing with select groups (buckets with a weight other than one), it should ignore the add message and must respond with an error message with the type OFPET_GROUP_MOD_FAILED and the code OFPGMFC_WEIGHT_UNSUPPORTED.

The specification doesn't define how the traffic distribution should be manipulated or adjusted when the port associated with a bucket goes down and is implementation-specific.

See also

- For more information on how the controller sends `OFPT_GROUP_MOD` messages, refer to the recipe, *Adding a new group entry in a group table* in *Chapter 4, Group Table and Meter Table Modification Messages (Part 2)* of this book
- Refer to the function `process_group_modify_message ()` in `of/openflow.c` file for the procedure to handle group entry modification messages from the controller

Deleting a group entry in a group table

When the controller wants to delete a group table entry, then it sends a group table modification message (`OFPT_GROUP_MOD`) to the switch. This group table modification message contains the necessary information required to delete the group entry which includes the flow group identifier, bucket list and so on.

The `OFPT_GROUP_MOD` message is used for all the group table entry operations such as adding a new group entry, deleting an existing group entry, and modifying a group entry in the group table.

How to do it...

The message format used by the controller to send the `OFPT_GROUP_MOD` is defined in the *Adding a new group entry in a group table* recipe in *Chapter 4, Group Table and Meter Table modification Messages (Part 1)*. Here, to delete a group table entry, the command field is set as `OFPGC_DELETE`.

While processing the group delete message by the switch, if there are no matching entries with a specified identifier present, then the switch should ignore this message and it need not send any error message back to the controller.

If the group entry presents in the group table then:

- The switch may prefer to check whether this group is being referenced by other group table entries (in case of chaining) before deleting the entry. If the switch cannot delete a group because it is referenced by another group, it must ignore the group delete message and must send an error message with the type `OFPET_GROUP_MOD_FAILED` and the code `OFPGMFC_CHAINED_GROUP`.
- The group entry should be deleted from the group table.
- All the flow entries which are using this group entry should also be removed.

If the controller wants to delete only the group entries but still wants to keep associated flow entries to point a group table entry, then the controller should send a group entry modification message instead of a group entry delete message. Refer to the recipe, *Modifying a group entry in a group table* from this chapter for more information regarding group entry modify messages.

When the switch receives a group delete message with the group identifier `OFPG_ALL`, the switch should delete all the group entries in the group table.

See also

- For more information regarding how the controller sends an `OFPT_GROUP_MOD` message, refer to the *Adding a new group entry in a group table* recipe in *Chapter 4, Group Table and Meter Table modification Messages (Part 2)* in this book
- Refer to the function `process_group_modify_message ()` in `of/openflow.c` file for the procedure to handle group entry modification messages from the controller

Modifying a group entry in a group table

When the controller wants to modify a group entry, the controller sends a group entry modification message (`OFPT_GROUP_MOD`) with the command value set as `OFPGC_MODIFY` to the switch. These flow table modification messages contain the information required to identify and modify an entry from a group table.

How to do it...

The message format that is used by the controller to send the OFPT_GROUP_MOD is defined in the *Adding a new group entry in a group table* recipe in *Chapter 4, Group Table and Meter Table modification Messages (Part 2)*. Here, to modify a group table entry, the command field is set as OFPGC_MODIFY.

When the switch receives a group modification message with the command OFPGC_MODIFY, it should fetch a group entry from the group table based on the group identifier.

If the switch can fetch a group entry, then the existing entry, along with type and action buckets, must be removed and a new entry should be created.

If the switch isn't able to fetch the corresponding group entry, then the switch must ignore this flow modification message and must send an error message with the type OFPET_GROUP_MOD_FAILED and the code OFPGMFC_UNKNOWN_GROUP.

See also

- For more information regarding how the controller sends OFPT_GROUP_MOD messages, refer to the *Adding a new group entry in a group table* recipe in *Chapter 4, Group Table and Meter Table modification Messages (part 2)* of this book
- Refer to the function process_group_modify_message () in of/openflow.c file for the procedure to handle group entry modification message from the controller

Adding a new meter in a meter table

When the controller wants to program a meter, then the controller sends a meter modification message (OFPT_METER_MOD) to the switch. This meter modification message contains the information required to program the meter table which includes meter identifier, bands and so on.

The OFPT_METER_MOD message is used for all the meter operations such as adding a new meter, deleting an existing meter, and modifying a meter.

How to do it...

The message format that is used by the controller to send the OFPT_METER_MOD is defined in *Adding a new meter in a meter table* recipe in *Chapter 4, Group Table and Meter Table modification Messages (Part 2).*

When the switch receives an OFPT_METER_MOD message to add a meter, the switch should perform the following check before adding the entry:

- If a meter is already present then the switch must ignore this add message and respond with an error message with the type OFPET_METER_MOD_FAILED and the code OFPMMFC_METER_EXISTS.
- If the switch cannot add the meter due to lack of space, then the switch must respond with an error message with the type OFPET_METER_MOD_FAILED and the code OFPMMFC_OUT_OF_METERS.
- If the switch cannot add the meter due to restrictions (hardware or otherwise) limiting the number of bands, then the switch must ignore the add message and must respond with an error message with the type OFPET_METER_MOD_FAILED and the code OFPMMFC_OUT_OF_METERS.

See also

- For more information on how the controller sends an OFPT_METER_MOD message, refer to the *Adding a new meter in a meter table* recipe in *Chapter 4, Group Table and Meter Table modification Messages (Part 2)*
- Refer to the function process_meter_modify_message () in of/openflow.c section for the procedure to handle meter entry modification messages from the controller

Deleting a meter entry

When the controller wants to delete a meter entry, it sends a meter modification message (OFPT_METER_MOD) to the switch. This meter modification message contains the information required to delete the meter which includes the meter identifier, bands and so on.

The `OFPT_METER_MOD` message is used for all the meter operations such as adding a new meter, deleting an existing meter, and modifying a meter.

How to do it...

The message format used by the controller to send the `OFPT_METER_MOD` is defined in *Adding a new meter in a meter table* recipe in *Chapter 4, Group Table and Meter Table modification Messages (Part 2)*. Here, to delete a meter entry, the command field is set as `OFPMC_DELETE`.

The procedure to construct the meter modification message for deleting a meter entry is similar to that of one explained in the previous recipe. However, deleting an entry controller need not set the bands in a modification message.

While processing the meter delete message, if there is no matching entry with the specified identifier, then the switch should ignore this message and it need not send any error message back to the controller.

If the meter entry presents in the meter table, then the following should be done:

- The meter entry should be deleted from the meter table.
- All the flow entries which are using this meter should also be removed.

When the switch receives the meter delete message with the meter identifier `OFPG_ALL`, then the switch should delete all the meter entries except the virtual meters.

See also

- For more information on how the controller sends an `OFPT_METER_MOD` message, refer to the recipe, *Adding a new meter in a meter table* recipe in *Chapter 4, Group Table and Meter Table modification Messages (Part 2)* of this book
- Refer to the function `process_meter_modify_message ()` in `of/openflow.c` section for the procedure to handle meter entry modification messages from the controller

Modifying a meter entry in a meter table

When the controller wants to modify a meter entry, the controller sends a meter modification message (OFPT_METER_MOD) with the command value set as OFPMC_MODIFY to the switch. This meter modification message contains the information required to identify and modify the meter.

[The OFPT_METER_MOD message is used for all the meter operations such as adding a new meter, deleting an existing meter, and modifying a meter.]

How to do it...

The message format used by the controller to send the OFPT_METER_MOD is defined in the *Adding a new meter in a meter table* recipe in *Chapter 4, Group Table and Meter Table modification Messages (Part 2)*. Here, to modify a meter entry, the command field is set as OFPMC_MODIFY.

When the switch receives a meter modification message with the command OFPMC_MODIFY, the switch should fetch the meter entry based on the meter identifier in the message.

If the switch can fetch a meter entry, then the existing entry, along with its type and bands, must be removed and a new entry should be created.

If the switch isn't able to fetch the corresponding meter entry, then the switch must ignore this meter modification message and must send an error message with the type OFPET_METER_MOD_FAILED and the code OFPMMFC_UNKNOWN_METER.

See also

- For more information on how the controller sends OFPT_METER_MOD messages, refer to the recipe, *Adding a new meter in a meter table* recipe in *Chapter 4, Group Table and Meter Table modification Messages (Part 2)*. of this book.
- Refer to the function process_meter_modify_message () in of/openflow.c section for the procedure to handle meter entry modification messages from the controller.

4

Group Table and Meter Table Modification Messages (Part 2)

This chapter describes in detail the controller procedure to program a group entry, a meter entry, and contains the following recipes:

- Adding a new group entry in a group table
- Deleting a group entry in a group table
- Modifying a group entry in a group table
- Adding a new meter in a meter table
- Deleting a meter entry
- Modifying a meter entry in a meter table

Introduction

The OpenFlow group table and meter table are two of the main components of the OpenFlow switch. The group table and meter tables are used in conjunction with the flow table entry for performing some special operations. The OpenFlow meters are used to implement simple QoS operations such as rate-limiting to complex QoS frameworks such as DiffServ.

For a detailed introduction to the group table, group table entries and various components of the group table, refer to the recipe, *Introduction* in *Chapter 4, Group Table and Meter Table Modification Messages (Part 1)*. Similarly, for a detailed introduction to the meter entry and various components of meter entry, refer to the recipe, *Introduction to the meter table and the meter entry* in *Chapter 4, Group Table and Meter Table Modification Messages (Part 1)*.

Adding a new group entry in a group table

When the controller wants to program a group table entry, the controller should send a group table modification message (`OFPT_GROUP_MOD`) to the switch. This group table modification message contains the information required to program the group table which includes the group identifier, bucket list and so on.

How to do it...

The message format that should be used by the controller to send `OFPT_GROUP_MOD` is as follows:

```
/* Group setup and teardown (controller -> datapath). */
struct ofp_group_mod {
struct ofp_header header;
uint16_t command;          /* One of OFPGC_*. */
uint8_t type;              /* One of OFPGT_*. */
uint8_t pad;                    /* Pad to 64 bits. */
uint32_t group_id;              /* Group identifier. */
struct ofp_bucket buckets[0]; /* The length of the bucket array
                                 * is inferred from the length field
                                 * in the header. */
};
```

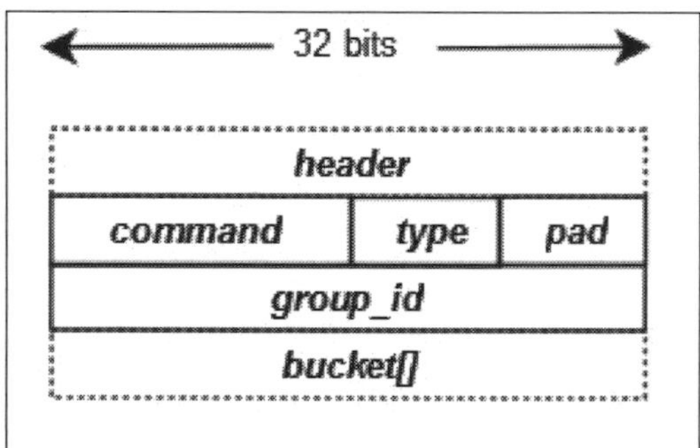

The `command` field represents the operation to be performed and is represented by the following enumeration:

```
/* Group commands */
enum ofp_group_mod_command {
OFPGC_ADD = 0,      /* New group. */
OFPGC_MODIFY = 1, /* Modify all matching groups. */
OFPGC_DELETE = 2, /* Delete all matching groups. */
};
```

For group entry addition, the controller should set this value to `OFPGC_ADD`.

The `type` field represents the type of group entry and takes the values as described in the following enumeration:

```
/* Group types. Values in the range [128, 255] are reserved
   for experimental use. */
enum ofp_group_type {
OFPGT_ALL = 0,        /* All (multicast/broadcast) group. */
OFPGT_SELECT = 1,     /* Select group. */
OFPGT_INDIRECT = 2, /* Indirect group. */
OFPGT_FF = 3,         /* Fast failover group. */
};
```

For a detailed description of various group types, refer to the *Introduction* in *Chapter 4, Group Table and Meter Table Modification Messages (Part 1)*.

The `group_id` field represents the identifier of the group table entry. The specification has defined the following special identifiers for the group:

```
/* Group numbering. Groups can use any number up to OFPG_MAX. */
enum ofp_group {
/* Last usable group number. */
OFPG_MAX = 0xffffff00,
/* Fake groups. */
OFPG_ALL = 0xfffffffc, /* Represents all groups for group
                        * delete commands. */
OFPG_ANY = 0xffffffff  /* Wildcard group used only for flow stats
                        * requests. Selects all flows regardless
                        * of group (including flows with no
                        * group).*/
};
```

The flags `OFPG_ALL` and `OFPG_ANY` don't have any significance in the group add messages and hence the controller need not set these flags.

The `buckets` field represents an array of buckets which contain a list of actions. The bucket list is defined as follows:

```
/* Bucket for use in groups. */
struct ofp_bucket {
uint16_t len;           /* Length the bucket in bytes, including
                         * this header and any padding to make it
                         * 64-bit aligned. */
uint16_t weight;        /* Relative weight of bucket. Only defined
                          for select groups. */
uint32_t watch_port;    /* Port whose state affects whether this
                         * bucket is live. Only required for fast
                         * failover groups. */
uint32_t watch_group;   /* Group whose state affects whether this
                         * bucket is live. Only required for fast
                         * failover groups. */
uint8_t pad[4];
struct ofp_action_header actions[0]; /* 0 or more actions
                         * associated with the bucket - The action
                         * list length is inferred from the length
                         * of the bucket. */
};
```

A group with the type indirect must contain exactly only one bucket, and for all other group types the bucket list can have more than one bucket.

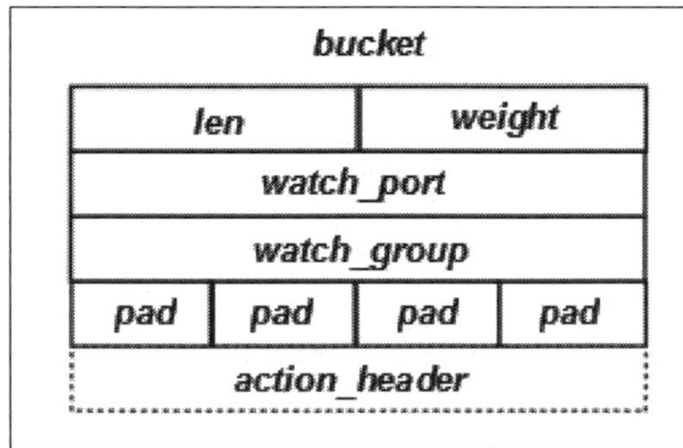

The `len` field should be set to the length of the buckets in bytes including this header.

The `weight` field should be set to a relative weight of the bucket in the list. This field is applicable only for a select group type. This field is used by the switch to determine the relative amount of traffic to be processed by this bucket. The amount of traffic to be processed by this bucket is defined by this bucket's weight divided by the sum of all the bucket weights in the group. Say the bucket *b* has a weight *x* and the total weight of all the buckets in the group is y, then the traffic processed by the bucket b will be *x/y*.

`watch_port` and `watch_group` represent the ports / groups whose liveliness controls whether this bucket is a candidate for traffic forwarding. This field should be set for a fast failover group and the controller can optionally set it for other group types.

The `actions` field should be set to the action list associated with the bucket. For more information regarding the action list and the action, refer to the recipe, *Introduction to the flow table and the flow entry* in *Chapter 3, Flow Table and Flow Entry Modification Messages (Part 1)*. When a bucket is selected for further processing, actions inside the action list will be executed by the switch.

How it works...

After sending `OFPT_GROUP_MOD`, the switch may send an error message to the controller when the switch isn't able to process the message successfully. The error messages that will be sent by the switch and their interpretation is described in detail in the following section:

- The switch sends an error message with the type `OFPET_BAD_ACTION`, when the action in any one of the buckets is not a valid action or not supported by the switch.
- The switch sends an error message with the type `OFPET_GROUP_MOD_FAILED` and the code `OFPGMFC_GROUP_EXISTS`, when a group entry is already present in the group table with the same group identifier.
- The switch sends an error message with the type `OFPET_GROUP_MOD_FAILED` and the code `OFPGMFC_INVALID_GROUP`, when the specified group type and its parameters are invalid.
- The switch sends an error message with the type `OFPET_GROUP_MOD_FAILED` and the code `OFPGMFC_OUT_OF_GROUPS`, when the switch cannot add a group entry due to lack of space.
- The switch sends an error message with the type `OFPET_GROUP_MOD_FAILED` and the code `OFPGMFC_OUT_OF_BUCKETS`, when the switch cannot add the group entry due to restrictions (hardware or otherwise) limiting the number of group buckets.

- The switch sends an error message with the type `OFPET_GROUP_MOD_FAILED` and the code `OFPGMFC_WATCH_UNSUPPORTED` when the switch cannot add a group because it does not support the proposed liveliness configuration.
- The switch sends an error message with the type `OFPET_GROUP_MOD_FAILED` and the code `OFPGMFC_WEIGHT_UNSUPPORTED` when the switch doesn't support unequal load sharing with select groups (buckets with weights other than 1).

See also

- For more information on how the switch processes group entry add messages, refer to the recipe, *Adding a new group entry in a group table* in *Chapter 4, Group Table and Meter Table Modification Messages(Part 1)* of this book

Deleting a group entry in a group table

When the controller wants to delete a group table entry, it should send a group table modification message (`OFPT_GROUP_MOD`) to the switch. This group table modification message contains the information required to delete the group table which includes the flow group identifier, bucket list, and so on.

> The `OFPT_GROUP_MOD` message is used for all the group table entry operations such as adding a new group entry, deleting an existing group entry, and modifying a group entry in a group table.

How to do it...

The message format that should be used by the controller to send `OFPT_GROUP_MOD` is defined in *Adding a new group entry in a group table* recipe of this chapter. Here, to delete a group table entry, the command field should be set to `OFPGC_DELETE`.

The procedure to construct the group modification message for deleting a group entry is similar to that of the one explained in the previous recipe. However, while deleting an entry, the controller need not set the group type in the modification message.

If the controller wants to delete only the group entries but still wants to keep the associated flow entries to point a group table entry, then the controller should send the group entry modification message instead of a group entry delete message. Refer to the recipe, *Modifying a group entry in a group table* for more information regarding the group entry modify message.

If the controller wants to delete all the entries from a group table, then it should set the identifier field as OFPG_ALL.

How it works...

While processing the group delete message with the switch, if there are no matching entries with a specified identifier present in the group table, then the switch ignores this message and it will not send any error message back to the controller.

See also

- For more information on how the switch processes group entry delete messages, refer to the recipe, *Deleting a group entry in a group table* in *Chapter 4, Group Table and Meter Table modification Messages (Part 1)* of this book

Modifying a group entry in a group table

When the controller wants to modify a group entry, it should send a group entry modification message (OFPT_GROUP_MOD) with a command value set to OFPGC_MODIFY to the switch. This flow table modification message contains the information required to identify and modify the entry from the group table.

The OFPT_GROUP_MOD message is used for all the flow entry operations such as adding a new flow entry, deleting an existing flow entry, and modifying a flow entry in a flow table.

How to do it...

The message format that should be used by the controller to send - OFPT_GROUP_MOD is defined in *Adding a new group entry in a group table* recipe of this chapter. Here, to modify a group table entry, the command field should be set to OFPGC_MODIFY.

The procedure to construct the group modification message for modifying a group entry is similar to that of the one explained in the previous recipe.

How it works...

When the switch receives a group modification message with the command `OFPGC_MODIFY`, the switch fetches a group entry from the group table based on the group identifier of the message.

If the switch can fetch a group entry, then the existing entry, along with type and action buckets, will be removed and a new entry will be created.

If the switch isn't able to fetch the corresponding group entry, then the switch sends a message to ignore this flow modification and sends an error message with the type `OFPET_GROUP_MOD_FAILED` and the code `OFPGMFC_UNKNOWN_GROUP`.

See also

- For more information on how the switch processes group entry modify messages, refer to the recipe, *Modifying a group entry in a group table* in *Chapter 4, Group Table and Meter Table Modification Messages (Part 1)* of this book

Adding a new meter in a meter table

The OpenFlow meter tables are used to implement simple QoS operations such as rate limiting to complex QoS frameworks such as DiffServ. For more information regarding the meter table, refer to the *Introduction* section in *Chapter 4, Group Table and Meter Table Modification Messages (Part 1).*

When the controller wants to program a meter, the controller should send a meter modification message (`OFPT_METER_MOD`) to the switch. This meter modification message contains the information required to program the meter table which includes the meter identifier, bands etc.

The `OFPT_METER_MOD` message is used for all the meter operations such as adding a new meter, deleting an existing meter, and modifying a meter.

How to do it...

The message format that should be used by the controller to send OFPT_METER_MOD is as follows:

```
/* Meter configuration. OFPT_METER_MOD. */
struct ofp_meter_mod {
struct ofp_header header;
uint16_t command;  /* One of OFPMC_*. */
uint16_t flags;    /* Bitmap of OFPMF_* flags. */
uint32_t meter_id; /* Meter instance. */
struct ofp_meter_band_header bands[0]; /* The band list length is
                                        * inferred from the length
                                        * field in the header. */
};
```

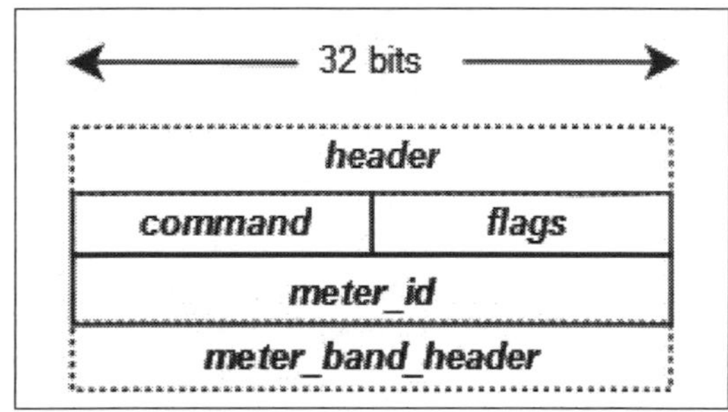

The command field represents the operation to be performed and is represented by the following enumeration:

```
/* Meter commands */
enum ofp_meter_mod_command {
OFPMC_ADD,    /* New meter. */
OFPMC_MODIFY, /* Modify specified meter. */
OFPMC_DELETE, /* Delete specified meter. */
};
```

For a group entry addition, the controller should set this value to OFPMC_ADD.

The `meter_id` field represents the identifier of the meter entry. The specification has defined the following virtual meter that can be associated with a flow:

```
/* Meter numbering. Flow meters can use any number up to OFPM_MAX. */
enum ofp_meter {
        /* Last usable meter. */
OFPM_MAX = 0xffff0000,
        /* Virtual meters. */
OFPM_SLOWPATH = 0xfffffffd,    /* Meter for slow datapath. */
OFPM_CONTROLLER = 0xfffffffe, /* Meter for controller
                               * connection. */
OFPM_ALL = 0xffffffff,        /* Represents all meters for stat
                               * requests commands. */
};
```

The meter `OFPM_SLOWPATH` and `OFPM_CONTROLLER` are termed as virtual meters and are provided to support previous versions of OpenFlow.

The `OFPM_CONTROLLER` meter is used to control the rate of packets sent to the controller as a packet-in message. So, when the controller wants to limit the number of packets sent by the switch to the controller, it should create this meter.

The `OFPM_SLOWPATH` meter is used to control the rate of packets which are being forwarded using the switch's slow path. So, when the controller wants to limit the number of packets sent by the switch's slow path, it should create this meter.

The OpenFlow specification recommends not to use these virtual meters. Instead, regular meters should be used.

The `flag` can be set with the combination of the following flag values:

```
/* Meter configuration flags */
enum ofp_meter_flags {
OFPMF_KBPS = 1 << 0, /* Rate value in kb/s (kilo-bit per
                      * second). */
OFPMF_PKTPS = 1 << 1, /* Rate value in packet/sec. */
OFPMF_BURST = 1 << 2, /* Do burst size. */
OFPMF_STATS = 1 << 3, /* Collect statistics. */
};
```

The controller should set the `flag` as `OFPMF_KBPS` when the rate value in the band is mentioned in **KBPS** (**Kilo-Bits Per Second**).

The controller should set the `flag` as `OFPMF_PKTPS` when the rate value in band is mentioned in **PPS** (**Packets Per Second**).

The controller should set the `flag` to `OFPMF_BURST`, when the controller wants to set the burst value. By default the burst size is kilobytes.

The `band` field should be set with the list of rate bands. While forwarding packets, only one band will be chosen by the switch based on the current rate of packets. If the current rate of packets exceeds the rate of multiple bands, then the band with the highest configured rate will be chosen by the switch. The bands are defined as follows:

The band field can contain any number of rate bands.

```
/* Common header for all meter bands */
struct ofp_meter_band_header {
uint16_t type;       /* One of OFPMBT_*. */
uint16_t len;        /* Length in bytes of this band. */
uint32_t rate;       /* Rate for this band. */
uint32_t burst_size; /* Size of bursts. */
};
```

The `rate` field should be set with the rate value above which the corresponding band applies to the packets. The rate value is in kbps unless the flag `OFPMF_PKTPS` is set, in which case the rate is defined in PPS.

The `burst_size` field should be set with the burst value. It defines the granularity of the meter so that if the packet or byte burst, if the length is greater than this `burst_size`, the meter rate will be applied.

The `type` field represents the action to be taken for the packets which are hitting this meter band and is set with one of the following values:

```
/* Meter band types */
enum ofp_meter_band_type {
OFPMBT_DROP = 1,                /* Drop packet. */
OFPMBT_DSCP_REMARK = 2,         /* Remark DSCP in the IP header. */
OFPMBT_EXPERIMENTER = 0xFFFF /* Experimenter meter band. */
};
```

The `type` field should be set with the value `OFPMBT_DROP` when the controller wants to drop packets which are exceeding the configured rate value, and uses the following structure:

```
/* OFPMBT_DROP band - drop packets */
struct ofp_meter_band_drop {
uint16_t type;        /* OFPMBT_DROP. */
uint16_t len;         /* Length is 16. */
uint32_t rate;        /* Rate for dropping packets. */
uint32_t burst_size; /* Size of bursts. */
uint8_t pad[4];
};
```

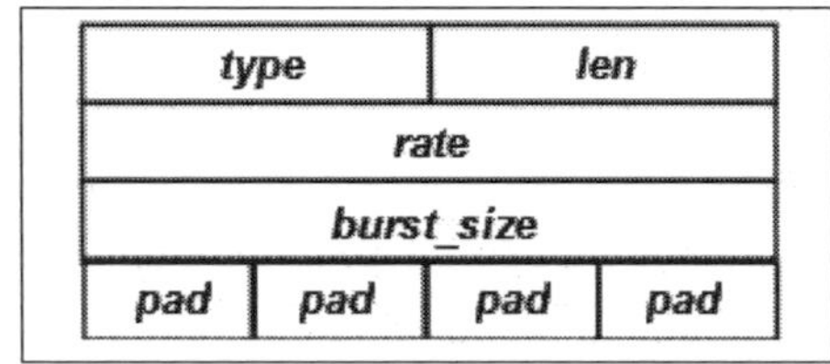

The `type` field should be set with the value `OFPMBT_DSCP_REMARK` when the controller wants to define a simple DiffServ policer that remarks the drop precedence of the DSCP field in the IP header of packets that exceed the band rate value, and uses the following structure:

```
/* OFPMBT_DSCP_REMARK band - Remark DSCP in the IP header */
struct ofp_meter_band_dscp_remark {
uint16_t type;        /* OFPMBT_DSCP_REMARK. */
uint16_t len;         /* Length is 16. */
uint32_t rate;        /* Rate for remarking packets. */
uint32_t burst_size; /* Size of bursts. */
uint8_t prec_level;  /* Number of drop precedence level to add. */
uint8_t pad[3];
};
```

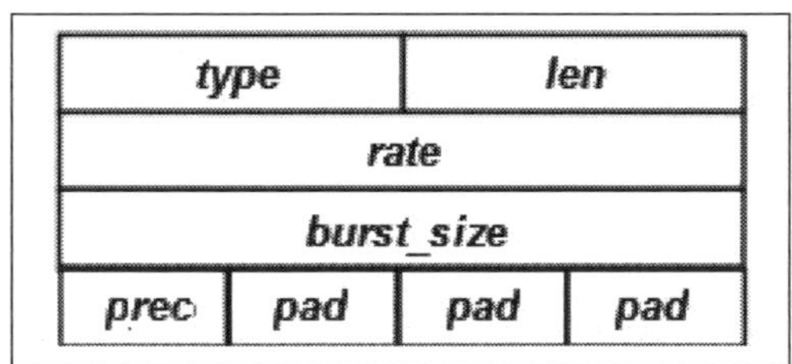

How it works...

After sending OFPT_METER_MOD, the switch may send an error message to the controller when the switch isn't able to process the message successfully. The error message that is sent by the switch and its interpretation is described in detail in the following section:

- The switch sends an error message with the type OFPET_METER_MOD_FAILED and the code OFPMMFC_METER_EXISTS when a meter is already present with the same meter ID.
- The switch sends an error message with the type OFPET_METER_MOD_FAILED and the code OFPMMFC_OUT_OF_METERS when the switch cannot add a meter due to lack of space or due to hardware restrictions.

See also

- For more information on how the switch processes meter entry add messages, refer to the recipe, *Adding a new meter in a meter table* in *Chapter 4, Group Table and Meter Table Modification Messages (Part 1)* of this book

Deleting a meter entry

When the controller wants to delete a meter entry, it should send a meter modification message (OFPT_METER_MOD) to the switch. This meter modification message contains the information required to delete the meter which includes the meter identifier, bands and so on.

The OFPT_METER_MOD message is used for all the meter operations such as adding a new meter, deleting an existing meter, and modifying a meter.

How to do it...

The message format that should be used by the controller to send OFPT_METER_MOD is defined in *Adding a new group entry in a group table* recipe of this chapter. Here, to delete a meter entry, the command field should be set OFPMC_DELETE.

The procedure to construct a meter modification message for deleting a meter entry is similar to that of the one explained in the previous recipe. However, while deleting an entry, the controller need not set the bands in a modification message.

If the controller wants to delete all the entries from the meter table except the virtual meters, then it should set the meter identifier field as `OFPG_ALL`.

How it works...

While processing a meter delete message with the switch, if there are no matching entries with the specified identifier, then the switch ignores this message and does not send any error message back to the controller.

If the meter entry presents in the meter table then the following will happen:

- The meter entry will be deleted from the group table
- All the flow entries which are using this meter will also be removed

See also

- For more information on how the switch processes meter entry delete messages, refer to the recipe, *Deleting a meter entry* in *Chapter 4, Group Table and Meter Table Modification Messages (Part 1)* of this book.

Modifying a meter entry in a meter table

When the controller wants to modify a meter entry, the controller should send a meter modification message (`OFPT_METER_MOD`) with the command value set as `OFPMC_MODIFY` to the switch. This meter modification message contains the information required to identify and modify the meter.

The `OFPT_METER_MOD` message is used for all the meter operations such as adding a new meter, deleting an existing meter, and modifying a meter.

How to do it...

The message format that should be used by the controller to send `OFPT_METER_MOD` is defined in *Adding a new group entry in a group table* recipe of this chapter. Here, to modify a meter entry, the command field should be set as `OFPMC_MODIFY`.

The procedure to construct a group modification message for modifying a meter entry is similar to that of the one explained in the previous recipe.

How it works...

When the switch receives a meter modification message with the command `OFPMC_MODIFY`, the switch fetches a meter entry based on the meter identifier.

If the switch can fetch a meter entry, then the existing entry along with the type and bands will be removed and a new entry will be created.

If the switch isn't able to fetch the corresponding meter entry, then the switch will ignore this flow modification message and send an error message with the type `OFPET_METER_MOD_FAILED` and the code `OFPMMFC_UNKNOWN_METER`.

See also

- For more information regarding how the switch processes meter entry modify messages, refer to the recipe, *Modifying a meter entry in a meter table* in *Chapter 4, Group Table and Meter Table Modification Messages (Part 1)* of this book

5
Handling Multipart Statistics Messages (Part 1)

This chapter describes multipart statistics messages in detail and contains the following recipes:

- Handling a multipart request message to get statistics of an individual flow table entry
- Handling a multipart request message to get statistics of a group/aggregate of flow table entries
- Handling a multipart request message to get statistics of a flow table
- Handling a multipart request message to get port statistics
- Handling a multipart request message to get port queue statistics
- Handling a multipart request message to get meter statistics
- Handling a multipart request message to get group statistics

Introduction

Multipart messages are used to encode OpenFlow request and reply messages that carry large amounts of data that can't fit into a single OpenFlow message. When the switch or controller has to send an OpenFlow message whose size exceeds 64 KB, then these messages can be encoded as a sequence of multipart messages. The sequence of multipart messages will be sent to the receiver, and the receiver should reassemble the OpenFlow message.

Multipart messages are typically used to send request and response messages for statistics messages and state information messages.

A request or reply message that spans across multiple multipart messages must use the same multipart `type` field and transaction ID (`xid`). The sequence of messages that are part of the same multipart message may be interleaved with other request or reply messages. However, the receiver should be able to reassemble these multipart messages, based on the transaction ID. The next chapter describes multipart state information messages in detail.

The message format that should be used by the switch to send a multipart reply message is defined as follows:

```
struct ofp_multipart_reply
{
  struct ofp_header header;
  uint16_t type; /* One of the OFPMP_* constants. */
  uint16_t flags; /* OFPMPF_REPLY_* flags. */
  uint8_t pad[4];
  uint8_t body[0]; /* Body of the reply. 0 or more bytes. */
};
```

The `type` field represents the type of the multipart message, and can take any one of the values described in the *Common OpenFlow multipart message types* section of *Appendix, Common OpenFlow Headers, Structures, and Error Code*. The `flag` field is used by the receiver to determine whether it should wait for more multipart messages before reassembling the received message. The `flag` field is defined as follows:

```
enum ofp_multipart_reply_flags {
OFPMPF_REPLY_MORE = 1 << 0     /* More replies to follow. */
};
```

The `body` field represents the information to be fetched from the switch, and its format depends on the type of the multipart message.

Handling a multipart request message to get statistics of an individual flow table entry

If the controller wants to get statistics for a particular flow entry, then it sends a `OFPMP_FLOW` multipart message (`ofp_multipart_request`) to the switch.

How to do it...

The message format that will be used by the controller to get the statistics of a flow entry using a multipart message is defined in the *Getting statistics of an individual flow table entry using multipart messages* recipe of *Chapter 5*, Handling *Multipart Statistics Messages (Part 2)*.

When the switch receives this `OFPMP_FLOW` message, it should first fetch the matching flow entry from its flow table. Once it fetches the matching flow entry, it should construct a reply message. The format of the reply message is defined in the *Introduction* section of this chapter.

The `type` field represents the type of multipart message and should be set to the value as `OFPMP_FLOW`. The `body` field should take the following format:

```
/* Body of reply to OFPMP_FLOW request. */
struct ofp_flow_stats {
uint16_t length;         /* Length of this entry. */
uint8_t table_id;        /* ID of table flow came from. */
uint8_t pad;
uint32_t duration_sec;   /* Time flow has been alive in seconds. */
uint32_t duration_nsec;  /* Time flow has been alive in nanoseconds
                          * beyond duration_sec. */
uint16_t priority;       /* Priority of the entry. */
uint16_t idle_timeout;   /* Number of seconds idle before
                          * expiration. */
uint16_t hard_timeout;   /* Number of seconds before expiration. */
uint16_t flags;          /* Bitmap of OFPFF_* flags. */
uint16_t importance;     /* Eviction precedence. */
uint8_t pad2[2];         /* Align to 64-bits. */
uint64_t cookie;         /* Opaque controller-issued identifier. */
uint64_t packet_count;   /* Number of packets in flow. */
uint64_t byte_count;     /* Number of bytes in flow. */
struct ofp_match match; /* Description of fields. Variable size.*/
};
```

The reply to the OFPMP_FLOW request is as follows:

- length: This field should be filled with length of the respective flow entry.
- table_id: This field should be filled with the flow table ID in which the matching flow entry was present.
- duration_sec: This and duration_nsec should be filled with the total duration from the time the port was configured in the OpenFlow pipeline to the current time. Their units are seconds and nanoseconds respectively.
- idle_timeout: This field should be filled with the idle_timeout value associated with the flow entry.
- hard_timeout: This field should be filled with the hard_timeout value associated with the respective flow entry. For more information regarding hard_timeout, refer to xxx.
- flag: This value should be set to the flags associated with the respective flow entry. For detailed information of this flag, refer to the *Adding a new flow entry to a flow table* recipe of *Chapter 3, Flow Table and Flow Entry Modification Messages (part 1).*
- importance: This field should be set with the eviction precedence associated with the flow entry.
- cookie: This value should be filled with the cookie value of the multipart request message.
- packet_count and byte_count: This should be filled with the number of packets and total number of bytes of data that have been forwarded by the flow entry respectively.

Here is the following figure which illustrates `OFPMP_FLOW` request:

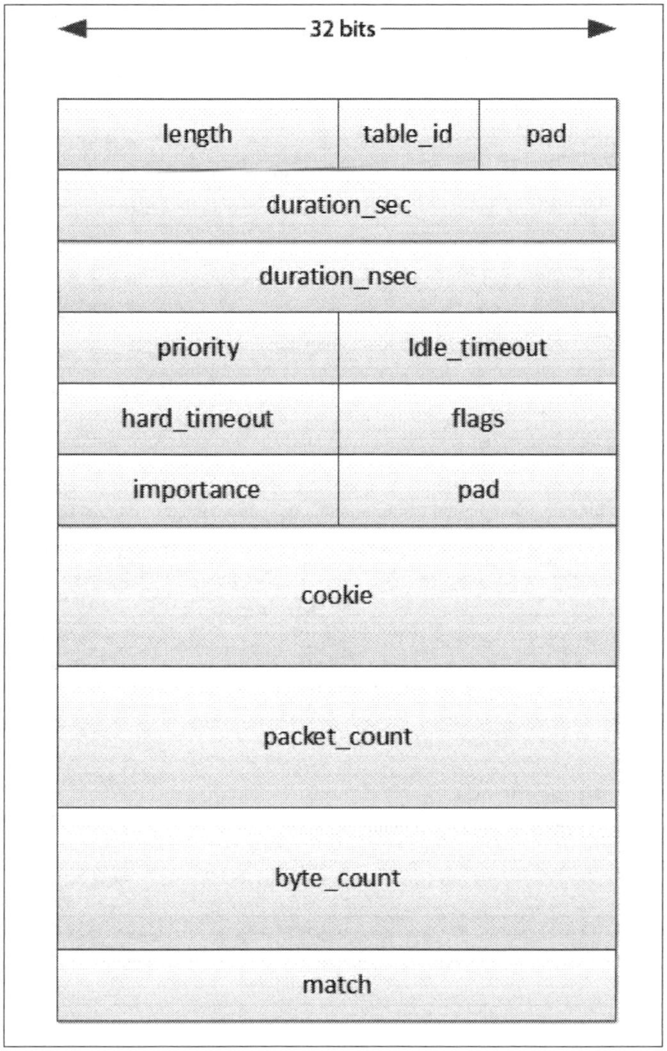

32 bits

length	table_id	pad
duration_sec		
duration_nsec		
priority	Idle_timeout	
hard_timeout	flags	
importance	pad	
cookie		
packet_count		
byte_count		
match		

Once the switch creates the reply message and fills the `message` field with the appropriate values, it should send the reply message to the controller. The format of the multipart reply message is defined in the *Introduction* section of this chapter.

After constructing the reply message, if the size of the reply message exceeds the maximum limit of OpenFlow messages (which is 64 KB), then the switch should send this message as a sequence of multiple reply messages, each having the same transaction ID (`xid`) and the `flag` field in the multipart reply message set to `OFPMPF_REPLY_MORE`. In the last message of the multipart sequence, the switch should unset this `flag` field.

See also

- For more information regarding how the controller sends the `OFPMP_FLOW` multipart message, refer to the *Getting statistics of an individual flow table entry using multipart messages* recipe of *Chapter 5, Handling Multipart State Information Messages (Part 2)*

Handling a multipart request message to get statistics of a group/aggregate of flow table entry

When the controller wants to get statistics for an aggregate or set of flow entries, it sends the `OFPMP_AGGREGATE` multipart message (`ofp_multipart_request`) to the switch.

How to do it...

The message format that will be used by the controller to get the statistics of the group/aggregate of flow entries is defined in the *Getting statistics of a group/aggregate of flow table entries using multipart messages* recipe of *Chapter 5, Handling Multipart State Information Messages (Part 2)*.

When the switch receives this `OFPMP_AGGREGATE` message, it should first fetch all the matching flow entries from its flow table. Once it fetches all the matching flow entries, it should construct a reply message. The format of the reply message is defined in the *Introduction* section of this chapter.

The `type` field represents the type of the multipart message and should be set with the value as `OFPMP_AGGREGATE`. The `body` field should take the following format:

```
/* Body of reply to OFPMP_AGGREGATE request. */
struct ofp_aggregate_stats_reply {
uint64_t packet_count; /* Number of packets in flows. */
```

```
uint64_t byte_count;    /* Number of bytes in flows. */
uint32_t flow_count;    /* Number of flows. */
uint8_t pad[4];         /* Align to 64 bits. */
};
```

The `packet_count` value and `byte_count` value should be filled with the number of packets and the total number of bytes of data that have been forwarded by the flow entries, respectively. The `flow_count` value should be set to the number of matching flow entries for which the counter values are being sent.

Once the switch creates the reply message and fills the `message` field with the appropriate values, it should send the reply message to the controller. The format of the multipart reply message is defined in the *Introduction* section of this chapter.

After constructing the reply message, if the size of the reply message exceeds the maximum limit of OpenFlow messages (which is 64 KB), then the switch should send this message as a sequence of multiple reply messages, each having the same transaction ID (`xid`) and the `flag` field in the multipart reply message set to `OFPMPF_REPLY_MORE`. In the last message of the multipart sequence, the switch should unset this flag.

See also

- For more information regarding how the controller sends the `OFPMP_AGGREGATE` multipart message, refer to the *Getting statistics of a group/aggregate of flow table entries using multipart messages* recipe of *Chapter 5, Handling Multipart State Information Messages (Part 2)*

Handling a multipart request message to get statistics of flow table

When the controller wants to get statistics of a flow table, it sends an `OFPMP_TABLE` multipart message (`ofp_multipart_request`) to the switch.

How to do it...

The message format that will be used by the controller to get the statistics of a flow table using multipart messages is defined in the *Getting statistics of a flow table using multipart messages* recipe of *Chapter 5, Handling Multipart State Information Messages (Part 2)*. When the switch receives this `OFPMP_TABLE` message, it should fetch the flow-table-related statistical information. Once it fetches this information, it should construct a reply message. The format of the reply message is defined in the *Introduction* section of this chapter.

The `type` field represents the type of multipart message and should be set with the value as `OFPMP_TABLE`. The `body` field should take the following format:

```
/* Body of reply to OFPMP_TABLE request. */
struct ofp_table_stats {
uint8_t table_id;       /* Identifier of table. Lower numbered
                         * tables are consulted first. */
uint8_t pad[3];         /* Align to 32-bits. */
uint32_t active_count; /* Number of active entries. */
uint64_t lookup_count; /* Number of packets looked up in table. */
uint64_t matched_count;/* Number of packets that hit table. */
};
```

The `active_count` field should be set to the number of active entries in the table. The `lookup_count` field should be set to the total number of packets lookups that happened in this table. Finally, the `matched_count` field should be set to the total number of packets that hit this table, as shown in the following figure:

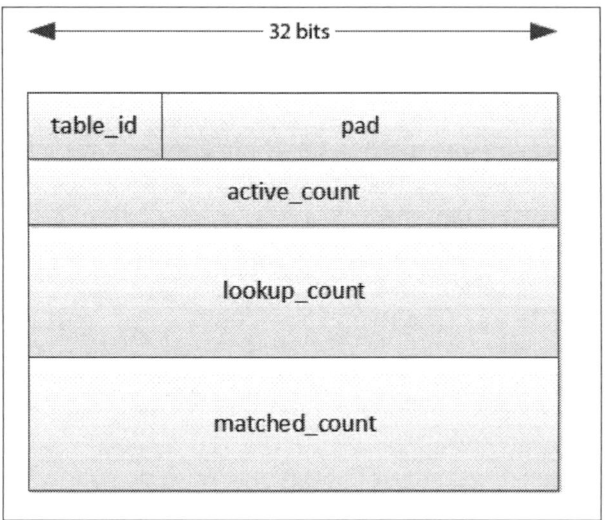

After constructing the reply message, if the size of the reply message exceeds the maximum limit of OpenFlow messages (which is 64 KB), the switch should send this message as a sequence of multiple reply messages, each having the same transaction ID (`xid`) and the `flag` field in the multipart reply message set to `OFPMPF_REPLY_MORE`. In the last message of the multipart sequence, the switch should unset this flag.

See also

For more information on how the controller sends an `OFPMP_TABLE` multipart message, refer to the *Getting statistics of a flow table using multipart messages* recipe of *Chapter 5, Handling Multipart State Information Messages (Part 2)*

Handling a multipart request message to get port statistics

When the controller wants to get statistics of an OpenFlow port, it sends the `OFPMP_PORT_STATS` multipart message (`ofp_multipart_request`) to the switch.

How to do it...

The message format that will be used by the controller to get the statistics of a port using a multipart message is defined in the *Getting port statistics using multipart messages* recipe of *Chapter 5, Handling Multipart State Information Messages (Part 2)*.

When the switch receives this `OFPMP_PORT_STATS` message, it should first fetch the matching port entry based on the `port_no` field. Once it fetches the matching port entries, it should construct a reply message. The format of the reply message is defined in the *Introduction* section of this chapter.

The `type` field represents the type of multipart message and should be set with the value as `OFPMP_PORT_STATS`. The `body` field should take the following format:

```
/* Body of reply to OFPMP_PORT_STATS request. If a counter is
unsupported,
* set the field to all ones. */
struct ofp_port_stats {
uint16_t length;        /* Length of this entry. */
uint8_t pad[2];         /* Align to 64 bits. */
uint32_t port_no;
uint32_t duration_sec;  /* Time port has been alive in seconds. */
uint32_t duration_nsec; /* Time port has been alive in nanoseconds
                         * beyond duration_sec. */
uint64_t rx_packets;    /* Number of received packets. */
uint64_t tx_packets;    /* Number of transmitted packets. */
uint64_t rx_bytes;      /* Number of received bytes. */
uint64_t tx_bytes;      /* Number of transmitted bytes. */
uint64_t rx_dropped;    /* Number of packets dropped by RX. */
```

```
uint64_t tx_dropped;     /* Number of packets dropped by TX. */
uint64_t rx_errors;      /* Number of receive errors. This is a
                          * super-set of more specific receive
                          * errors and should be greater than or
                          * equal to the sum of all rx_*_err values
                          * in properties. */
uint64_t tx_errors;      /* Number of transmit errors. This is a
                          * super-set of more specific transmit
                          * errors and should be greater than or
                          * equal to the sum of all tx_*_err values
                          * (none currently defined.) */
/* Port description property list - 0 or more properties */
struct ofp_port_desc_prop_header properties[0];
};
```

Let's cover the `body` field in detail:

- `duration_sec` and `duration_nsec`: These should be filled with the total duration from the time the port was configured in the OpenFlow pipeline to the current time, in seconds and nanoseconds, respectively. The total duration in nanoseconds can be computed as duration *sec* × *109 + duration nsec*. Implementations are required to provide precision up to seconds, but higher precision is encouraged.
- `rx_packets` and `rx_bytes`: These fields should be filled with the total number of packets and bytes received by this port respectively.
- `tx_packets` and `tx_bytes`: These fields should be filled with the total number of packets and bytes sent from this port respectively.
- `rx_dropped` and `tx_dropped`: These fields should be filled with the total number of packets dropped while receiving and sending respectively.
- `rx_errors` and `tx_errors`: This field should be filled with the number of receive errors and send errors on this particular port.

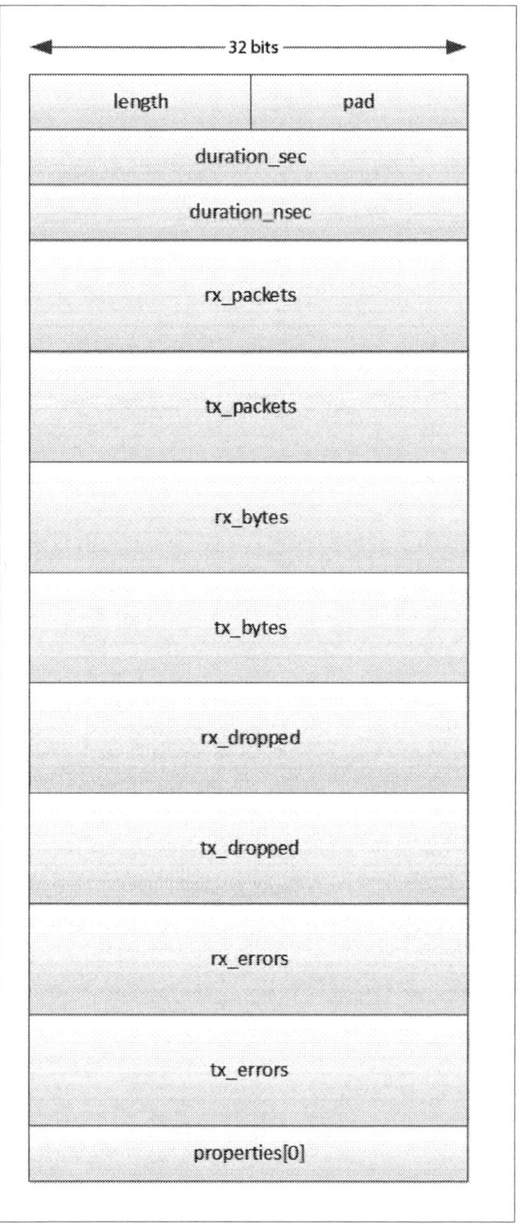

- `properties`: This field should contain the properties of all the ports whose statistical information is included in this multipart reply message.

If the port type is `Ethernet`, then this field should be filled with the following format:

```
/* Ethernet port stats property. */
struct ofp_port_stats_prop_ethernet {
uint16_t type;          /* OFPPSPT_ETHERNET. */
uint16_t length;        /* Length in bytes of this property. */
uint8_t pad[4];         /* Align to 64 bits. */
uint64_t rx_frame_err; /* Number of frame alignment errors. */
uint64_t rx_over_err;  /* Number of packets with RX overrun. */
uint64_t rx_crc_err;   /* Number of CRC errors. */
uint64_t collisions;   /* Number of collisions. */
};
```

The `type` field represents the type of port, which is defined as follows:

```
/* Port stats property types.
*/
enum ofp_port_stats_prop_type {
OFPPSPT_ETHERNET = 0,           /* Ethernet property. */
OFPPSPT_OPTICAL = 1,            /* Optical property. */
OFPPSPT_EXPERIMENTER = 0xFFFF, /* Experimenter property. */
};
```

For Ethernet ports, the `type` field should be filled with value as `OFPPSPT_ETHERNET`, which is `0`. Ethernet ports consist of the following fields:

- `rx_frame_err`: This field should be set to the number of frame alignment errors, if any
- `rx_over_err`: This field should be set to the number of frame overrun errors, if any
- `rx_crc_err`: This field should be set to the number of CRC errors, if any
- `collisions`: This field should be set to the number of detected collisions, if any

If the port type is `optical` port, then this field should be filled in the following format:

```
/* Optical port stats property. */
struct ofp_port_stats_prop_optical {
uint16_t type;          /* OFPPSPT_OPTICAL. */
uint16_t length;        /* Length in bytes of this property. */
uint8_t pad[4];         /* Align to 64 bits. */
uint32_t flags;         /* Features enabled by the port. */
uint32_t tx_freq_lmda; /* Current TX Frequency/Wavelength */
uint32_t tx_offset;    /* TX Offset */
uint32_t tx_grid_span; /* TX Grid Spacing */
uint32_t rx_freq_lmda; /* Current RX Frequency/Wavelength */
```

```
uint32_t rx_offset;     /* RX Offset */
uint32_t rx_grid_span; /* RX Grid Spacing */
uint16_t tx_pwr;        /* Current TX power */
uint16_t rx_pwr;        /* Current RX power */
uint16_t bias_current; /* TX Bias Current */
uint16_t temperature;  /* TX Laser Temperature */
};
```

For optical ports, the type field should be filled with value as `OFPPSPT_OPTICAL`, which is `1`. The optical ports consist of the following fields:

- `tx_freq_lmda`: This field should be set to the current `tx` frequency in MHz or wavelength in `nm*100`
- `tx_offset`: This field should be set to the `tx` offset value
- `tx_grid_span`: This field should be set to the `tx` grid spacing value
- `rx_freq_lmda`: This field should be set to the current `rx` frequency or wavelength
- `rx_offset`: This field should be set to the `rx` offset value
- `rx_grid_span`: This field should be set to the `rx` grid spacing value
- `tx_pwr`: This field should be set to the `tx` power value in `dBm*10`
- `rx_pwr`: This field should be set to `rx` power value in `dBm*10`
- `bias_current`: This field should be set to the `tx` bias current value in `mA*10`
- `temperature`: This field should be set to the `tx` laser temperature in `C*10`

The flag value should be set with validity information containing the validity of tune and the power and bias of both the `tx` and `rx` sides. It takes the following values:

```
/* Flags is one of OFPOSF_ below */
enum ofp_port_stats_optical_flags {
OFPOSF_RX_TUNE = 1 << 0, /* Receiver tune info valid */
OFPOSF_TX_TUNE = 1 << 1, /* Transmit tune info valid */
OFPOSF_TX_PWR = 1 << 2,  /* TX Power is valid */
OFPOSF_RX_PWR = 1 << 4,  /* RX power is valid */
OFPOSF_TX_BIAS = 1 << 5, /* Transmit bias is valid */
OFPOSF_TX_TEMP = 1 << 6, /* TX Temp is valid */
};
```

If the value of the `port_no` field in the request message is `OFPP_ANY`, then the switch should fetch the statistics of all the ports in the system and send the reply message containing the statistics of all the ports.

After constructing the reply message, if the size of the reply message exceeds the maximum limit of OpenFlow messages (which is 64 KB), then the switch should send this message as a sequence of multiple reply messages, each having the same transaction ID (`xid`) and the `flag` field in the multipart reply message set to `OFPMPF_REPLY_MORE`. In the last message of the multipart sequence, the switch should unset this flag.

See also

- For more information on how the controller sends an `OFPMP_PORT_STATS` multipart message, refer to the *Getting port statistics using multipart messages* recipe of *Chapter 5, Handling Multipart State Information Messages (Part 2)*

Handling a multipart request message to get port queue statistics

When the controller wants to get port queue statistics of one or more queues in one or more OpenFlow ports, it sends the `OFPMP_QUEUE_STATS` multipart message (`ofp_multipart_request`) to the switch.

How to do it...

The message format that will be used by the controller to get the statistics of a port queue using a multipart message is defined in the *Getting port queue statistics using multipart messages* recipe of *Chapter 5, Handling Multipart State Information Messages (Part 2).*

When the switch receives this message, it should first fetch the matching queue entry based on the `queue_id` and `port_no` fields in the request message. Once it fetches the matching queue entries, it should construct a reply message. The format of the reply message is defined in the *Introduction* section of this chapter.

The `type` field represents the type of multipart message and should be set with the value as `OFPMP_QUEUE_STATS`. The `body` field should take the following format:

```
/* Body of reply to OFPMP_QUEUE_STATS request. */
struct ofp_queue_stats {
uint16_t length;        /* Length of this entry. */
uint8_t pad[6];         /* Align to 64 bits. */
uint32_t port_no;       /* Port the queue is attached to. */
uint32_t queue_id;      /* Queue i.d */
uint64_t tx_bytes;      /* Number of transmitted bytes. */
uint64_t tx_packets;    /* Number of transmitted packets. */
uint64_t tx_errors;     /* Number of packets dropped due to
                         * overrun. */
```

```
uint32_t duration_sec; /* Time queue has been alive in seconds. */
uint32_t duration_nsec;/* Time queue has been alive in
                        * nanoseconds beyond duration_sec. */
struct ofp_queue_stats_prop_header properties[0];
            /* List of properties. */
};
```

The body field consists of the following fields:

- port_no: This field should be filled with the port_no value from the request message
- queue_id: This field should be filled with the queue_id value from the request message
- tx_packets and tx_bytes: These should be filled with the number of packets and the total number of bytes of data that has been forwarded by this queue, respectively

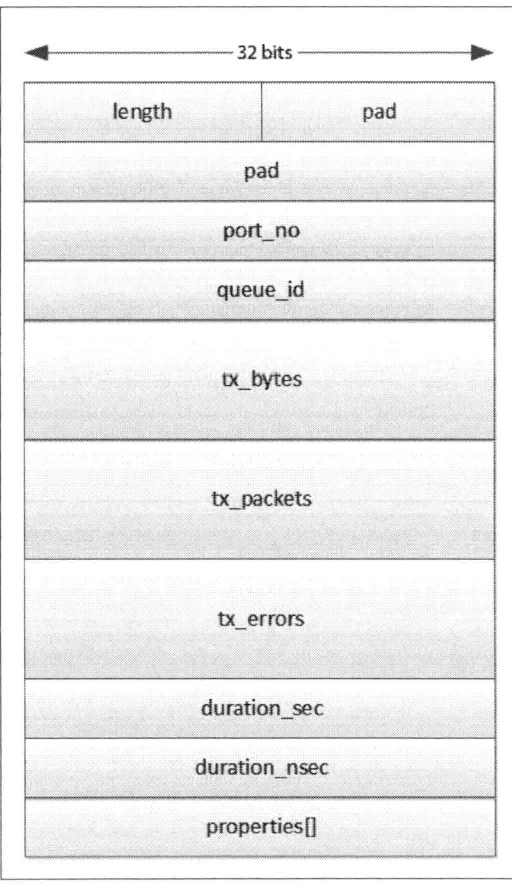

- `duration_sec` and `duration_nsec`: These should be filled with the total duration from the time queue was configured to the current time, in seconds and nanoseconds respectively
- `properties`: This field should contain the properties of all the queues whose statistical information is included in this multipart reply message

The specification has defined only one property for the queue as an experimenter property, and is defined as follows:

```
/* Experimenter queue property description. */
struct ofp_queue_stats_prop_experimenter {
uint16_t type;          /* OFPQSPT_EXPERIMENTER. */
uint16_t length;        /* Length in bytes of this property. */
uint32_t experimenter; /* Experimenter ID which takes the same
                         * form as in struct
                         * ofp_experimenter_header. */
uint32_t exp_type;      /* Experimenter defined. */
/* Followed by:
* - Exactly (length - 12) bytes containing the experimenter data, *
then Exactly (length + 7)/8*8 - (length) (between 0 and 7)
* bytes of all-zero bytes */
uint32_t experimenter_data[0];
};
```

Here, the `experimenter` value should be the experimenter ID, and the experimenter data contains the data part.

> If the value of the `queue_id` field in the request message is `OFPQ_ANY`, then the switch should fetch the statistics of all the queues of a given port, or all the ports (based on the `port_no` field value), and send the reply message containing the statistics of all the queues.

After constructing the reply message, if the size of the reply message exceeds the maximum limit of OpenFlow messages (which is 64 KB), then the switch should send this message as a sequence of multiple reply messages, each having the same transaction ID (`xid`) and the flag field in the multipart reply message set to `OFPMPF_REPLY_MORE`. In the last message of the multipart sequence, the switch should unset this flag.

See also

- For more information on how the controller sends the `OFPMP_QUEUE_STATS` multipart message, refer to the *Getting port queue statistics using multipart messages* recipe of *Chapter 5, Handling Multipart State Information Messages (Part 2)*

Handling a multipart request message to get meter statistics

When the controller wants to get statistics of an OpenFlow meter entry, it sends an `OFPMT_METER` multipart message (`ofp_multipart_request`) to the switch.

How to do it...

The message format that will be used by the controller to get the statistics of a meter using multipart messages is defined in the *Getting meter statistics using multipart messages* recipe of *Chapter 5, Handling Multipart State Information Messages (Part 2)*.

When the switch receives this `OFPMT_METER` message, it should first fetch the matching meter entry based on the `meter_id` field. If the `meter_id` field contains the value as `OFPM_ALL`, then the switch should fetch all the meters in the system. Once it fetches the matching entries, it should construct a reply message. The format of the reply message is defined in the *Introduction* section of this chapter.

The `type` field represents the type of multipart message and should be set with the value as `OFPMT_METER`. The `body` field should take the following format:

```
/* Body of reply to OFPMP_METER request. Meter statistics. */
struct ofp_meter_stats {
uint32_t meter_id;         /* Meter instance. */
uint16_t len;              /* Length in bytes of this stats. */
uint8_t pad[6];
uint32_t flow_count;       /* Number of flows bound to meter. */
uint64_t packet_in_count; /* Number of packets in input. */
uint64_t byte_in_count;/* Number of bytes in input. */
uint32_t duration_sec; /* Time meter has been alive in seconds. */
```

```
uint32_t duration_nsec;/* Time meter has been alive in nanoseconds
                        * beyond duration_sec. */
struct ofp_meter_band_stats band_stats[0];
/* The band_stats length is inferred from the length field. */
};
```

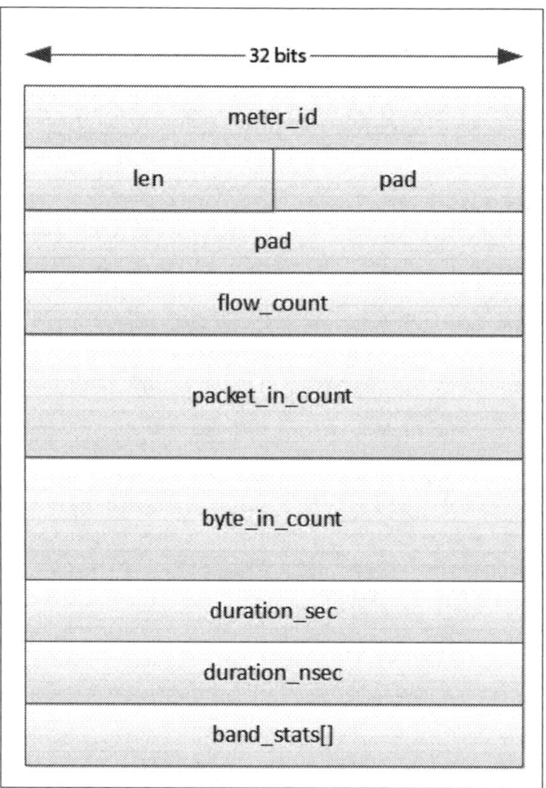

The reply to the `OFPMP_METER` request is as follows:

- `flow_count`: This field should be set to the number of flows associated with the meter
- `packet_in_count`: This and the `byte_in_count` field should be filled with the total number of packets and bytes (respectively) received, processed and forwarded by this meter
- `duration_sec` and `duration_nsec`: These should be filled with the total duration from the time this meter was configured to the current time in seconds and nanoseconds, respectively

- `band_stat`: This field should be filled with the statistics of all bands in a meter entry, and takes the following format:

```
/* Statistics for each meter band */
struct ofp_meter_band_stats {
uint64_t packet_band_count; /* Number of packets in band. */
uint64_t byte_band_count;   /* Number of bytes in band. */
};
```

- `packet_band_count` and `byte_band_count`: These fields should be filled with the total number of packets and bytes received, processed, and forwarded by this band

If the value of the `meter_id` field in the request message is `OFPMM_ALL`, then the switch should fetch the statistics of all the meter entries in the system, and send the reply message containing the statistics of all the meter entries.

After constructing the reply message, if the size of the reply message exceeds the maximum limit of OpenFlow messages (which is 64 KB), then the switch should send this message as a sequence of multiple reply messages, each having the same transaction ID (`xid`) and the `flag` field in the multipart reply message set to `OFPMPF_REPLY_MORE`. In the last message of the multipart sequence, the switch should unset this flag.

See also

- For more information on how the controller sends the `OFPMT_METER` multipart message, refer to the *Getting meter statistics using multipart messages* recipe of *Chapter 5, Handling Multipart State Information Messages (Part 2)* of this book

Handling a multipart request message to get group statistics

When the controller wants to get statistics of an OpenFlow group entry, it sends the `OFPMP_GROUP` multipart message (`ofp_multipart_request`) to the switch.

How to do it...

The message format that will be used by the controller to get the statistics of a group entry using multipart messages is defined in the *Getting group statistics using multipart messages* recipe of *Chapter 5, Handling Multipart State Information Messages (Part 2)*.

When the switch receives this `OFPMP_GROUP` message, it should first fetch the matching group entry based on the `group_id` field. If the `group_id` field contains the value as `OFPG_ALL`, then the switch should fetch all group entries in the system. Once it fetches the matching entries, it should construct a reply message. The format of the reply message is defined in the *Introduction* section of this chapter.

The `type` field represents the type of multipart message and should be set with the value as `OFPMP_GROUP`. The `body` field should take the following format:

```
/* Body of reply to OFPMP_GROUP request. */
struct ofp_group_stats {
uint16_t length;        /* Length of this entry. */
uint8_t pad[2];         /* Align to 64 bits. */
uint32_t group_id;      /* Group identifier. */
uint32_t ref_count;     /* Number of flows or groups that directly
                         * forward to this group. */
uint8_t pad2[4];        /* Align to 64 bits. */
uint64_t packet_count; /* Number of packets processed by group. */
uint64_t byte_count;    /* Number of bytes processed by group. */
uint32_t duration_sec; /* Time group has been alive in seconds. */
uint32_t duration_nsec;/* Time group has been alive in nanoseconds
                         * beyond duration_sec. */
struct ofp_bucket_counter bucket_stats[0];
/* One counter set per bucket. */
};
```

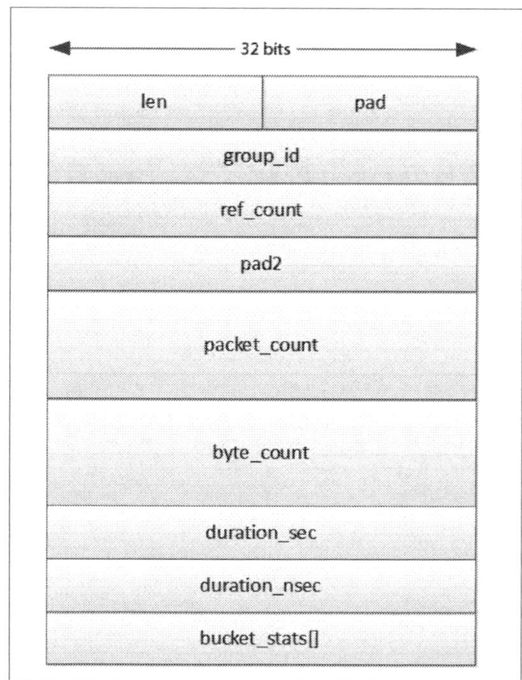

- `packet_count` and `byte_count`: These fields should be filled with the total number of packets and bytes received, processed and forwarded by this group
- `duration_sec` and `duration_nsec`: These should be filled with the total duration from the time this group was configured to the current time, in seconds and nanoseconds respectively
- `bucket_stat`: This field should be filled with the statistics of all buckets in a group entry, and it takes the following format:

```
/* Used in group stats replies. */
struct ofp_bucket_counter {
uint64_t packet_count; /* Number of packets processed by
                        * bucket. */
uint64_t byte_count;   /* Number of bytes processed by bucket. */
};
```

- `packet_count` and `byte_count`: These fields should be filled with the total number of packets and bytes received, processed, and forwarded by this bucket

If the value of the `group_id` field in the request message is `OFPMG_ALL`, then the switch should fetch the statistics of all the group entries in the system and send the reply message containing the statistics of all the group entries.

After constructing the reply message, if the size of the reply message exceeds the maximum limit of OpenFlow messages (which is 64 KB), then the switch should send this message as a sequence of multiple reply messages, each having the same transaction ID (`xid`) and the `flag` field in the multipart reply message set to `OFPMPF_REPLY_MORE`. In the last message of the multipart sequence, the switch should unset this flag.

See also

- For more information on how the controller sends the `OFPMP_GROUP` multipart message, refer to the *Getting group statistics using multipart messages* recipe of *Chapter 5, Handling Multipart State Information Messages (Part 2)*

5

Handling Multipart Statistics Messages (Part 2)

This chapter describes in detail about multipart statistics messages and contains the following recipes:

- Getting statistics of an individual flow table entry using multipart messages
- Getting statistics of group/aggregate of flow table entries using multipart messages
- Getting statistics of flow table using multipart messages
- Getting port statistics using multipart messages
- Getting port queue statistics using multipart messages
- Getting group statistics using multipart messages
- Getting meter statistics using multipart messages

The multipart messages are used to encode the OpenFlow request and reply messages which carry large amount of data that can't be fit into a single OpenFlow message. When the switch / controller has to send a OpenFlow message whose size exceeds 64Kb, these messages can be encoded as a sequence of multipart messages. The sequence of multipart message will be sent to the receiver and the receiver should re-assemble the OpenFlow message.

The multipart messages are typically used for sending the request and response messages for statistics message and state information messages.

A request or reply message which spans across multiple multipart messages must use same multipart `type` and transaction ID (`xid`). The sequence of messages which are part of the same multipart message may be interleaved with other request or reply messages. However, the receiver should be able to re-assemble these multipart messages based on the transaction ID.

The next chapter describes in detail about multipart state information messages.

The message format that should be used by controller for sending the multipart request message is as follows:

```
struct ofp_multipart_request {
struct ofp_header header;
uint16_t type;          /* One of the OFPMP_* constants. */
uint16_t flags;         /* OFPMPF_REQ_* flags. */
uint8_t pad[4];
uint8_t body[0];        /* Body of the request. 0 or more bytes. */
};
```

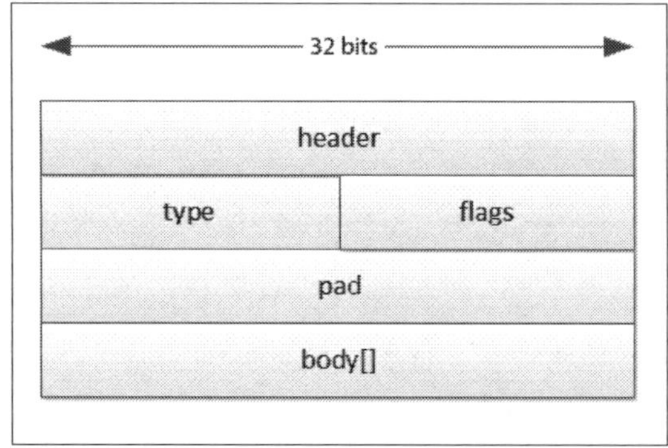

The `type` field represents the type of the multipart message and can take any one the following values as described in appendix *Common OpenFlow multipart message types*. For getting the statistics of a flow entry, the controller should set the `type` field as `OFPMP_FLOW`.

The `flag` field is used by the receiver to determine whether it should wait for more multipart messages before reassembling the received message. The `flag` field is defined as follows:

```
enum ofp_multipart_request_flags {
OFPMPF_REQ_MORE = 1 << 0 /* More requests to follow. */
};
```

The `body` field represents the information to be sent to the controller and its format depends on the type of the multipart message.

Getting statistics of an individual flow table entry using multipart messages

When the controller wants to get statistics for a particular flow entry, it should send OFPMP_FLOW multipart message (ofp_multipart_request) to switch.

How to do it...

The message format that should be used by controller for sending the multipart request message is defined in the *Introduction* section of this chapter.

For getting the statistics of a flow entry, the controller should set the type field as OFPMP_FLOW.

The body field should be filled with the following structure:

```
/* Body for ofp_multipart_request of type OFPMP_FLOW. */
struct ofp_flow_stats_request {
uint8_t table_id;    /* ID of table to read (from ofp_table_stats),
                      * OFPTT_ALL for all tables. */
uint8_t pad[3];      /* Align to 32 bits. */
uint32_t out_port;   /* Require matching entries to include this
                      * as an output port. A value of OFPP_ANY
                      * indicates no restriction. */
uint32_t out_group; /* Require matching entries to include this
                      * as an output group. A value of OFPG_ANY
                      * indicates no restriction. */
uint8_t pad2[4];     /* Align to 64 bits. */
uint64_t cookie;     /* Require matching entries to contain this
                      * cookie value */
uint64_t cookie_mask; /* Mask used to restrict the cookie bits
                        * that must match. A value of 0 indicates
                        * no restriction. */
struct ofp_match match; /* Fields to match. Variable size. */
};
```

The table_id field should be set with flow table to be used.

The match_field should contain the description of the flow entry to be matched. The controller could set the wildcard and mask fields which will be used by the switch while matching the flow entry. Refer to the *Introduction* section of *Chapter 3, Flow Table and Flow Entry Modification Messages (Part 1)* for more information regarding the flow match.

The `out_port` and `out_group` fields are optional values. If the controller want to add some constraint of the flow entry based on its output action, then the controller could set these values. When these fields are set, the switch applies constraint while matching the flow entry. When these values are set, the switch will select the flow entry whose action contains Output with value as `out_port` or Group with group ID as `out_group`. This is an additional constraint along with the constraints mentioned in `ofp_match_structs`. To disable this output filtering, these fields should be set with `OFPP_ANY` and `OFPG_ANY`.

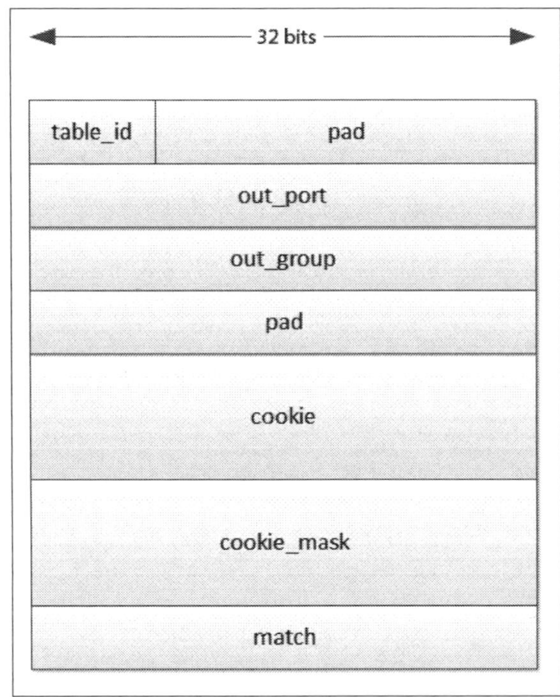

If the controller wants to filter the flow entries from flow table and then fetch the statistics of the flow entry based on this filter, the `cookie` field and `cookie_mask` field should be filled with the value which was generated at the time of adding the flow entry in the flow table. Using the `cookie` field and cookie `mask` field, the switch fetches the flow entry from the flow.

After sending the multipart request message, the controller should wait for the reply message from switch. If the size of the reply message exceeds the maximum limit of OpenFlow message (which is 64KB), then the switch sends this message as a sequence of multiple reply messages with `flag` field in multipart message header set as `OFPMPF_REPLY_MORE`. If the controller receives the reply message with this flag set, then the controller should buffer the sequence of multipart messages till it receives the last message in the sequence. As the switch sends the sequence of multipart message with same transaction ID (`xid`), the controller should map all the messages in the sequence and should decode the message to get the actual statistics information from the message.

How it works...

When the switch receives this `OFPMP_FLOW` message, the switch first fetches the matching flow entry from its flow table. Once it fetches the matching flow entry, it constructs a reply message and sends the reply message back to controller. Refer to recipe *Handling a multipart request message to get statistics of an individual flow table entry* of *Chapter 5, Handling Multipart Statistics Messages (Part 1)* for more information regarding the format of the reply message.

Getting statistics of group/aggregate of flow table entries using multipart messages

When the controller wants to get statistics for aggregate or set of flow entries, it should send `OFPMP_AGGREGATE` multipart message (`ofp_multipart_request`) to switch.

How to do it...

The message format that should be used by controller for sending the multipart request message is defined in the *Introduction* section of this chapter.

For getting the statistics of a flow entry, the controller should set the `type` field as `OFPMP_AGGREGATE`.

The `body` field should be filled with the following structure:

```
/* Body for ofp_multipart_request of type OFPMP_AGGREGATE. */
struct ofp_aggregate_stats_request {
uint8_t table_id;      /* ID of table to read (from
                        * ofp_table_stats) OFPTT_ALL for
                        * all tables. */
uint8_t pad[3];        /* Align to 32 bits. */
uint32_t out_port;     /* Require matching entries to include this
                        * as an output port. A value of OFPP_ANY
                        * indicates no restriction. */
uint32_t out_group;    /* Require matching entries to include this
                        * as an output group. A value of OFPG_ANY
                        * indicates no restriction. */
uint8_t pad2[4];       /* Align to 64 bits. */
uint64_t cookie;       /* Require matching entries to contain this
                        * cookie value */
uint64_t cookie_mask;/* Mask used to restrict the cookie bits that
                        * must match. A value of 0 indicates
                        * no restriction. */
struct ofp_match match; /* Fields to match. Variable size. */
};
```

The `table_id` should be set with the ID of flow table to be used.

The `match_field` should contain the description of the flow entry to be matched. The controller could set the wildcard and `mask` fields which will be used by the switch while matching the flow entry. Refer to the *Introduction* section of *Chapter 3, Flow Table and Flow Entry Modification Messages (Part 1)* for more information regarding the flow match.

The `out_port` and `out_group` fields are optional values. If the controller wants to add some constraint of the flow entry based on its output action, then the controller could set these values. When these fields are set, the switch applies constraint while matching the flow entry. When these values are set, the switch will select the flow entry whose action contains Output with value as `out_port` or Group with group ID as `out_group`.

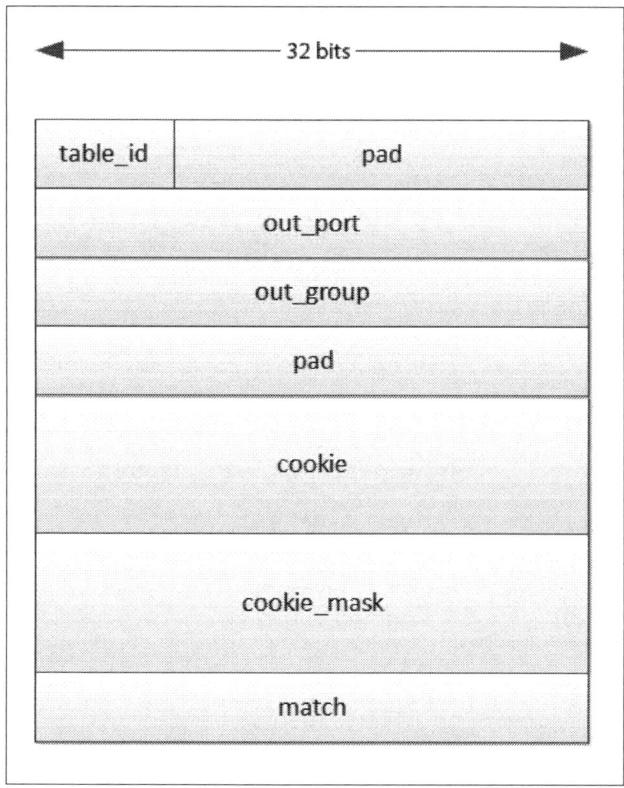

If the controller wants to filter the flow entries from flow table and then fetch the statistics of the flow entry based on this filter, the `cookie` field and `cookie_mask` field should be filled with the value which was generated at the time of adding the flow entry in the flow table. Using the `cookie` field and cookie mask filed, the switch fetches the flow entry from the flow table.

After sending the multipart request message, the controller should wait for the reply message from switch. If the size of the reply message exceeds the maximum limit of OpenFlow message (which is 64KB), then the switch sends this message as a sequence of multiple reply messages with `flag` field in multipart message header set as `OFPMPF_REPLY_MORE`. If the controller receives the reply message with this flag set, then the controller should buffer the sequence of multipart messages till it receives the last message in the sequence. As the switch sends the sequence of multipart message with same transaction ID (`xid`), the controller should map all the messages in the sequence and should decode the message to get the actual statistics information from the message.

How it works...

When the switch receives this `OFPMP_AGGREGATE` message, the switch first fetches all the matching flow entries from its flow table. Once it fetches all the matching flow entries, it constructs a reply message and sends the reply message back to controller.

Refer to recipe *Handling a multipart request message to get statistics of an individual flow table entry* of *Chapter 5, Handling Multipart Statistics Messages (Part 1)* for more information regarding the format of the reply message.

Getting statistics of flow table using multipart messages

When the controller wants to get statistics of a flow table, it should send `OFPMP_TABLE` multipart message (`ofp_multipart_request`) to switch.

How to do it...

The message format that should be used by controller for sending the multipart request message is defined in the *Introduction* section of this Chapter.

For getting the statistics of a flow entry, the controller should set the `type` field as `OFPMP_TABLE`.

The `body` field should be left empty.

After sending the multipart request message, the controller should wait for the reply message from switch. If the size of the reply message exceeds the maximum limit of OpenFlow message (which is 64KB) then the switch sends this message as a sequence of multiple reply messages with `flag` field in multipart message header set as `OFPMPF_REPLY_MORE`. If the controller receives the reply message with this flag set, then the controller should buffer the sequence of multipart messages till it receives the last message in the sequence. As the switch sends the sequence of multipart message with same transaction ID (xid), the controller should map all the messages in the sequence and should decode the message to get the actual statistics information from the message.

How it works...

When the switch receives this `OFPMP_TABLE` message, it fetches the flow table related statistics information. Once it fetches statistics information, it constructs a reply message and sends the reply message back to controller. Refer to recipe *Handling multipart request message to get statistics of an individual flow table entry* of *Chapter 5, Handling a Multipart Statistics Messages (Part 1)* for more information regarding the format of the reply message.

Getting port statistics using multipart messages

When the controller wants to get statistics of an OpenFlow port, it should send `OFPMP_PORT_STATS` multipart message (`ofp_multipart_request`) to switch.

How to do it...

The message format that should be used by controller for sending the multipart request message is defined in the *Introduction* section of this Chapter.

For getting the statistics of a flow entry, the controller should set the `type` field as `OFPMP_PORT_STATS`.

The `body` field should be filled with the following message format:

```
/* Body for ofp_multipart_request of type OFPMP_PORT_STATS. */
struct ofp_port_stats_request {
uint32_t port_no; /* OFPMP_PORT message must request statistics
                   * either for a single port (specified in
                   * port_no) or for all ports (if port_no ==
                   * OFPP_ANY). */
uint8_t pad[4];
};
```

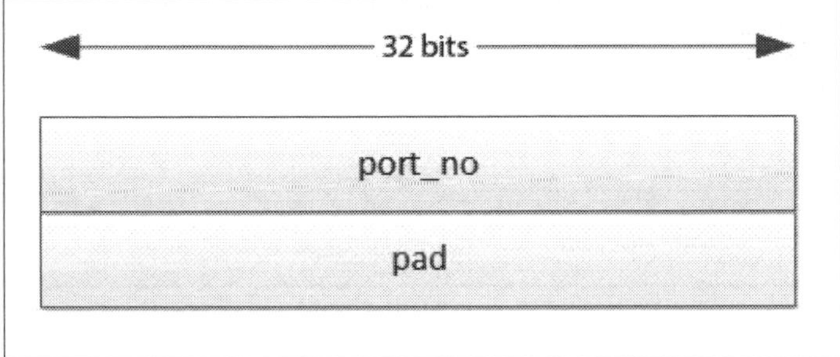

The `port_no` field should be filled with the port number whose statistics are to be fetched by the switch. If the controller wants to get statistics of all the ports in the system, then this value should be set to `OFPP_ANY`.

After sending the multipart request message, the controller should wait for the reply message from switch. If the size of the reply message exceeds the maximum limit of OpenFlow message (which is 64KB) then the switch sends this message as a sequence of multiple reply messages with `flag` field in multipart message header set as `OFPMPF_REPLY_MORE`. If the controller receives the reply message with this flag set, then the controller should buffer the sequence of multipart messages till it receives the last message in the sequence. As the switch sends the sequence of multipart messages with same transaction ID (`xid`), the controller should map all the messages in the sequence and should decode the message to get the actual statistics information from the message.

How it works...

When the switch receives this `OFPMP_PORT_STATS` message, the switch first fetches the matching port entry based on the `port_no` field. Once it fetches the matching port entries, it constructs a reply message and sends the reply message back to controller.

Getting port queue statistics using multipart messages

When the controller wants to get port queue statistics of one or more queues in one or more OpenFlow ports, it should send `OFPMP_QUEUE_STATS` multipart message (`ofp_multipart_request`) to switch.

How to do it...

The message format that should be used by controller for sending the multipart request message is defined in the *Introduction* section of this Chapter.

For getting the statistics of a flow entry, the controller should set the `type` field as `OFPMP_QUEUE_STATS`.

The `body` field should be filled with the following message format:

```
/* Body for ofp_multipart_request of type OFPMP_QUEUE_STATS. */
struct ofp_queue_stats_request {
uint32_t port_no;    /* All ports if OFPP_ANY. */
uint32_t queue_id;  /* All queues if OFPQ_ALL. */
};
```

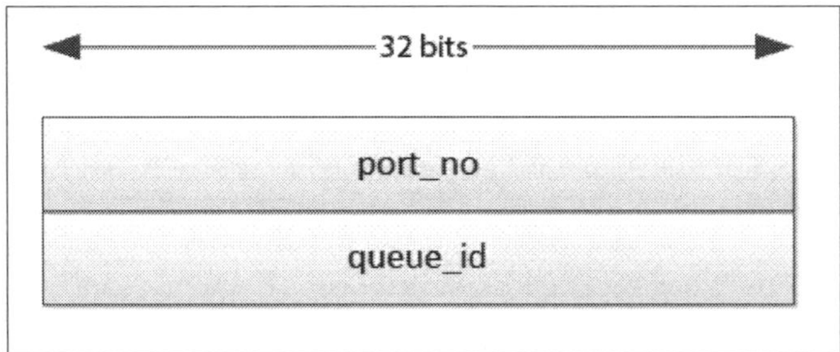

The `port_no`. field should be filled with the port number whose queue statistics are to be fetched by the switch. If the controller wants to get queue statistics of all the ports in the system, then this value should be set to `OFPP_ANY`.

The `queue_id` field should be filled with the queue in a port whose statistics to be fetched by the switch. If the controller wants to get statistics of all the queues in a port, then this value should be set to `OFPP_ANY`.

After sending the multipart request message, the controller should wait for the reply message from switch. If the size of the reply message exceeds the maximum limit of OpenFlow message (which is 64KB) then the switch sends this message as a sequence of multiple reply messages with `flag` field in multipart message header set as `OFPMPF_REPLY_MORE`. If the controller receives the reply message with this flag set, then the controller should buffer the sequence of multipart messages till it receives the last message in the sequence. As the switch sends the sequence of multipart message with same transaction ID (xid), the controller should map all the messages in the sequence and should decode the message to get the actual statistics information from the message.

How it works...

When the switch receives this message, the switch first fetches the matching queue entry based on the `queue_id` and `port_no` field in the request message. Once it fetches the matching queue entries, it constructs a reply message and sends the reply message back to controller.

Refer to recipe *Handling a multipart request message to get statistics of an individual flow table entry* of *Chapter 5, Handling Multipart Statistics Messages (Part 1)* for more information regarding the format of the reply message.

Getting meter statistics using multipart messages

When the controller wants to get statistics of an OpenFlow meter entry, it should send `OFPMT_METER` multipart message (`ofp_multipart_request`) to switch.

How to do it...

The message format that should be used by controller for sending the multipart request message is defined in the Introduction section of this chapter. For getting the statistics of a flow entry, the controller should set the `type` field as `OFPMT_METER`.

The `body` field should be filled with the following message format:

```
/* Body of OFPMP_METER and OFPMP_METER_CONFIG requests. */
struct ofp_meter_multipart_request {
uint32 t meter_id; /* Meter instance, or OFPM_ALL. */
uint8_t pad[4];    /* Align to 64 bits. */
};
```

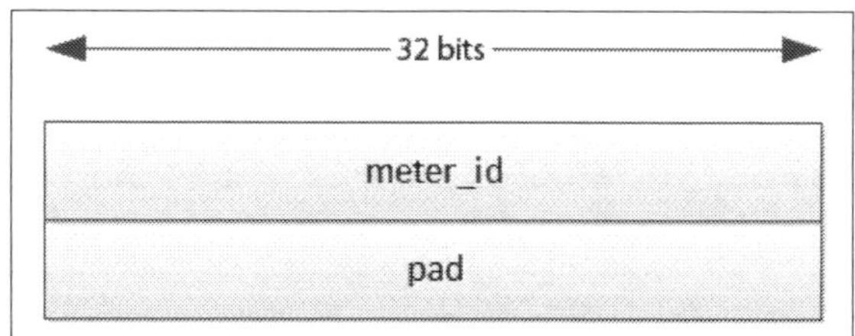

The `meter_id` field should be filled with the meter ID whose statistics are to be fetched by the switch. If the controller wants to get statistics of all the meters in the system, then this value should be set to `OFPM_ALL`.

After sending the multipart request message, the controller should wait for the reply message from switch. If the size of the reply message exceeds the maximum limit of OpenFlow message (which is 64KB) then the switch sends this message as a sequence of multiple reply messages with flag field in multipart message header set as `OFPMPF_REPLY_MORE`. If the controller receives the reply message with this flag set, then the controller should buffer the sequence of multipart messages till it receives the last message in the sequence. As the switch sends the sequence of multipart message with same transaction ID (`xid`), the controller should map all the messages in the sequence and should decode the message to get the actual statistics information from the message.

How it works...

When the switch receives this `OFPMP_METER` message, the switch first fetches the matching meter entry based on the meter_id field, then constructs a reply message and sends the reply message back to controller.

Refer to recipe *Handling a multipart request message to get statistics of an individual flow table entry* of *Chapter 5, Handling Multipart Statistics Messages (Part 1)* for more information regarding the format of the reply message.

Getting group statistics using multipart messages

When the controller wants to get statistics of an OpenFlow group entry, it should send `OFPMP_GROUP` multipart message (`ofp_multipart_request`) to switch.

How to do it...

The message format that should be used by controller for sending the multipart request message is defined in the *Introduction* section of this Chapter.

For getting the statistics of a group entry the controller should set the `type` field as `OFPMP_GROUP`.

After sending the multipart request message, the controller should wait for the reply message from switch. If the size of the reply message exceeds the maximum limit of OpenFlow message (which is 64KB) then the switch sends this message as a sequence of multiple reply messages with `flag` field in multipart message header set as `OFPMPF_REPLY_MORE`. If the controller receives the reply message with this flag set, then the controller should buffer the sequence of multipart messages till it receives the last message in the sequence. As the switch sends the sequence of multipart message with same transaction ID (`xid`), the controller should map all the messages in the sequence and should decode the message to get the actual statistics information from the message.

How it works...

When the switch receives this `OFPMP_GROUP` message, the switch first fetches the matching group entry based on the `group_id` field, followed by constructing a reply message and sending the reply message back to controller.

Refer to recipe *Handling a multipart request message to get statistics of an individual flow table entry* of *Chapter 5, Handling Multipart Statistics Messages (Part 1)* for more information regarding the format of the reply message.

6
Handling Multipart State Information Messages (Part 1)

This chapter describes multipart state information messages in detail, and contains the following recipes:

- Getting information about the switch using multipart messages
- Getting the group description using multipart messages
- Getting the group feature using multipart messages
- Getting the meter configuration using multipart messages
- Getting the meter feature using multipart messages
- Getting the table feature using multipart messages
- Getting the port description using multipart messages
- Getting the table description using multipart messages
- Getting the queue description using multipart messages
- Configuring the flow monitor using multipart messages
- Experimenter multipart messages

Introduction

The multipart messages are used to encode OpenFlow request and reply messages, which carry large amount of data that can't be fitted into a single OpenFlow message. For more information regarding multipart messages and the message formats that will be used by the controller for sending the multipart request message, refer to the *Introduction* section in *Chapter 5, Handling Multipart Statistics Messages (Part 1)*. The chapter also describes multipart statistics information messages in detail.

Getting information about the switch using multipart messages

When the controller wants to get information about switch details like the manufacturer, serial number, hardware revision, software revision, description and so on, it sends an `OFPMP_DESC` multipart message (`ofp_multipart_request`) to switch.

How to do it...

When the switch receives this `OFPMP_DESC` message, it should insert the information, as shown in the following structure and should pack this structure in the body field of the multipart reply message and send the reply message back to the controller. For more information on the procedure to construct and send the multipart reply message to the controller, refer to the *Introduction* section of *Chapter 5, Handling Multipart Statistics Messages (Part 1)*.

The `body` field should take the following format:

```
/* Body of reply to OFPMP_DESC request. Each entry is a NULL-
terminated
* ASCII string. */
struct ofp_desc {
char mfr_desc[DESC_STR_LEN]; /* Manufacturer description. */
char hw_desc[DESC_STR_LEN];  /* Hardware description. */
char sw_desc[DESC_STR_LEN];       /* Software description. */
char serial_num[SERIAL_NUM_LEN]; /* Serial number. */
char dp_desc[DESC_STR_LEN];       /* Human readable description
                                   * of datapath. */
};
```

All the values in the structure should be ASCII formatted and padded with null terminated byte (0).

The fields of OFPMP_DESC are as follows:

- mfr_desc: This field should be filled with NULL terminated manufacturer information
- hw_desc: This field should be filled with NULL terminated hardware description
- sw_desc: This field should be filled with NULL terminated software description

The values of DESC_STR_LEN and SERIAL_NUM_LEN are 256 and 32, respectively.

- dp_desc: This field should be filled with NULL terminated datapath description

See also

- For more information on how the controller sends an OFPMP_DESC message to switch, refer to the recipe *Getting information about the switch using multipart message* in *Chapter 6, Handling Multipart State Information Messages (Part 2)*

Getting group description using multipart messages

When the controller wants to fetch the details of all the group entries installed in the switch, it sends an OFPMP_GROUP_DESC multipart message (ofp_multipart_request) to switch.

How to do it...

When the switch receives this OFPMP_GROUP_DESC message, the switch should first fetch all the group entries from its group table. Once it fetches all the group entries, it should insert the information as shown in the following structure and should pack this structure in the body field of the multipart reply message, and send the reply message back to the controller. For more information regarding the procedure to construct and send the multipart reply message, refer to the *Introduction* section in *Chapter 5, Handling Multipart State Information Messages (Part 1)*.

The body field should take the following format:

```
/* Body of reply to OFPMP_GROUP_DESC request. */
struct ofp_group_desc {
uint16_t length;                /* Length of this entry. */
uint8_t type;                   /* One of OFPGT_*. */
uint8_t pad;                    /* Pad to 64 bits. */
uint32_t group_id;              /* Group identifier. */
struct ofp_bucket buckets[0]; /* List of buckets - 0 or more. */
};
```

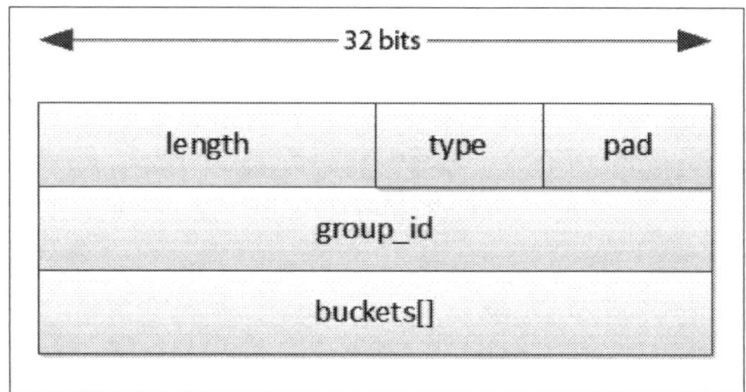

The fields of OFPMP_GROUP_DESC are as follows:

- group_id: This field represents the identifier of the group table entry.
- buckets: This field represents an array of buckets which contains a list of actions. For more information regarding this bucket field and the format of this bucket field, refer to the recipe *Adding a new group entry in a group table* in *Chapter 4, Group Table and Meter Table modification Messages (Part 1)*.

See also

- For more information on how the controller sends an OFPMP_DESC message to the switch, refer to the recipe *Getting the group description using multipart messages* in *Chapter 6, Handling Multipart State Information Messages (Part 2)*

Getting group feature using multipart messages

When the controller wants to fetch the features supported by group table in the switch, it sends an `OFPMP_GROUP_FEATURES` multipart message (`ofp_multipart_request`) to switch.

How to do it...

When the switch receives this `OFPMP_GROUP_FEATURES`, the switch should insert the information as shown in the following structure and should pack this structure in the body field of the multipart reply message and send the reply message back to the controller. For more information regarding the procedure to construct the multipart reply message, refer to the *Introduction* section of *Chapter 5, Handling Multipart State Information Messages (Part 1)*.

The `body` field should take the following format:

```
/* Body of reply to OFPMP_GROUP_FEATURES request. Group features. */
struct ofp_group_features {
uint32_t types;        /* Bitmap of OFPGT_* values supported. */
uint32_t capabilities; /* Bitmap of OFPGFC_* capability
                        * supported. */
uint32_t max_groups[4];/* Maximum number of groups for each
                        * type. */
uint32_t actions[4];   /* Bitmaps of OFPAT_* that are
                        * supported. */
};
```

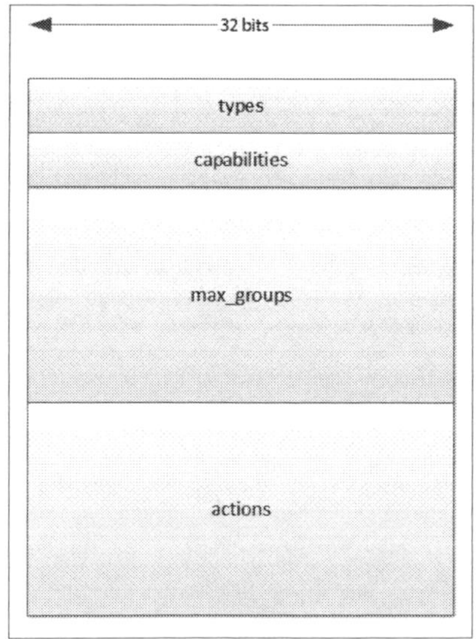

The fields of `OFPMP_GROUP_FEATURES` are as follows:

- `type`: This field should be filled with group type which is defined in the recipe *Adding a new group entry in a group table* in *Chapter 4, Group Table and Meter Table modification Messages (Part 1)*.
- `capabilities`: This field should be filled with one or more values of the following enumeration based on the capability of the switch:

```
/* Group configuration flags */
enum ofp_group_capabilities {
OFPGFC_SELECT_WEIGHT = 1 << 0,     /* Support weight for select
                                    * groups */
OFPGFC_SELECT_LIVENESS = 1 << 1,  /* Support liveness for select
                                    * groups */
OFPGFC_CHAINING = 1 << 2,          /* Support chaining groups */
OFPGFC_CHAINING_CHECKS = 1 << 3,  /* Check chaining for loops and
                                     * delete */
};
```

- `max_groups`: This field should be filled with maximum number of groups supported by this switch for each type of group. For example, if the switch supports x number of groups of type `OFPGT_ALL`, then the `max_groups[0]` should be filled with value as x.
- `action`: This field should be filled with the supported actions of each type of group. This should take one or more values of `OFPAT_ *` and is defined in *Appendix, Common OpenFlow Structures*.

See also

- For more information on how the controller sends an `OFPMP_GROUP_FEATURES` message to the switch, refer to the recipe *Getting the group feature using multipart message* in *Chapter 6, Handling Multipart State Information Messages (Part 2)*

Getting meter configuration using multipart messages

When the controller wants to fetch the configuration detail of one or more meters in the switch, it sends an `OFPMT_METER_CONFIG` multipart message (`ofp_multipart_request`) to the switch.

How to do it...

When the switch receives this `OFPMT_METER_CONFIG` message, the switch should first fetch the meter entry from the meter table using `meter_id`, then it should insert the information as shown in the following structure, and pack this structure in the body field of the multipart reply message. For more information regarding the procedure to construct and the multipart reply message refer to the *Introduction* section of *Chapter 5, Handling Multipart Statistics Messages (Part 1)*.

The `body` field should take the following format:

```
/* Body of reply to OFPMP_METER_CONFIG request. Meter configuration.
*/
struct ofp_meter_config {
uint16_t length;                        /* Length of this entry. */
uint16_t flags;                         /* All OFPMC_* that apply */
uint32_t meter_id;                      /* Meter instance. */
struct ofp_meter_band_header bands[0];/* The bands length is
                                         * inferred from the
                                         * length field. */
};
```

The fields of `OFPMP_METER_CONFIG` are as follows:

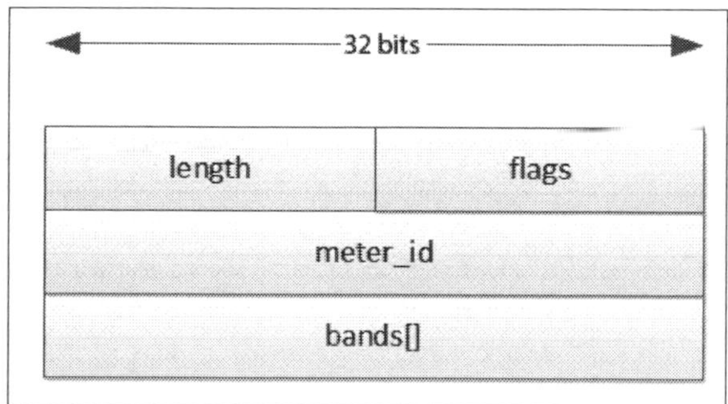

See also

- For more information on how the controller sends an `OFPMT_METER_CONFIG` message to switch, refer to the recipe *Getting the meter configuration using multipart messages* in *Chapter 6, Handling Multipart State Information Messages (Part 2)*

Getting the meter feature using multipart messages

When the controller wants to fetch the features of the meter table in the switch, it sends `OFPMT_METER_FEATURES` multipart message (`ofp_multipart_request`) to switch.

How to do it...

When the switch receives this `OFPMP_METER_FEATURES`, the switch should insert the information as shown in the following structure and should pack this structure in body field of multipart reply message and send the reply message back to controller. For more information regarding the procedure to construct and send the multipart reply message, refer to the *Introduction* section of *Chapter 5, Handling Multipart Statistics Messages (Part 1)*.

The `body` field should take the following format:

```
/* Body of reply to OFPMP_METER_FEATURES request. Meter features. */
struct ofp_meter_features {
uint32_t max_meter;  /* Maximum number of meters. */
uint32_t band_types;   /* Bitmaps of OFPMBT_* values supported. */
uint32_t capabilities; /* Bitmaps of "ofp_meter_flags". */
uint8_t max_bands;     /* Maximum bands per meters */
uint8_t max_color;     /* Maximum color value */
uint8_t pad[2];
};
```

The fields of `OFPMP_METER_FEATURES` are as follows:

- `max_meter`: This field should be filled with the maximum number of meters supported by this switch
- `band_type`: This field should be filled with band type, which is defined in *Appendix, Common OpenFlow Structures*

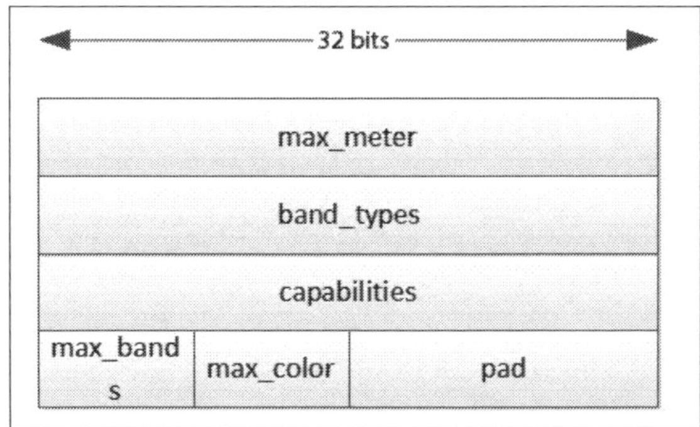

- `capabilities`: This field should be filled with one or more values of the following enumeration based on the capability of the switch:

```
/* Meter configuration flags */
enum ofp_meter_flags {
OFPMF_KBPS = 1 << 0,   /* Rate value in kb/s */
OFPMF_PKTPS = 1 << 1, /* Rate value in packet/sec. */
OFPMF_BURST = 1 << 2, /* Do burst size. */
OFPMF_STATS = 1 << 3, /* Collect statistics. */
};
```

- `max_bands`: This should be filled with the maximum number of bands supported in each meter by this switch.
- `max_color`: This should be filled with the maximum color value supported by this switch.

See also

- For more information on how the controller sends an `OFPMP_METER_FEATURES` message to the switch, refer to the recipe *Getting the meter feature using multipart messages* in *Chapter 6, Handling Multipart State Information Messages (Part 2)*

Getting the table feature using multipart messages

The table feature multipart messages are used by the controller for the following:

- To query the capabilities of existing tables in the switch
- To reconfigure the tables in the switch with a new configuration

How to do it...

When the switch receives this `OFPMP_TABLE_FEATURES` message, the switch should examine whether the multipart request message has a body field or not. If the request doesn't have any body field, then the switch should construct a reply message which contains the array of `ofp_table_features` structure and send the reply message back to the controller. The array size is determined by the number of flow tables present in the switch. The reply message that should be sent from the switch to the controller takes a similar format to the request message, as defined in the recipe *Getting the table feature using multipart message* in *Chapter 6, Handling Multipart State Information Messages (Part 2)*.

If the request message sent by the controller has the body field filled with the array of structure `ofp_table_features`, then the switch should apply the configurations, as mentioned in these messages, to the corresponding flow table, which results in configuring the entire pipeline of the flow table. This results in applying the table configurations of all the flow tables in the system, or none (if there is any error). If the configuration message doesn't contain one or more flow tables supported by the switch, then these flow tables should be removed from the pipeline stages of the switch.

See also

- For more information regarding how the controller sends an `OFPMP_TABLE_FEATURES` message to the switch, refer to the recipe *Getting the table feature using multipart message* in *Chapter 6, Handling Multipart State Information Messages (Part 2)*

Getting port description using multipart messages

When the controller wants to fetch the details of all the ports in the switch, it sends an `OFPMP_PORT_DESCRIPTION` multipart message (`ofp_multipart_request`) to the switch.

How to do it...

When the switch receives this `OFPMP_PORT_DESCRIPTION` message, the switch should first fetch all the OpenFlow ports present in the system. Once it fetches all the port information, the switch should fill the information as shown in the following structure and should pack this structure in the body field of the multipart reply message and send the reply message back to the controller. For more information regarding the procedure to construct and send the multipart reply message, refer to the *Introduction* section of *Chapter 5, Handling Multipart Statistics Messages (Part 1)*.

The code description of the port is as follows:

```
/* Description of a port */
struct ofp_port {
uint32_t port_no;
uint16_t length;
uint8_t pad[2];
uint8_t hw_addr[OFP_ETH_ALEN];
uint8_t pad2[2];                  /* Align to 64 bits. */
char name[OFP_MAX_PORT_NAME_LEN]; /* Null-terminated */
```

```
uint32_t config;                    /* Bitmap of OFPPC_* flags. */
uint32_t state;                     /* Bitmap of OFPPS_* flags. */
   /* Port description property list - 0 or more properties */
struct ofp_port_desc_prop_header properties[0];
};
```

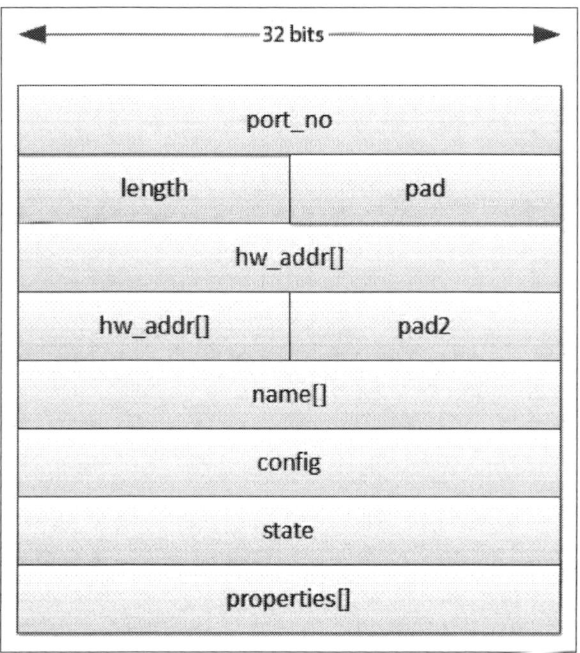

The description of the port as follows:

- `port_no`: This field should be filled with the port identifier of the port. The `port_no` uniquely identifies the port in the switch.
- `hw_addr`: This should be filled with the MAC address of the port.
- `name`: This field should be filled with the name of the interface. The name should be in a human-readable format with null terminated string.

The values of `OFP_ETH_ALEN` and `OFP_MAX_PORT_NAME_LEN` are 6 and 16, respectively.

- `config_field`: This should be filled with the configuration information related to the port and is described in the following enumeration:

```
/* Flags to indicate behavior of physical port. These flags are
* used in ofp_port to describe the current configuration. They are
* used in the ofp_port_mod message to configure the port's
* behavior.
*/
enum ofp_port_config {
OFPPC_PORT_DOWN = 1 << 0,    /* Port is administratively down. */
OFPPC_NO_RECV = 1 << 2,      /* Drop all packets received by
                              * port. */
OFPPC_NO_FWD = 1 << 5,       /* Drop packets forwarded to port. */
OFPPC_NO_PACKET_IN = 1 << 6 /* Do not send packet-in msgs for
port. */
};
```

- `state`: This field should be filled with the running status of the port and is described in the following enumeration:

```
/* Current state of physical port. These are not configurable from
 * the controller.
 */
enum ofp_port_state {
OFPPS_LINK_DOWN = 1 << 0, /* No physical link present. */
OFPPS_BLOCKED = 1 << 1,   /* Port is blocked */
OFPPS_LIVE = 1 << 2,      /* Live for Fast Failover Group. */
};
```

- `properties`: This field should be filled with the list of port properties which describes various configurations and state information of the port. Refer to *Appendix, Port Structures* for more information regarding the properties field structure.

See also

- For more information on how the controller sends an `OFPMP_PORT_DESCRIPTION` message to the switch, refer to the recipe *Getting port description using multipart messages* in *Chapter 6, Handling Multipart State Information Messages (Part 2)*

Getting table description using multipart messages

When the controller wants to fetch the configuration details of all the flow tables in the switch, it sends an `OFPMP_TABLE_DESC` multipart message (`ofp_multipart_request`) to the switch.

How to do it...

When the switch receives this `OFPMP_TABLE_DESC` message, the switch should first fetch table configurations. Once it fetches this information, the switch should insert the information as shown in the following structure and should pack this structure in body field of multipart reply message and send the reply message back to the controller. For more information regarding the procedure to construct and send the multipart reply message, refer to the *Introduction* section of *Chapter 5, Handling Multipart Statistics Messages (Part 1)*.

The `body` field should take the following format:

```
/* Body of reply to OFPMP_TABLE_DESC request. */
struct ofp_table_desc {
uint16_t length;    /* Length is padded to 64 bits. */
uint8_t table_id;   /* Identifier of table. Lower numbered tables
                     * are consulted first. */
uint8_t pad[1];     /* Align to 32-bits. */
uint32_t config;    /* Bitmap of OFPTC_* values. */
  /* Table Mod Property list - 0 or more. */
struct ofp_table_mod_prop_header properties[0];
};
```

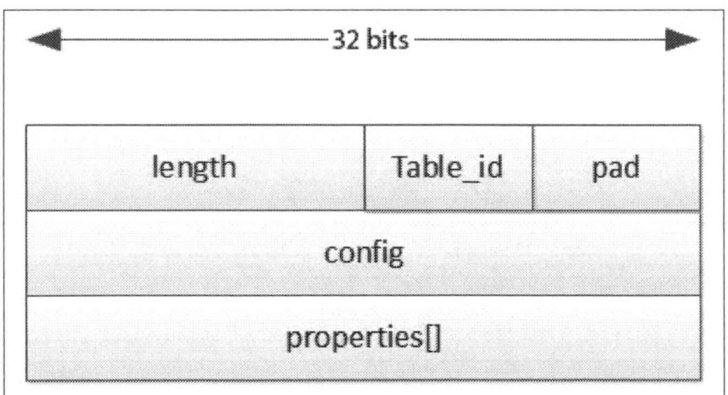

The `ofp_table_desc` structure is similar to the `ofp_table_mod` structure and hence the same procedure could be used to fill this structure too. For the actual procedure to fill this information refer to the recipe *Adding new flow entry in flow table* in *Chapter 3, Flow Table and Flow Entry Modification Messages (Part 1)*.

See also

- For more information on how the controller sends an `OFPMP_TABLE_DESC` message to switch, refer to the recipe *Getting the table description using multipart messages* in *Chapter 6, Handling Multipart State Information Messages (Part 2)*

Getting queue description using multipart messages

When the controller wants to fetch the details of the queues attached to OpenFlow ports in the switch, it sends an `OFPMP_QUEUE_DESC` multipart message (`ofp_multipart_request`) to the switch.

How to do it...

When the switch receives this `OFPMP_QUEUE_DESC` message, the switch should first fetch the queue information based on the `port_no` and `queue_id` fields in the multipart request message. Once it fetches the queue information, the switch should insert the information as shown in the following structure and should pack this structure in the body field of the multipart reply message and send the reply message back to the controller. For more information regarding the procedure to construct and the multipart reply message, refer to the *Introduction* section of *Chapter 5, Handling Multipart Statistics Messages (Part 1)*.

The `body` field should take the following format:

```
/* Body of reply to OFPMP_QUEUE_DESC request. */
struct ofp_queue_desc {
uint32_t port_no;  /* Port this queue is attached to. */
uint32_t queue_id; /* id for the specific queue. */
uint16_t len;    /* Length in bytes of this queue desc. */
uint8_t pad[6]; /* 64-bit alignment. */
struct ofp_queue_desc_prop_header properties[0];
    /* List of properties. */
};
```

The fields of OFPMP_QUEUE_DESC are as follows:

- port_no and queue_id: These fields should be filled with the port identifier and queue identifier of the queues whose details are being sent in this reply message.

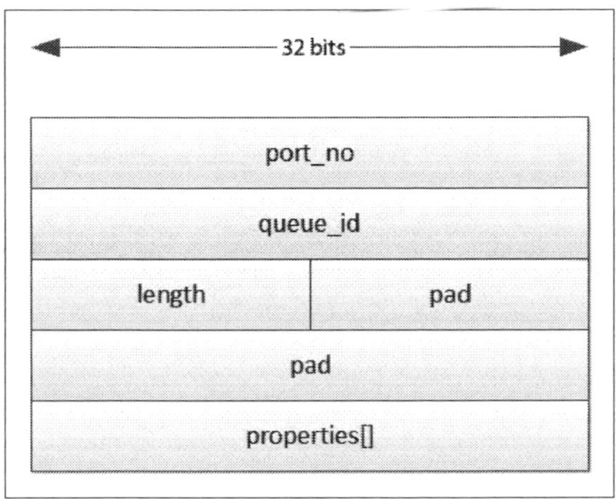

- properties: This field should be filled with the list of property of the queue. The specification has defined the properties as described in the following enumeration:

```
enum ofp_queue_desc_prop_type {
OFPQDPT_MIN_RATE = 1,          /* Minimum datarate guaranteed. */
OFPQDPT_MAX_RATE = 2,          /* Maximum datarate. */
OFPQDPT_EXPERIMENTER = 0xffff /* Experimenter defined property. */
};
```

- OFPQDPT_MIN_RATE: This property is defined, as shown in the following structure:

```
/* Min-Rate queue property description. */
struct ofp_queue_desc_prop_min_rate {
uint16_t type;   /* OFPQDPT_MIN_RATE. */
uint16_t length; /* Length is 8. */
uint16_t rate;   /* In 1/10 of a percent; >1000 -> disabled. */
uint8_t pad[2];  /* 64-bit alignment */
};
```

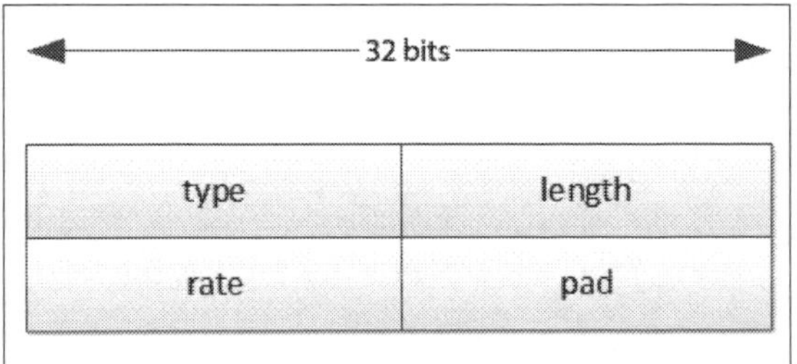

- type: This field should be filled with OFPQDPT_MIN_RATE
- length: This field should be filled with the value 8
- rate: This field should be filled with the queue rate in 1/10 of percent

If the rate is not configured, then the rate field should be set with OFPQ_MIN_RATE_UNCFG which is 0xffff.

- OFPQDPT_MAX_RATE: This property is defined, as shown in the following structure:

```
/* Min-Rate queue property description. */
struct ofp_queue_desc_prop_min_rate {
uint16_t type;    /* OFPQDPT_MIN_RATE. */
uint16_t length; /* Length is 8. */
uint16_t rate;    /* In 1/10 of a percent; >1000 -> disabled. */
uint8_t pad[2];   /* 64-bit alignment */
};
```

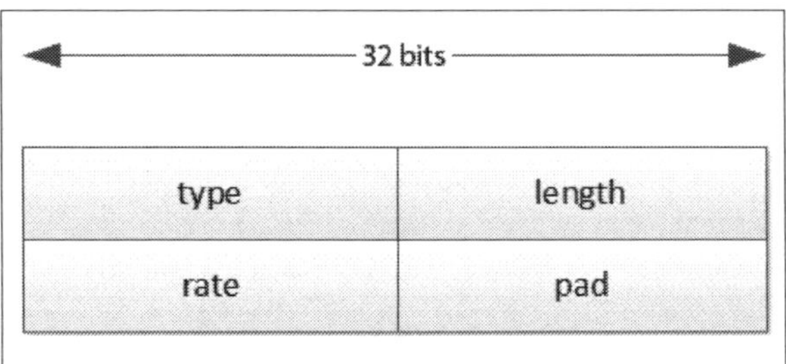

- type: This field should be filled with OFPQDPT_MAX_RATE
- length: This field should be filled with the value 8
- rate: This field should be filled with the queue rate in 1/10 of percent

If the rate is not configured, then the rate field should be set with OFPQ_MAX_RATE_UNCFG which is 0xffff.

See also

- For more information on how the controller sends OFPMP_QUEUE_DESC message to the switch, refer to the recipe *Getting the queue description using multipart messages* in *Chapter 6, Handling Multipart State Information Messages (Part 2)*

Configuring Flow monitor using multipart messages

Flow monitoring is a mechanism provided by OpenFlow specification to send an asynchronous event to the controller whenever there is any change in the flow entry. The Flow monitoring mechanism will be very useful in multi-controller deployment, wherein any change in the flow entry by one controller can be intimated to the other controllers in the system.

When the controller wants to configure a flow monitor, it sends an `OFPMP_FLOW_MONITOR` multipart message (`ofp_multipart_request`) to switch.

How to do it...

When the switch receives the `OFPMP_FLOW_MONITOR` message with the command field set as `OFPFMC_ADD`, the switch should check whether there is any monitor entry already configured in the system with the same `monitor_id`. If there is an entry already present, then the switch should respond with an error message.

After which, the switch should examine the flags field and perform the action as follows:

- `OFPFMF_INITIAL`: This is set, then the switch should construct a reply message containing all the flow entries which will match the flow monitor.
- `OFPFMF_ADD`: This is set, then the flow monitor should be installed in the switch which generates an asynchronous event to the controller whenever a new flow entry matching this flow monitor is added.
- `OFPFMF_REMOVED`: This is set, then the flow monitor should be installed in the switch which generates an asynchronous event to the controller whenever the existing flow entry matching this flow monitor gets deleted.
- `OFPFMF_MODIFY`: This is set, then the flow monitor should be installed in the switch which generates an asynchronous event to the controller whenever a flow entry matching this flow monitor gets modified.

The `OFPT_FLOW_REMOVED` and `OFPFMF_REMOVED` messages are two independent notification mechanisms.

- `OFPFMF_INSTRUCTIONS`: This is set, then while generating the asynchronous flow event the switch should add the flow entry instructions.

- `OFPFMF_NO_ABBREV`: This is set, then the switch shouldn't generate the update message with abbreviated flow updates. If this flag is unset, then the switch should generate the abbreviated flow update message to the controller which installs the flow entry.
- `OFPFMF_ONLY_OWN`: This flag is set, then the switch should generate the flow updates to a controller only for the flow which is created by this controller.

When the switch receives the `OFPMP_FLOW_MONITOR` message with the command field set as `OFPFMC_DELETE`, the switch should try to check whether there is any monitor entry already configured in the system with the same `monitor_id`. If there is an entry already present, then the switch should delete this flow monitor entry and should stop generating the flow monitor events.

The `OFPFMC_MODIFY` is similar to `OFPFMC_DELETE` and `OFPFMC_ADD` and hence the switch should invoke the flow monitor delete routine first, followed by invoking the flow monitor add routine.

Once the switch finishes its internal processing of this multipart request message, the switch should fill the information, as shown in the following structure and should pack this structure in the body field of the multipart reply message and send the reply message back to the controller. For more information regarding the procedure to construct the multipart reply message, refer to the *Introduction* section of *Chapter 5, Handling Multipart Statistics Messages (Part 1)*. The transaction ID of this multipart reply message should be the same as that of the multipart request message.

Otherwise, the multipart reply message has to be generated by the switch asynchronously whenever a flow table entry matching the flow monitor gets changed. The transaction ID (`xid`) of this multipart message must be set with the value 0. When multiple flow entries which match a flow monitor are modified using a single flow modify message, the switch should generate a notification message which is a multipart reply message containing a flow update for all the flow entries.

The message format that should be used to generate the multipart reply message for flow notification is as follows:

```
/* OFPMP_FLOW_MONITOR reply header.
 *  The body of an OFPMP_FLOW_MONITOR reply is an array of
 * variable-length structures, each of which begins with this
 * header. The 'length' member may be used to traverse the array,
 * and the 'event' member may be used to determine the particular
 * structure. Every instance is a multiple of 8 bytes long.
 */
```

```
struct ofp_flow_update_header {
uint16_t length;   /* Length of this entry. */
uint16_t event;    /* One of OFPFME_*. */
/* ...other data depending on 'event'... */
};
```

The event field should be filled with flow update type which is defined in the following enumeration:

```
/* 'event' values in struct ofp_flow_update_header. */
enum ofp_flow_update_event {
        /* struct ofp_flow_update_full. */
OFPFME_INITIAL = 0,  /* Flow present when flow monitor created. */
OFPFME_ADDED = 1,    /* Flow was added. */
OFPFME_REMOVED = 2,  /* Flow was removed. */
OFPFME_MODIFIED = 3, /* Flow instructions were changed. */
      /* struct ofp_flow_update_abbrev. */
OFPFME_ABBREV = 4,   /* Abbreviated reply. */
      /* struct ofp_flow_update_header. */
OFPFME_PAUSED = 5,   /* Monitoring paused(out of buffer space). */
OFPFME_RESUMED = 6,  /* Monitoring resumed. */
};
```

The `event` field should be set with `OFPFME_ADDED`, `OFPFME_REMOVED` or `OFPFME_MODIFIED` when a flow entry matching the flow monitor is added, deleted or modified, respectively.

The `event` field should be set with a value as `OFPFME_INITIAL` when the switch received a multipart request message to add a flow notification with the `OFPFMF_INITIAL` flag set.

The `body` part of `OFPFME_INITIAL`, `OFPFME_ADDED`, `OFPFME_REMOVED` or `OFPFME_MODIFIED` should be filled with the following structure:

```
/* OFPMP_FLOW_MONITOR reply for OFPFME_INITIAL, OFPFME_ADDED,
 * OFPFME_REMOVED, and OFPFME_MODIFIED. */
struct ofp_flow_update_full {
uint16_t length;        /* Length is 32 + match + instructions. */
uint16_t event;         /* One of OFPFME_*. */
uint8_t table_id;       /* ID of flow's table. */
uint8_t reason;         /* OFPRR_* for OFPFME_REMOVED,else zero */
uint16_t idle_timeout;  /* Number of seconds idle before
                         * expiration. */
uint16_t hard_timeout;  /* Number of seconds before expiration. */
uint16_t priority;      /* Priority of the entry. */
```

```
uint8_t zeros[4];         /* Reserved, currently zeroed. */
uint64_t cookie;          /* Opaque controller-issued identifier. */
struct ofp_match match; /* Fields to match. Variable size. */
/* Instruction set.
 * If OFPFMF_INSTRUCTIONS was not specified, or 'event' is
 * OFPFME_REMOVED, no instructions are included.
 */
struct ofp_instruction instructions[0];
};
```

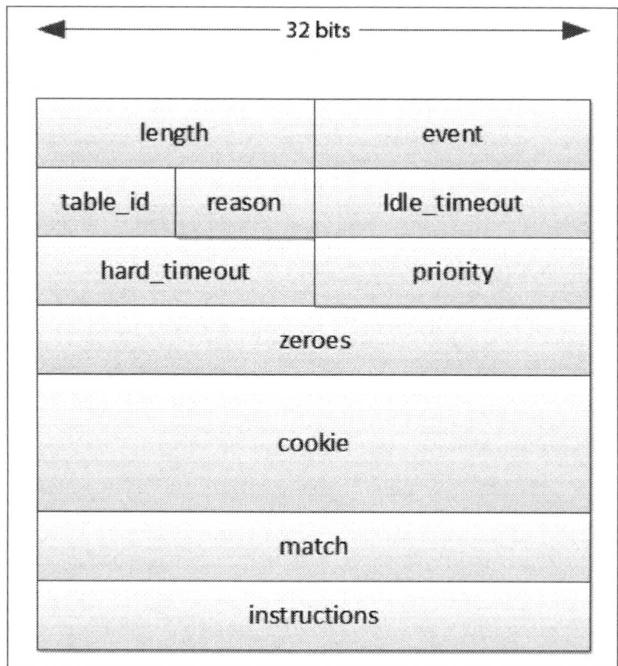

The fields in the structure are similar to the `OFPT_FLOW_REMOVED` message and should be filled with the flow modification message that created/modified the flow entry. For more information on the flow modification message, refer to *Adding new flow entry in flow table* recipe in *Chapter 3, Flow Table and Flow Entry Modification Messages (Part 1)*.

For `OFPFME_REMOVED`, the reason field should be set with the reason for removal which is defined in *Sending flow-removed message to controller* recipe in *Chapter 2, Symmetric Messages & Asynchronous Messages (Part 1)*.

The `event` field should be set with `OFPFME_ABBREV` when the switch sends an abbreviated flow update message to the controller and it takes the following message format:

```
/* OFPMP_FLOW_MONITOR reply for OFPFME_ABBREV.
 * When the controller does not specify OFPFMF_OWN in a monitor
 * request, any flow tables changes due to the controller's own
 * requests (on the same OpenFlow channel) will be abbreviated,
 * when possible, to this form, which simply specifies the 'xid'
 * of the OpenFlow request (e.g. an OFPT_FLOW_MOD) that caused the
 * change. Some changes cannot be abbreviated and will be sent in
 * full.
 */
struct ofp_flow_update_abbrev {
uint16_t length; /* Length is 8. */
uint16_t event;  /* OFPFME_ABBREV. */
uint32_t xid;    /* Controller-specified xid from flow_mod. */
};
```

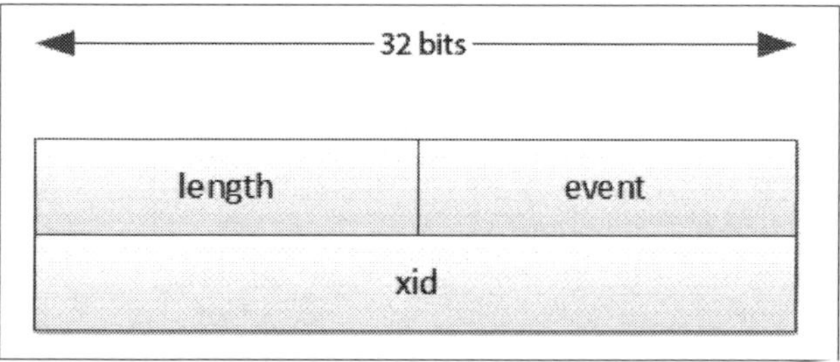

After constructing the reply message with the appropriate format and filling the message field with the appropriate value, the switch should send the reply message back to the controller. For more information regarding the procedure to construct and send the multipart reply message, refer to the *Introduction* section of *Chapter 5, Handling Multipart Statistics Messages (Part 1)*.

See also

- For more information on how the controller sends `OFPMP_FLOW_MONITOR` message to the switch, refer to the recipe *Configuring Flow monitor using multipart message* in *Chapter 6, Handling Multipart State Information Messages (Part 2)*

Experimenter multipart messages

When the switch wants to send experimenter-specific multipart message, it should send an `OFPMP_EXPERIMENTER` multipart message (`ofp_multipart_request`) to controller.

How to do it...

The message format that should be used by the switch for forming the multipart message is defined in the *Introduction* section of *Chapter 5, Handling Multipart Statistics Messages (Part 1)*.

The `body` field should be filled with the following structure:

```
/* Body for ofp_multipart_request/reply of type
 * OFPMP_EXPERIMENTER. */
struct ofp_experimenter_multipart_header {
uint32_t experimenter; /* Experimenter ID. */
uint32_t exp_type;     /* Experimenter defined. */
/* Experimenter-defined arbitrary additional data. */
};
```

The `experimenter` field should be filled with an experimenter ID and the `exp_type` field should be filled with an experimenter type.

The `body` field could be filled with experimenter-defined values.

6
Handling Multipart State Information Messages (Part 2)

This chapter describes in detail about multipart state information messages and contains the following recipes:

- Getting information about the switch using multipart messages
- Getting the group description using multipart messages
- Getting the group feature using multipart messages
- Getting the meter configuration using multipart messages
- Getting the meter feature using multipart messages
- Getting the table feature using multipart messages
- Getting the port description using multipart messages
- Getting the table description using multipart messages
- Getting the queue description using multipart messages
- Configuring the flow monitor using multipart messages
- Experimenter multipart message

Introduction

Multipart messages are used to encode OpenFlow request and reply messages, which carry a large amount of data that can't be fitted into a single OpenFlow message. For more information regarding multipart messages and the message formats that will be used by the controller to send the multipart request message, refer to the *Introduction* section in *Chapter 5, Handling Multipart Statistics Messages (Part 2)*. The chapter also describes in detail about multipart statistics information messages.

Getting information about the switch using multipart messages

When the controller wants to get information about the switch (details such as manufacturer, serial number, hardware revision, software revision, description, and so on), it sends the `OFPMP_DESC` multipart message (`ofp_multipart_request`) to the switch.

How to do it...

In order to get information about the switch, the controller should send a multipart request message with the `type` field set as `OFPMP_DESC`. The message format that should be used by the controller to form the multipart request message is defined in the *Introduction* section in *Chapter 5, Handling Multipart Statistics Messages (Part 2)*.

The `body` field should be left empty.

After sending the multipart request message to the switch, the controller should wait for the reply message from the switch. Once the controller receives the reply message, they should parse the reply message and should either store the data present in the reply message in their data structure, or invoke a callback API to inform the application, based on the implementation.

See also

- For more information regarding how the switch sends a reply message to the controller, refer to the *Getting information about the switch using multipart message* recipe in *Chapter 6, Handling Multipart State Information Messages (Part 1)*

Getting the group description using multipart messages

When the controller wants to fetch the details of all the group entries installed in the switch, they should send the `OFPMP_GROUP_DESC` multipart message (`ofp_multipart_request`) to the switch.

How to do it...

To get information about the group entries in switch, the controller should send a multipart request message with the `type` field set as `OFPMP_GROUP_DESC`. The message format that should be used by the controller to form the multipart request message is defined in the *Introduction* section in *Chapter 5, Handling Multipart Statistics Messages (Part 2)*.

The `body` field should be left empty.

After sending the multipart request message to the switch, the controller should wait for the reply message from the switch. The format of the reply message is described in detail in the *Getting the group description using multipart messages* recipe in *Chapter 6, Handling Multipart State Information Messages (Part 1)*. Once the controller receives the reply message, they should parse the reply message and should either store the data present in the reply message in their data structure, or invoke a callback API to inform the application, based on the implementation.

See also

- For more information regarding how the switch sends a reply message to the controller, refer to the *Getting the group description using multipart messages* recipe in *Chapter 6, Handling Multipart State Information Messages (Part 1)*

Getting the group feature using multipart messages

When the controller wants to fetch the features supported by the group table in the switch, they should send the `OFPMP_GROUP_FEATURES` multipart message (`ofp_multipart_request`) to switch.

How to do it...

To get information about the group features supported by switch, the controller should send a multipart request message the with `type` field set as `OFPMP_GROUP_FEATURES`. The message format that should be used by the controller to form the multipart request message is defined in the *Introduction* section in *Chapter 5, Handling Multipart Statistics Messages (Part 2)*.

The `body` field should be left empty.

After sending the multipart request message to the switch, the controller should wait for the reply message from the switch. Once the controller receives the reply message, they should parse the reply message and should either store the data present in the reply message in their data structure, or invoke a callback API to inform the application, based on the implementation.

See also

- For more information on how the switch sends a reply message to the controller, refer to the *Getting the group feature using multipart message* recipe in *Chapter 6, Handling Multipart State Information Messages (Part 1)*

Getting the meter configuration using multipart messages

When the controller wants to fetch the configuration details of one or more meters in the switch, it should send the `OFPMT_METER_CONFIG` multipart message (`ofp_multipart_request`) to the switch.

How to do it...

To get the configuration details of one or more meter entries in the switch, the controller should send a multipart request message with the `type` field set as `OFPMT_METER_CONFIG`. The message format that should be used by the controller to form the multipart request message is defined in the *Introduction* section in *Chapter 5, Handling Multipart Statistics Messages (Part 2)*.

The `body` field should be filled with the following structure by the controller:

```
/* Body of OFPMP_METER and OFPMP_METER_CONFIG requests. */
struct ofp_meter_multipart_request {
uint32_t meter_id;  /* Meter instance, or OFPM_ALL. */
uint8_t pad[4];     /* Align to 64 bits. */
};
```

The `meter_id` field should be filled with the meter ID. The `meter_id` field is defined in detail in the *Adding a new meter to a meter table* recipe in *Chapter 4, Group Table and Meter Table Modification Messages (Part 1)*.

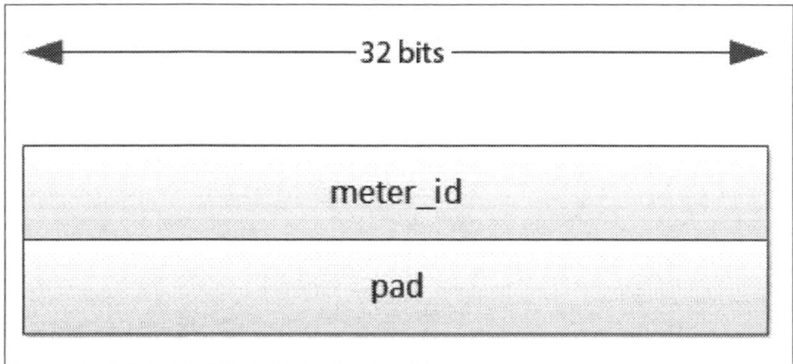

After sending the multipart request message to the switch, the controller should wait for the reply message from the switch. Once the controller receives the reply message, they should parse the reply message and should either store the data present in the reply message in their data structure, or invoke a callback API to inform the application, based on the implementation.

See also

- For more information regarding how the switch sends a reply message to the controller, refer to the *Getting the meter configuration using multipart message* recipe in *Chapter 6, Handling Multipart State Information Messages (Part 1)*

Getting the meter feature using multipart messages

When the controller wants to fetch the features of the meter table in the switch, it should send the `OFPMT_METER_FEATURES` multipart message (`ofp_multipart_request`) to the switch.

How to do it...

To get information about the meter features supported by the switch, the controller should send a multipart request message with the `type` field set as `OFPMT_METER_FEATURES`. The message format that should be used by the controller to form the multipart request message is defined in the *Introduction* section in *Chapter 5, Handling Multipart Statistics Messages (Part 2)*.

The `body` field should be left empty.

After sending the multipart request message to the switch, the controller should wait for the reply message from the switch. Once the controller receives the reply message, they should parse the reply message and should either store the data present in the reply message in their data structure, or invoke a callback API to inform the application, based on the implementation.

See also

- For more information regarding how the switch sends a reply message to the controller, refer to the *Getting the meter feature using multipart message* recipe in *Chapter 6, Handling Multipart State Information Messages (Part 1)*

Getting the table feature using multipart messages

The table feature multipart messages are used by the controller for the following:

- To query the capabilities of the existing tables in the switch
- To reconfigure the tables in the switch

How to do it...

To get information about the table features or to reconfigure the flow tables, the controller should send a multipart request message with the `type` field set as `OFPMP_TABLE_FEATURES`. The message format that should be used by the controller to form the multipart request message is defined in the *Introduction* section in *Chapter 5, Handling Multipart Statistics Messages (Part 2)*.

If the controller wants to get only the features of the tables in the switch, then they should send the multipart request message with the `body` field left empty.

If the controller wants to reconfigure the tables, then they should add array of one or more `ofp_table_features` structures, one for each flow table, in the following structure format:

```
/* Body for ofp_multipart_request of type OFPMP_TABLE_FEATURES.
 * Body of reply to OFPMP_TABLE_FEATURES request. */
struct ofp_table_features {
uint16_t length;    /* Length is padded to 64 bits. */
uint8_t table_id;   /* Identifier of table. Lower numbered tables
                     * are consulted first. */
uint8_t pad[5];     /* Align to 64-bits. */
char name[OFP_MAX_TABLE_NAME_LEN];
uint64_t metadata_match; /* Bits of metadata table can match. */
uint64_t metadata_write; /* Bits of metadata table can write. */
```

```
uint32_t capabilities;    /* Bitmap of OFPTC_* values. */
uint32_t max_entries;     /* Max number of entries supported. */
        /* Table Feature Property list */
struct ofp_table_feature_prop_header properties[0];
};
```

The `table_id` field should be filled with the identifier of the table that needs to be reconfigured.

The `name` field should be filled with the `table_name` field.

The `metadata_match` field should be filled with bits of the `metadata` field that this table matches. If the controller wants to match the full `metadata` field, then it should set this value as `0xFFFFFFFFFFFFFFFF`.

The `metadata_match` field should be filled with bits of the `metadata` field that this table can write, using the `OFPIT_WRITE_METADATA` instruction. If the controller wants to write the full `metadata` field, then it should set this value as `0xFFFFFFFFFFFFFFFF`.

The `capabilities` field should be set with the flag values that are defined in *Modifying a flow table with eviction enabled* recipe in *Chapter 3, Flow Table and Flow Entry Modification Messages (Part 1)*.

The `max_entries` field should be set with the maximum number of entries allowed in the table.

The `properties` field should be filled with the list of table feature properties that describes the capabilities of the table as follows:

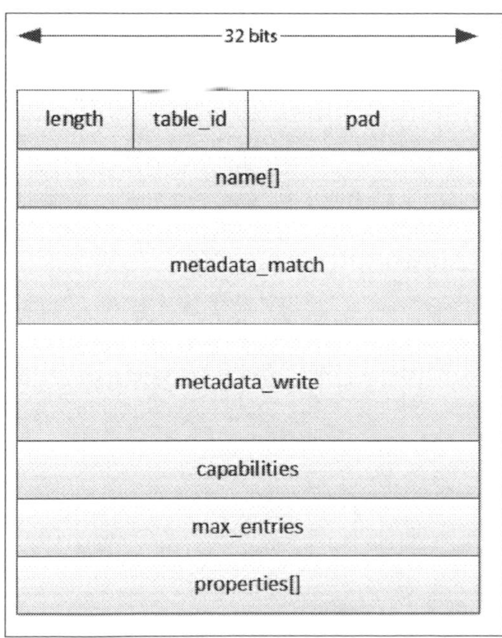

```
/* Table Feature property types.
 * Low order bit cleared indicates a property for a regular
 * Flow Entry.
 * Low order bit set indicates a property for the Table-Miss
 * Flow Entry.
 */
enum ofp_table_feature_prop_type {
OFPTFPT_INSTRUCTIONS = 0, /* Instructions property. */
OFPTFPT_INSTRUCTIONS_MISS = 1,  /* Instructions for table-miss. */
OFPTFPT_NEXT_TABLES = 2,        /* Next Table property. */
OFPTFPT_NEXT_TABLES_MISS = 3,   /* Next Table for table-miss. */
OFPTFPT_WRITE_ACTIONS = 4,      /* Write Actions property. */
OFPTFPT_WRITE_ACTIONS_MISS = 5, /* Write Actions for table-miss */
OFPTFPT_APPLY_ACTIONS = 6,      /* Apply Actions property. */
OFPTFPT_APPLY_ACTIONS_MISS = 7, /* Apply Actions for table-miss */
OFPTFPT_MATCH = 8,              /* Match property. */
OFPTFPT_WILDCARDS = 10,         /* Wildcards property. */
OFPTFPT_WRITE_SETFIELD = 12,    /* Write Set-Field property. */
OFPTFPT_WRITE_SETFIELD_MISS = 13,   /* Write Set-Field for
                                     * table-miss. */
OFPTFPT_APPLY_SETFIELD = 14,        /* Apply Set-Field property.*/
OFPTFPT_APPLY_SETFIELD_MISS = 15,   /* Apply Set-Field for
                                     * table-miss. */
OFPTFPT_TABLE_SYNC_FROM = 16,       /* Table synchronization
                                     * property. */
OFPTFPT_EXPERIMENTER = 0xFFFE,      /* Experimenter property. */
OFPTFPT_EXPERIMENTER_MISS = 0xFFFF, /* Experimenter for
                                     * table-miss. */
};
```

The `property` value with the `_MISS` suffix describes the table miss flow entry, and the one that doesn't have the `_MISS` suffix represents the normal flow entry.

The `property` values with `OFPTFPT_INSTRUCTIONS` and `OFPTFPT_INSTRUCTIONS_MISS` represent the lists of instructions that can be supported by this table's normal flow entry and miss flow entry, respectively. These properties use the following structure:

```
/* Instructions property */
struct ofp_table_feature_prop_instructions {
uint16_t type;     /* One of OFPTFPT_INSTRUCTIONS,
                    * OFPTFPT_INSTRUCTIONS_MISS. */
```

```
uint16_t length;  /* Length in bytes of this property. */
/* Followed by:
 * - Exactly (length - 4) bytes containing the instruction
 * ids, then Exactly (length + 7)/8*8 - (length) (between 0 and 7)
 * bytes of all-zero bytes
 */
struct ofp_instruction_id instruction_ids[0];
   /* List of instructions */
};
```

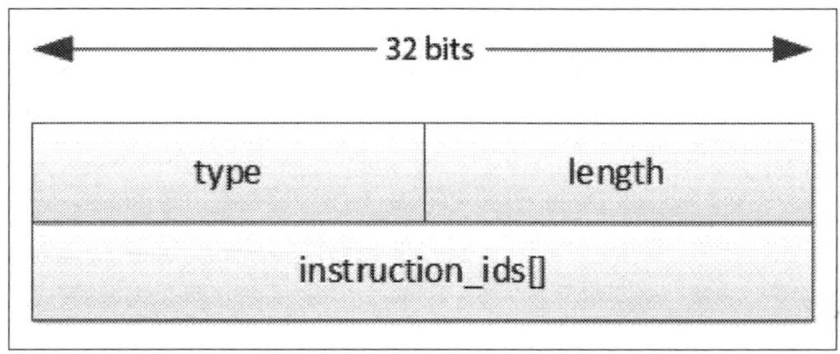

The `instruction_ids` field should be filled with the list of instructions supported by the table that is defined as the following structure:

```
/* Instruction ID */
struct ofp_instruction_id {
uint16_t type;       /* One of OFPIT_*. */
uint16_t len;        /* Length is 4 or experimenter defined. */
uint8_t exp_data[0]; /* Optional experimenter id + data. */
};
```

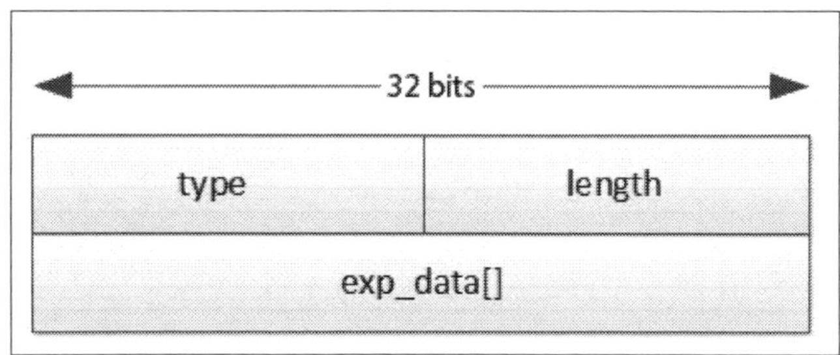

The `type` field should be set with the instruction type. For more information regarding the instruction type, refer to section *Appendix, Common OpenFlow Structures*.

The `property` values with `OFPTFPT_NEXT_TABLES` and `OFPTFPT_NEXT_TABLES_MISS` represent the array of tables that can be reached directly, using the `OFPIT_GOTO_TABLE` instruction, by this table's normal flow entry and miss flow entry, respectively. Therefore, this value should be filled by the controller accordingly.

The `property` value with `OFPTFPT_TABLE_SYNC_FROM` represents the array of tables that this table is synchronizing its content from, so this value should be filled by the controller accordingly.

The `OFPTFPT_NEXT_TABLES`, `OFPTFPT_NEXT_TABLES_MISS`, and `OFPTFPT_TABLE_SYNC_FROM` properties use the following structure:

```
/* Next Tables and Table Synchronise From properties */
struct ofp_table_feature_prop_tables {
uint16_t type;    /* One of OFPTFPT_NEXT_TABLES,
                   * OFPTFPT_NEXT_TABLES_MISS,
                   * OFPTFPT_TABLE_SYNC_FROM. */
uint16_t length; /* Length in bytes of this property. */
/* Followed by:
* - Exactly (length - 4) bytes containing the table_ids, then
* - Exactly (length + 7)/8*8 - (length) (between 0 and 7)
* bytes of all-zero bytes */
uint8_t table_ids[0]; /* List of table ids. */
};
```

The `table_ids` field should be set with the identifiers of the next tables or the synchronization table based on the `type` field, so this value should be filled by the controller accordingly. For more information regarding table synchronization, refer to the *Flow table synchronizations* recipe in *Chapter 3, Flow Table and Flow Entry Modification Messages (Part 1)*.

The `property` values with `OFPTFPT_WRITE_ACTIONS` and `OFPTFPT_WRITE_ACTIONS_MISS` represent the array of actions supported using the `OFPIT_WRITE_ACTIONS` instruction by this table's normal flow entry and miss flow entry, respectively. Therefore, this value should be filled by the controller accordingly.

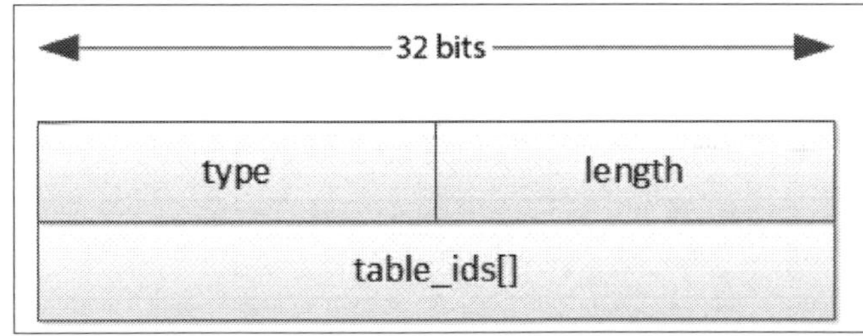

The `property` values with `OFPTFPT_APPLY_ACTIONS` and `OFPTFPT_APPLY_ACTIONS_MISS` represent the array of actions supported using the `OFPIT_APPLY_ACTIONS` instruction by this table's normal flow entry and miss flow entry, respectively. Therefore, this value should be filled by the controller accordingly.

The `OFPTFPT_APPLY_ACTIONS`, `OFPTFPT_APPLY_ACTIONS_MISS`, `OFPTFPT_APPLY_ACTIONS`, and `OFPTFPT_APPLY_ACTIONS_MISS` properties use the following structure:

```
/* Actions property */
struct ofp_table_feature_prop_actions {
uint16_t type;    /* One of OFPTFPT_WRITE_ACTIONS,
                   * OFPTFPT_WRITE_ACTIONS_MISS,
                   * OFPTFPT_APPLY_ACTIONS,
                   * OFPTFPT_APPLY_ACTIONS_MISS. */
uint16_t length; /* Length in bytes of this property. */
/* Followed by:
 * - Exactly (length - 4) bytes containing the action_ids, then
 * - Exactly (length + 7)/8*8 - (length) (between 0 and 7)
 * bytes of all-zero bytes
 */
struct ofp_action_id action_ids[0]; /* List of actions */
};
```

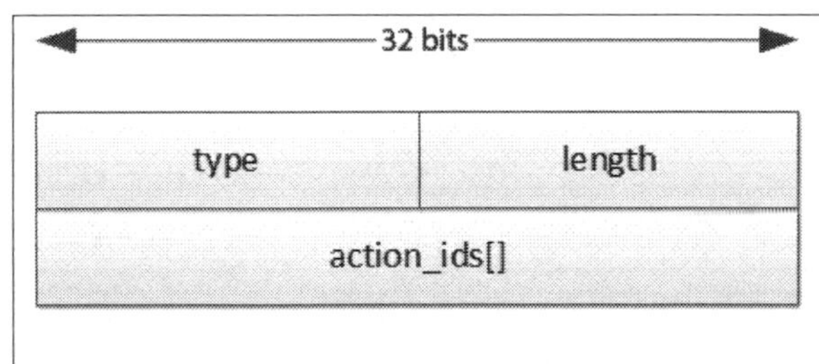

The `action_ids` field should be filled with the list of actions supported by the table that is defined as shown in the following structure:

```
/* Action ID */
struct ofp_action_id {
uint16_t type;        /* One of OFPAT_*. */
uint16_t len;         /* Length is 4 or experimenter defined. */
```

```
uint8_t exp_data[0]; /* Optional experimenter id + data. */
};
```

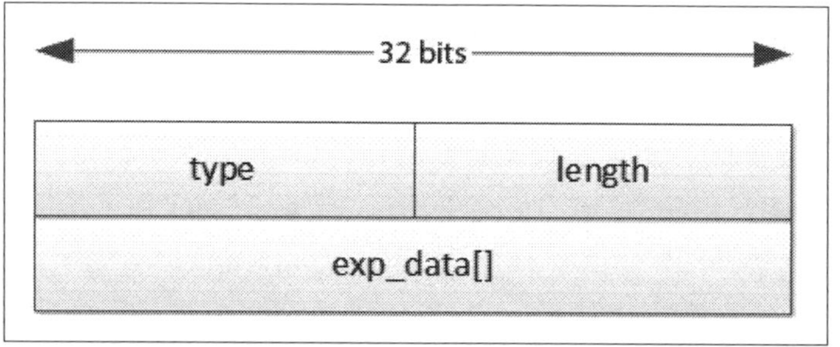

The `type` field should be set with the action type. For more information regarding the action type, refer to *Appendix, Common OpenFlow Structures*.

The `property` value with `OFPTFPT_MATCH` represents the list of fields in the incoming packet that can be matched against the entries in that table, so this value should be filled by the controller accordingly.

The `property` value with `OFPTFPT_WILDCARDS` represents the list of fields in the incoming packet that can be matched against the entries in that table with wildcard matching, so this value should be filled by the controller accordingly.

The `property` values with `OFPTFPT_WRITE_SETFIELD` and `OFPTFPT_WRITE_SETFIELD_MISS` represent the Set-Field action type supported using the `OFPIT_WRITE_ACTIONS` instruction by this table's normal flow entry and miss flow entry, respectively. Therefore, this value should be filled by the controller accordingly.

The `property` values with `OFPTFPT_APPLY_SETFIELD` and `OFPTFPT_APPLY_SETFIELD_MISS` represent the Set-Field action type supported using the `OFPIT_APPLY_ACTIONS` instruction by this table's normal flow entry and miss flow entry, respectively. Therefore, this value should be filled by the controller accordingly.

The `OFPTFPT_MATCH`, `OFPTFPT_WILDCARDS`, `OFPTFPT_WRITE_SETFIELD`, `OFPTFPT_WRITE_SETFIELD_MISS`, `OFPTFPT_APPLY_SETFIELD`, and `OFPTFPT_APPLY_SETFIELD_MISS` properties use the following structure:

```
/* Match, Wildcard or Set-Field property */
struct ofp_table_feature_prop_oxm {
uint16_t type;    /* One of OFPTFPT_MATCH,
                   * OFPTFPT_WILDCARDS,
                   * OFPTFPT_WRITE_SETFIELD,
                   * OFPTFPT_WRITE_SETFIELD_MISS,
                   * OFPTFPT_APPLY_SETFIELD,
```

```
                    * OFPTFPT_APPLY_SETFIELD_MISS.
                    */
uint16_t length; /* Length in bytes of this property. */
/* Followed by:
* - Exactly (length - 4) bytes containing the oxm_ids, then
* - Exactly (length + 7)/8*8 - (length) (between 0 and 7)
* bytes of all-zero bytes */
uint32_t oxm_ids[0]; /* Array of OXM headers */
};
```

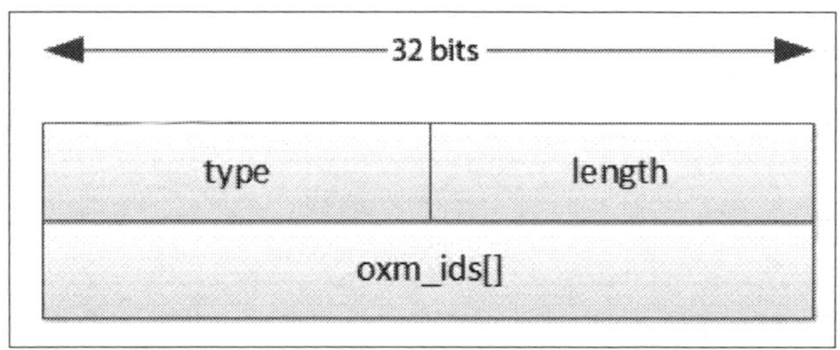

The `oxm_ids` field is the list of supported OXM types. For more information regarding the OXM, refer to the *Introduction* section in *Chapter 3, Flow Table and Flow Entry Modification Messages (Part 1)*.

The `OFPTFPT_EXPERIMENTER` and `OFPTFPT_EXPERIMENTER_MISS` properties use the following structure:

```
/* Experimenter table feature property */
struct ofp_table_feature_prop_experimenter {
uint16_t type;          /* One of OFPTFPT_EXPERIMENTER,
                         * OFPTFPT_EXPERIMENTER_MISS. */
uint16_t length;        /* Length in bytes of this property. */
uint32_t experimenter; /* Experimenter ID which takes the same
                         * form as in struct
                         * ofp_experimenter_header. */
uint32_t exp_type;      /* Experimenter defined. */
/* Followed by:
 * - Exactly (length - 12)bytes containing the experimenter data then
 * - Exactly (length + 7)/8*8 - (length) (between 0 and 7)
 * bytes of all-zero bytes */
uint32_t experimenter_data[0];
};
```

The `experimenter` field should be filled with the experimenter ID, and `exp_type` should be filled with the experimenter type.

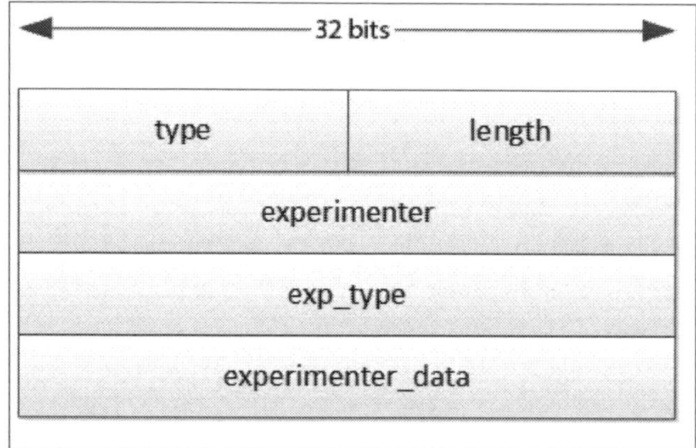

The `experimenter_data` field should be filled with the vendor-defined experimenter data.

The multipart table feature request message or reply message should meet the following requirements:

- The `table_id` field in every `ofp_table_features` should be unique.
- The `properties` field in the `ofp_table_features` structure must contain exactly one of each of the `ofp_table_feature_prop_type` properties, with two exceptions:
    - The `_MISS` suffix property can be ignored if the action for the `_MISS` property is the same as the regular entries.
    - The `experimenter` properties can be ignored or included multiple times.

After sending the multipart request message to the switch, the controller should wait for the reply message from the switch. The message format of the reply message is described in detail in the *Getting the table feature using multipart message* recipe in *Chapter 6, Handling Multipart State Information Messages (Part 1)*. Once the controller receives the reply message, they should parse the reply message and should either store the data present in the reply message in their data structure, or invoke a callback API to inform the application, based on the implementation.

See also

- For more information regarding how the switch sends a reply message to the controller, refer to the *Getting the table feature using multipart message* recipe in *Chapter 6, Handling Multipart State Information Messages (Part 1)*

Getting the port description using multipart messages

When the controller wants to fetch the details of all the ports in the switch, they should send the `OFPMP_PORT_DESCRIPTION` multipart message (`ofp_multipart_request`) to the switch.

How to do it...

In order to get information about the port description from the switch, the controller should send a multipart request message with the `type` field set as `OFPMP_PORT_DESCRIPTION`. The message format that should be used by the controller to form the multipart request message is defined in the *Introduction* section in *Chapter 5, Handling Multipart Statistics Messages (Part 2)*.

The `body` field should be left empty.

After sending the multipart request message to the switch, the controller should wait for the reply message from the switch. Once the controller receives the reply message, they should parse the reply message and should either store the data present in the reply message in their data structure, or invoke a callback API to inform the application, based on the implementation.

See also

- For more information on how the switch sends a reply message to the controller, refer to the *Getting port description using multipart messages* recipe in *Chapter 6, Handling Multipart State Information Messages (Part 1)*

Getting the table description using multipart messages

When the controller wants to fetch the configuration details of all the flow tables in the switch, it should send the `OFPMP_TABLE_DESC` multipart message (`ofp_multipart_request`) to the switch.

How to do it...

To get information about the flow table description from the switch, the controller should send a multipart request message with the `type` field set as `OFPMP_TABLE_DESC`. The message format that should be used by the controller to form the multipart request message is defined in the *Introduction* section in *Chapter 5, Handling Multipart Statistics Messages (Part 2)*.

The `body` field should be left empty.

After sending the multipart request message to the switch, the controller should wait for the reply message from the switch. Once the controller receives the reply message, they should parse the reply message and should either store the data present in the reply message in their data structure, or invoke a callback API to inform the application, based on the implementation.

See also

- For more information on how the switch sends a reply message to the controller, refer to the *Getting the table description using multipart messages* recipe in *Chapter 6, Handling Multipart State Information Messages (Part 1)*

Getting the queue description using multipart messages

When the controller wants to fetch the details of the queues attached to the OpenFlow ports in the switch, they should send the `OFPMP_QUEUE_DESC` multipart message (`ofp_multipart_request`) to the switch.

How to do it...

In order to get information about the queue from the switch, the controller should send a multipart request message with the `type` field set as `OFPMP_QUEUE_DESC`. The message format that will be used by the controller to form the multipart request message is defined in the *Introduction* section in *Chapter 5, Handling Multipart Statistics Messages (Part 2)*.

The `body` field of the multipart request message should be filled with the following structure by the controller:

```
/* Body for ofp_multipart_request of type OFPMP_QUEUE_DESC. */
struct ofp_queue_desc_request {
uint32_t port_no;  /* All ports if OFPP_ANY. */
uint32_t queue_id; /* All queues if OFPQ_ALL. */
};
```

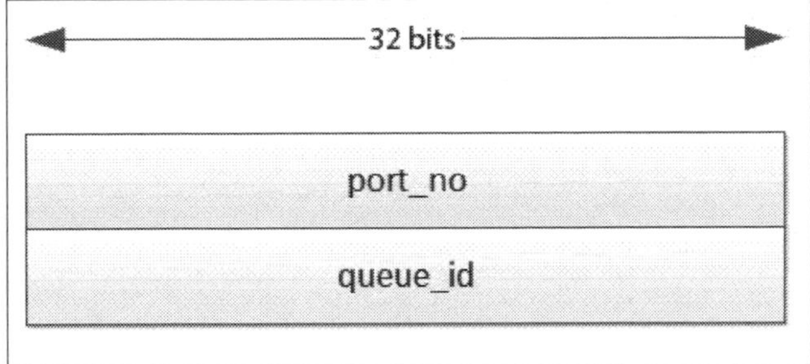

The `port_no` field represents the port on which the queue is attached, and `queue_id` represents the queue ID.

After sending the multipart request message to the switch, the controller should wait for the reply message from the switch. Once the controller receives the reply message, they should parse the reply message and should either store the data present in the reply message in their data structure, or invoke a callback API to inform the application, based on the implementation.

See also

- For more information regarding how the switch sends a reply message to the controller, refer to the *Getting the queue description using multipart messages* recipe in *Chapter 6, Handling Multipart State Information Messages (Part 1)*

Configuring the flow monitor using multipart messages

Flow monitoring is a mechanism provided by OpenFlow specification to send an asynchronous event to a controller whenever there is any change in the flow entry. The flow monitoring mechanism will be very useful in multicontroller deployment, wherein any change in the flow entry by one controller can be made known to other controllers in the system.

When the controller wants to configure a flow monitor, they should send the `OFPMP_FLOW_MONITOR` multipart message (`ofp_multipart_request`) to the switch.

How to do it...

In order to configure the flow monitor entry in the switch, the controller should send a multipart request message with the `type` field set as `OFPMP_FLOW_MONITOR`. The message format that should be used by the controller to form the multipart request message is defined in the *Introduction* section in *Chapter 5, Handling Multipart Statistics Messages (Part 2)*.

The `body` field should be filled with the following structure by the controller:

```
/* Body for ofp_multipart_request of type OFPMP_FLOW_MONITOR.
 * The OFPMP_FLOW_MONITOR request's body consists of an array of
 * zero or more instances of this structure. The request arranges
 * to monitor the flows that match the specified criteria, which
 * are interpreted in the same way as for OFPMP_FLOW.
 *
 * 'id' identifies a particular monitor for the purpose of
 * allowing it to be canceled later with OFPFMC_DELETE. 'id' must
 * be unique among existing monitors that have not already been
 * canceled.
*/
struct ofp_flow_monitor_request {
uint32_t monitor_id;     /* Controller-assigned ID for this
                          * monitor. */
uint32_t out_port;       /* Required output port, if not
                          * OFPP_ANY. */
uint32_t out_group;      /* Required output port, if not
                          * OFPG_ANY. */
uint16_t flags;          /* OFFMF_*. */
uint8_t table_id;        /* One table's ID or OFPTT_ALL
                          * (all tables). */
uint8_t command;         /* One of OFPFMC_*. */
struct ofp_match match; /* Fields to match. Variable size. */
};
```

The `monitor_id` field uniquely identifies a monitor in a controller connection. Therefore, the controller should set this with a unique value.

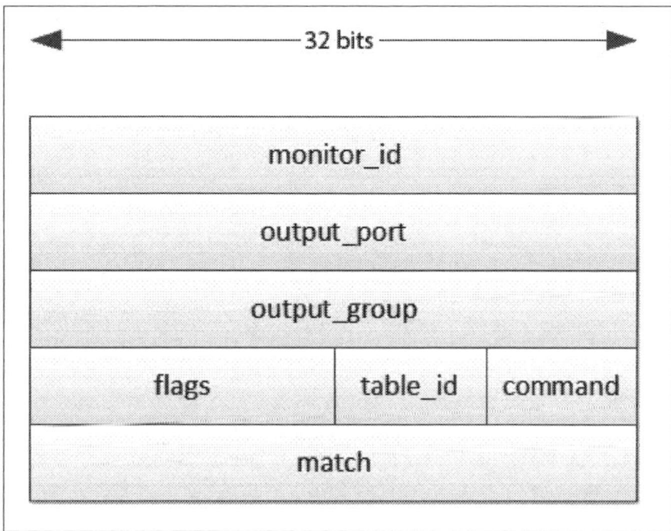

The `command` field represents whether the monitor is to be created, modified, or deleted, and will be set with one of the values as defined in the following enumeration:

```
/* Flow monitor commands */
enum ofp_flow_monitor_command {
OFPFMC_ADD = 0,     /* New flow monitor. */
OFPFMC_MODIFY = 1, /* Modify existing flow monitor. */
OFPFMC_DELETE = 2, /* Delete/cancel existing flow monitor. */
};
```

The `table_id` field should be set with the table ID of the flow table to be monitored.

The `match` field should be set with the fields to be matched with the flow entry for which this monitor is to be applied. For more information regarding the field match, refer to the *Introduction* section in *Chapter 3, Flow Table and Flow Entry Modification Messages (Part 1)*.

The `out_port` and `out_group` fields are optional fields that could be set by the controller to reduce the scope of the flow monitor.

The `flags` field has a significance only for the `OFPFMC_ADD` message type and should be set with one of the values defined in the following enumeration:

```
/* 'flags' bits in struct of_flow_monitor_request. */
enum ofp_flow_monitor_flags {
         /* When to send updates. */
OFPFMF_INITIAL = 1 << 0,       /* Initially matching flows. */
OFPFMF_ADD = 1 << 1,           /* New matching flows as they
                                * are added. */
OFPFMF_REMOVED = 1 << 2,       /* Old matching flows as they are
                                * removed. */
OFPFMF_MODIFY = 1 << 3,        /* Matching flows as they are
                                * changed. */
      /* What to include in updates.*/
OFPFMF_INSTRUCTIONS = 1 << 4,  /* If set, instructions are
                                * included. */
OFPFMF_NO_ABBREV = 1 << 5,     /* If set, include own changes in
                                * full. */
OFPFMF_ONLY_OWN = 1 << 6,      /* If set, don't include other
                                * controllers. */
};
```

The controller should set the `flags` field and perform the action as follows:

- `OFPFMF_INITIAL` should be set to get all the flow entries that are matched against the flow monitor
- `OFPFMF_ADD` should be set to install a flow monitor in the switch, which generates an asynchronous event whenever a new flow entry matching this flow monitor is added
- `OFPFMF_REMOVED` should be set to install a flow monitor in the switch, which generates an asynchronous event whenever an existing flow entry matching this flow monitor is deleted
- `OFPFMF_MODIFY` should be set to install a flow monitor in the switch, which generates an asynchronous event whenever a flow entry matching this flow monitor is modified
- `OFPFMF_INSTRUCTIONS` should be set to instruct the switch to add the flow entry instruction along with the multipart reply message while generating the asynchronous flow event
- `OFPFMF_NO_ABBREV` should be set to instruct the switch not to generate the update message with abbreviated flow updates. If this flag is unset, then the switch will generate the abbreviated flow update message to the controller that installs the flow entry
- `OFPFMF_ONLY_OWN` should be set to generate the flow updates from the switch only for the flows that are created by this controller

After sending the multipart request message to the switch, the controller should wait for the reply message from the switch. Once the controller receives the reply message, they should parse the reply message and should either store the data present in the reply message in their data structure, or invoke a callback API to inform the application, based on the implementation.

See also

- For more information regarding how the switch sends a reply message to the controller, refer to the *Configuring the flow monitor using multipart messages* recipe in *Chapter 6, Handling Multipart State Information Messages (Part 1)*

Experimenter multipart message

When the controller wants to send an experimenter-specific multipart message, they should send the `OFPMP_EXPERIMENTER` multipart message (`ofp_multipart_request`) to the switch.

How to do it...

The message format that should be used by the controller to form the multipart request message is defined in the *Introduction* section in *Chapter 5, Handling Multipart Statistics Messages (Part 2)*.

The `body` field should be filled with the following structure:

```
/* Body for ofp_multipart_request/reply of type
 * OFPMP_EXPERIMENTER. */
struct ofp_experimenter_multipart_header {
uint32_t experimenter; /* Experimenter ID. */
uint32_t exp_type;     /* Experimenter defined. */
/* Experimenter-defined arbitrary additional data. */
};
```

The `experimenter` field should be filled with the experimenter ID and the `exp_type` field should be filled with the experimenter type.

The `body` field should be filled with the experimenter-defined values.

7
Handling Bundle Messages (Part 1)

This chapter describes bundle messages in detail and contains the following recipes:

- Creation of a bundle
- Adding messages to a bundle
- Closing a bundle
- Committing or executing all the operations inside a bundle
- Discarding a bundle

Introduction

OpenFlow specification has defined a way to configure the switch in a transactional manner using bundle messages. The bundle message consists of a sequence of OpenFlow modification messages that is sent from the controller to the switch, which should be applied as a single operation. The bundle operates in an all or nothing fashion, i.e. if all the operations inside the bundle are successful, then the operations inside the bundle will be applied, otherwise none of the operations will be applied.

> The term **Bundle message** refers to the OpenFlow bundle message and the term **Bundle** refers to the set of OpenFlow messages present in `OFPT_BUNDLE_ADD_MESSAGE` with same bundle ID.

There are four stages in the OpenFlow bundle mechanism which are as follows:

- Creation of a bundle wherein the controller instructs the switch to create a bundle.
- Adding one or more OpenFlow messages inside the bundle using bundle add message. This stage involves parsing, pre-validating and storing the OpenFlow message inside the bundle without applying the operations.
- Closing the bundle wherein the bundle created in the switch will be closed.
- Finally committing/executing the message operations inside the bundle.

As the messages inside the bundles are pre-validated during the staging process, the possibility of an error message occurring during the commit stage is minimal.

The switch should support sending and processing of an echo request message, echo reply message, and asynchronous message during the creation and population of the bundle. It should not wait till the bundle closes the message.

When the switch has multiple controller connections or auxiliary connections, it should maintain separate bundle staging areas for each connection. This helps the switch to create and populate multiple bundles in parallel.

The switch might also support maintaining multiple bundle staging areas for a single controller connection with a different `bundle_id`. This is an optional feature.

The switch can also implement locking the objects referenced by the bundle. If any OpenFlow message either from the same controller or a different controller tries to modify this object, then the switch should reject this message and should return an error.

Creation of a bundle

When the controller wants the switch to create a bundle then the controller sends an `OFPT_BUNDLE_CONTROL` message with the `type` field set as `OFPBCT_OPEN_REQUEST`.

The `message` field that will be used by the controller to create a bundle is described in the *Introduction* section of *Chapter 7, Handling Bundle Messages (Part 2)*.

How to do it...

When the switch receives the `OFPBCT_OPEN_REQUEST` message, the switch must perform the following validations before creating a bundle:

- If the bundle request message is received by the switch over an unreliable connection, then the switch should respond as error message `ofp_error_msg` with the type as `OFPET_BUNDLE_FAILED`, and code as `OFPBFC_OUT_OF_BUNDLES`.

- If the bundle ID refers to an existing bundle over an existing connection, then the switch should send an error message `ofp_error_msg` with the type as `OFPET_BUNDLE_FAILED`, and code as `OFPBFC_BAD_ID`.
- If the switch isn't able to support the feature mentioned in the `flag` field, then the switch should send an error message ofp_error_msg with the type as `OFPET_BUNDLE_FAILED`, and code as `OFPBFC_BAD_FLAGS`.
- If the switch can't create a bundle because of some internal reasons such as less memory or too many bundles opened, then the switch should send an error message `ofp_error_msg` with type as `OFPET_BUNDLE_FAILED` and code as `OFPBFC_OUT_OF_BUNDLES`.

When all the above mentioned validations are successful, then the switch should do the following:

- Create a bundle with a key as the bundle ID present in the `OFPBCT_OPEN_REQUEST` message and the connection ID.
- Store the bundle parameters such as flags and property list (if present) in its data structure for future operations.
- Send the `OFPT_BUNDLE_CONTROL` message back to the controller with the type as `OFPBCT_OPEN_REPLY`.

Adding messages to a bundle

When the controller wants to add new OpenFlow message to a bundle, the controller sends `OFPT_BUNDLE_ADD_MESSAGE` message.

Getting started

The controller should have created the bundle as described in *Creation of a bundle* recipe of this chapter, before sending the bundle add message to a switch.

How to do it...

When the switch receives the `OFPT_BUNDLE_ADD_MESSAGE` message, the switch should first fetch the bundle (which was created already by, an `OFPBCT_OPEN_REQUEST` message) using the `bundle_id` and `connection_id` pair wherein the `bundle_id` is the bundle identifier present in the message, and the connection ID is the identifier of the received connection. The connection ID is used in the case of bundle parallelism, wherein separate bundle staging areas will be maintained for each controller connection.

Once the bundle is fetched, the switch should perform the following bundle related validations:

- If the switch can't fetch a bundle using these key pairs, then the switch should create a new bundle using the values present in this `OFPT_BUNDLE_ADD_MESSAGE` message. For the detailed procedure to create a new bundle, refer to the recipe *Creation of a bundle* of this Chapter.
- If the fetched bundle is already in a closed state, then the switch should send an error message `ofp_error_msg` with the type as `OFPET_BUNDLE_FAILED`, and code as `OFPBFC_BUNDLE_CLOSED`.
- The switch should match the `flag` field present in `OFPT_BUNDLE_ADD_MESSAGE` message to the `flag` field which is already stored in its internal data structure, which was created by the `OFPBCT_OPEN_REQUEST` message. If these fields are not matching, then the switch should send an error message `ofp_error_msg` with the type as `OFPET_BUNDLE_FAILED` and code as `OFPBFC_BAD_FLAGS`.

Once the above mentioned validations are successful, the switch should fetch the OpenFlow message present in the `OFPT_BUNDLE_ADD_MESSAGE` message and should perform the following validations related to the OpenFlow message:

- The switch should validate whether the OpenFlow message present in the `OFPT_BUNDLE_ADD_MESSAGE` message is supported by the bundle operation or not. If the switch doesn't support this message type, then it should send an error message `ofp_error_msg` with the type as `OFPET_BUNDLE_FAILED` and code as `OFPBFC_MSG_UNSUP`.
- The switch should validate the consistency of this OpenFlow message with the messages already stored in the bundle, and if there is any issue, then the switch should send an error message `ofp_error_msg` with the type as `OFPET_BUNDLE_FAILED` and code as `OFPBFC_MSG_CONFLICT`.
- The switch should validate the `length` field present in the OpenFlow message, and if it is not valid, then the switch should send an error message `ofp_error_msg` with the type as `OFPET_BUNDLE_FAILED` and code as `OFPBFC_MSG_BAD_LEN`.
- The switch can optionally check the `xid` present in the received OpenFlow message with the `xids` of all the messages already present in bundle.
- The Switch should perform the pre-validation of the message present in the `OFPT_BUNDLE_ADD_MESSAGE` message. The pre-validation includes syntax checking, features supported by the switch and optional resource availability. If these validations fail, then the switch should send an error message to the controller with the `xid` field in the error message set to the `xid` of the message present in `OFPT_BUNDLE_ADD_MESSAGE` message.

Once all these validations are successful, the switch should add the message present in `OFPT_BUNDLE_ADD_MESSAGE` message to the bundle for further processing.

Closing a bundle

When the controller wants to finish recording the bundle messages, it sends an `OFPT_BUNDLE_CONTROL` message with the `type` field set as `OFPT_BUNDLE_CLOSE_REQUEST`.

Getting started

The controller should have created the bundle as described in the *Creation of a bundle* recipe, before sending the bundle close message to a switch.

The `message` field that will be used for bundle operations is described in the *Introduction* section of *Chapter 7, Handling Bundle Messages (Part 2)*. This is an optional message and the controller does not need to send this message; instead, it can directly send the bundle commit message. For more information regarding the bundle commit message, refer to the recipe *Committing or executing all the operations inside a bundle* in this Chapter.

How to do it...

When the switch receives an `OFPBCT_CLOSE_REQUEST` message, the switch should fetch the bundle (which was created already by the `OFPBCT_OPEN_REQUEST` message) using the `bundle_id` and `connection_id` pair wherein the `bundle_id` is the bundle identifier present in the message, and the connection id is the identifier of the received connection. Once the bundle is fetched, the switch should perform the following bundle related validations:

- If the switch can't fetch a bundle using these key pairs, then the switch should send an error message `ofp_error_msg` with the type as `OFPET_BUNDLE_FAILED` and code as `OFPBFC_BAD_ID`.
- If the fetched bundle is already in a closed state, then the switch should send an error message `ofp_error_msg` with the type as `OFPET_BUNDLE_FAILED` and code as `OFPBFC_BUNDLE_CLOSED`
- The switch should match the `flag` field present in an `OFPBCT_CLOSE_REQUEST` message to the `flag` field which is already stored in its internal data structure, which was created by an `OFPBCT_OPEN_REQUEST` message. If these fields are not matching, then the switch should send an error message `ofp_error_msg` with the type as `OFPET_BUNDLE_FAILED` and code as `OFPBFC_BAD_FLAGS`.

Once all these validations are successful, then switch should close the bundle and send an `OFPT_BUNDLE_CONTROL` message back to controller with the type as `OFPBCT_CLOSE_REPLY`.

Committing or executing all the operations inside a bundle

When the controller wants to execute/apply all the operations in the bundle, it sends an `OFPT_BUNDLE_CONTROL` message with the `type` field set as `OFPBCT_COMMIT_REQUEST`.

Getting started

The controller should have created the bundle as described in the *Creation of a bundle* recipe, before sending the bundle commit message to a switch.

The `message` field that will be used for bundle operations is described in the *Introduction* section of *Chapter 7, Handling Bundle Messages (Part 2)*.

How to do it...

When the switch receives an `OFPBCT_COMMIT_REQUEST` message, the switch should fetch the bundle (which was created already by the `OFPBCT_OPEN_REQUEST` message) using a `bundle_id` and `connection_id` pair wherein the bundle_id is the bundle identifier present in the message, and the connection ID is the identifier of the received connection. Once the bundle is fetched, the switch should perform the following bundle related validations:

- If the switch can't fetch a bundle using these key pairs, then the switch should send an error message `ofp_error_msg` with the type as `OFPET_BUNDLE_FAILED`, and code as `OFPBFC_BAD_ID`.
- The switch should match the `flag` field present in the `OFPBCT_COMMIT_REQUEST` message to the flag filed which is already stored in its internal data structure, which was created by the `OFPBCT_OPEN_REQUEST` message. If these fields are not matching, then the switch should send an error message `ofp_error_msg` with the type as `OFPET_BUNDLE_FAILED`, and code as `OFPBFC_BAD_FLAGS`.

Once it fetches the bundle, the switch should verify the flag associated with the bundle.

- If the flag contains `OFPBF_ORDERED`, then the switch must strictly apply/execute the OpenFlow messages present in the bundle, in the order they are added in the bundle.
- If the flag contains `OFPBF_ATOMIC`, then the switch must commit the bundle with atomicity at packet level also. The atomicity in packet is explained as: the given packet should be either processed completely or never process from its initial stage, which can either be packet from input port or packet from the packet-out message.

Irrespective of the `flag` field, the switch should apply the messages in the bundle in an all or nothing fashion. If one or more messages present in the bundle cannot be applied properly, then the bundle commit fails, and all the messages present in the bundle should be discarded completely without being applied, followed by sending an error message `ofp_error_msg` for the individual messages which fail in the bundle commit process. The error message should contain the `xid` field with the `xid` value of the individual messages. If multiple messages are generating errors then the switch might choose to send the first error message or can send all the error messages to the controller and is implementation-specific. Once the error messages for the individual messages are sent, the switch should send a bundle error message with the type as `OFPET_BUNDLE_FAILED`, and code as `OFPBFC_MSG_FAILED`.

The switch should consider the bundle commit successful only when all the messages inside the bundle are committed successfully.

If the bundle doesn't contain any messages, then the bundle commit should be considered as successful.

Once all these validations are successful and the switch successfully applies all the messages in the bundle, it should send a bundle message with the `type` field as `OFPBCT_CLOSE_REPLY` to the controller.

Whether the bundle commit is successful or not, the switch should discard the bundle. For more information regarding the bundle discard, refer to the recipe *Discarding a bundle* in this chapter.

Discarding a bundle

When the controller wants to discard all the operation/messages in the bundle, it sends an `OFPT_BUNDLE_CONTROL` message with the `type` field set as `OFPBCT_DISCARD_REQUEST`.

Getting started

The controller should have created the bundle as described in the *Creation of a bundle* recipe, before sending the bundle discard message to a switch.

The `message` field that will be used for bundle operations are described in the *Introduction* section of this chapter.

How to do it...

When the switch receives an `OFPBCT_DISCARD_REQUEST` message, the switch should fetch the bundle (which was created already by the `OFPBCT_OPEN_REQUEST` message) using a `bundle_id` and `connection_id` pair wherein the `bundle_id` is the bundle identifier present in the message, and the connection id is the identifier of the received connection. Once the bundle is fetched, the switch should perform the following bundle related validations:

- If the switch can't fetch a bundle using these key pairs, the switch should send an error message `ofp_error_msg` with the type as `OFPET_BUNDLE_FAILED` and code as `OFPBFC_BAD_ID`.
- Once it fetches the bundle, the switch should discard all the messages present inside the bundle and should send a bundle message back to the controller with the `type` field set as `OFPBCT_DISCARD_REPLY`.

7
Handling Bundle Messages (Part 2)

This chapter describes in detail the OpenFlow bundling mechanisms and contains the following recipes:

- Creation of a bundle
- Adding messages to a bundle
- Closing a bundle
- Committing or executing all the operations inside a bundle
- Discarding a bundle

Introduction

The OpenFlow specification has provided a mechanism for the controller to apply a set of configuration/message actions on a switch in a transactional manner. This is defined as an OpenFlow Bundle and the messages used for this are Bundle messages. A bundle consists of a sequence of OpenFlow modification messages which are sent from the controller wherein all the messages present in the bundle operate in an all or nothing fashion, i.e. if all the operations inside the bundle are successful, then the operations inside the bundle will be applied, otherwise none of the operations will be applied.

There are four stages in the OpenFlow bundle mechanism, which are as follows:

- Bundle initiation from the controller
- Adding one or more OpenFlow messages inside the bundle using bundle add message
- Closing the bundle
- Finally committing/executing the messages inside the bundle

The following example illustrates the bundle operations with the following sequence of OpenFlow messages:

- OFPBCT_OPEN_REQUEST bundle_id
- OFPT_BUNDLE_ADD_MESSAGE bundle_id modification 1
- OFPT_BUNDLE_ADD_MESSAGE bundle_id
- OFPT_BUNDLE_ADD_MESSAGE bundle_id modification n
- OFPBCT_CLOSE_REQUEST bundle_id
- OFPBCT_COMMIT_REQUEST bundle_id

In the above mentioned bundle sequence, the first message to be sent from the controller to initiate bundle processing is `OFPBCT_OPEN_REQUEST`.

Followed by this open message, the controller should send a sequence of OpenFlow messages to be processed as a bundle using `OFPT_BUNDLE_ADD_MESSAGE`.

Then the controller can optionally choose to close the bundle using an `OFPBCT_CLOSE_REQUEST` message followed by `OFPBCT_COMMIT_REQUEST` to apply/commit all the OpenFlow operations present inside the bundle.

For the above mentioned bundle operations, the controller should use a bundle control message (`OFPT_BUNDLE_CONTROL`). The `OFPT_BUNDLE_CONTROL` message takes the following format:

```
/* Message structure for OFPT_BUNDLE_CONTROL. */
struct ofp_bundle_ctrl_msg {
struct ofp_header header;
uint32_t bundle_id; /* Identify the bundle. */
uint16_t type;      /* OFPBCT_*. */
uint16_t flags;     /* Bitmap of OFPBF_* flags. */
          /* Bundle Property list. */
struct ofp_bundle_prop_header properties[0]; /* Zero or more
properties. */
};
```

The `bundle_id` represents the identifier of the bundle, which is a 32-bit integer and should be unique over the connection during the bundle lifetime.

The `type` filed represents the type of the bundle message as follows:

```
/* Bundle control message types */
enum ofp_bundle_ctrl_type {
OFPBCT_OPEN_REQUEST = 0,
OFPBCT_OPEN_REPLY = 1,
```

```
OFPBCT_CLOSE_REQUEST = 2,
OFPBCT_CLOSE_REPLY = 3,
OFPBCT_COMMIT_REQUEST = 4,
OFPBCT_COMMIT_REPLY = 5,
OFPBCT_DISCARD_REQUEST = 6,
OFPBCT_DISCARD_REPLY = 7,
};
```

The `flag` field represents the bundle flags and is defined as follows:

```
/* Bundle configuration flags. */
enum ofp_bundle_flags {
OFPBF_ATOMIC = 1 << 0, /* Execute atomically. */
OFPBF_ORDERED = 1 << 1, /* Execute in specified order. */
};
```

The `properties` field represents the list of bundle properties and is used only for experimental purposes now.

Creation of a bundle

When the controller wants to create a bundle, the controller should send an `OFPT_BUNDLE_CONTROL` message with the `type` field set as `OFPBCT_OPEN_REQUEST`.

How to do it...

The `message` field that should be used by the controller to create a bundle is described in the *Introduction* section of this chapter.

The `bundle_id` field is a 32-bit integer and should be filled with an arbitrary value and it represents the identifier of the bundle in both controller and switch. The controller might create multiple bundles, each identified by unique `bundle_id` to provide bundle parallelism in the switch. The controller could apply any of them in any order by specifying its `bundle_id` in a commit message.

The `flag` field should be filled with either `OFPBF_ATOMIC` (value 1) or `OFPBF_ORDERED` (value 2), or both, or none:

- If the controller wants the switch to apply the OpenFlow messages (inside the bundle) in the order in which it is sending, then the controller should set the `OFPBF_ORDERED` flag.
- If the controller wants to apply/commit the bundle with packet level atomicity, then the controller should set the `OFPBF_ATOMIC` flag.

The properties field should be left empty unless the experimenter property is to be used.

Once the controller sends the OFPBCT_OPEN_REQUEST message to the switch, the controller should wait for the response message from the switch. The controller may either receive an OFPBCT_OPEN_REPLY message or ofp_error_msg with the type as OFPET_BUNDLE_FAILED. The operations to be performed when the controller receives the error message are defined as follows:

- If the error code is OFPBFC_BAD_ID, then the controller should re-verify whether the bundle_id sent in OFPBCT_OPEN_REQUEST message is proper.
- If the error code is OFPBFC_BAD_FLAGS, then it implies that the switch doesn't support the flag field mentioned in the OFPBCT_OPEN_REQUEST message. The controller could either choose to send a new OFPBCT_OPEN_REQUEST message with a modified flag value or discard the opening of a new bundle.
- If the error code is OFPBFC_OUT_OF_BUNDLES, then it implies that the switch was not able to open the bundle because of some internal error.

Adding messages to a bundle

When the controller wants to add a new OpenFlow message to a bundle, the controller should send an OFPT_BUNDLE_ADD_MESSAGE message.

Getting started

The controller should have created the bundle as described in the *Creation of a bundle* recipe before sending the bundle add message to a switch.

How to do it...

The OFPT_BUNDLE_ADD_MESSAGE message contains an OpenFlow message whose operation needs to be executed/performed by the switch in a bundled fashion. The message format that should be used by the controller to add an OpenFlow message to a bundle is described as follows:

```
/* Message structure for OFPT_BUNDLE_ADD_MESSAGE.
* Adding a message in a bundle is done with. */
struct ofp_bundle_add_msg {
struct ofp_header header;
uint32_t bundle_id;        /* Identify the bundle. */
uint16_t pad;              /* Align to 64 bits. */
uint16_t flags;            /* Bitmap of OFPBF_* flags. */
struct ofp_header message; /* Message added to the bundle. */
```

```
/* If there is one property or more, 'message' is followed by:
 * - Exactly (message.length + 7)/8*8 - (message.length) (between
 * 0 and 7) bytes of all-zero bytes */
    /* Bundle Property list. */
 struct ofp_bundle_prop_header properties[0];
    /* Zero or more properties. */
};
```

The `bundle_id` field should be filled with the bundle identifier. This `bundle_id` should refer to a bundle which was created by the controller earlier, using an `OFPBCT_OPEN_REQUEST` message.

The `flag` field should be filled with either `OFPBF_ATOMIC` (value 1) or `OFPBF_ORDERED` (value 2), or both, or none.

The `flag` field should be same as that of the `flag` field in the `OFPBCT_OPEN_REQUEST` message, which was used to create the bundle.

The `message` field should be filled with the OpenFlow message to be bundled. The `xid` field in this message should be same as that of the `xid` field value of this `OFPT_BUNDLE_ADD_MESSAGE` bundle message.

The `properties` field should be left empty unless the experimenter property is to be used.

Once the controller sends the `OFPT_BUNDLE_ADD_MESSAGE` message to the switch, the controller need not wait for any response message from the switch. However, the controller might receive an `ofp_error_msg`. The operations to be performed when the controller receives the error message are defined as follows:

- If the error code is `OFPBFC_BUNDLE_CLOSED`, then the controller should verify whether it has already sent a bundle close message to the switch with the same bundle ID.
- If the error code is `OFPBFC_BAD_FLAGS`, then the controller should verify that the `flag` field set in this message is the same as that of the `OFPBCT_OPEN_REQUEST` message. If not, it could choose to send a new `OFPT_BUNDLE_ADD_MESSAGE` message with the same `flag` field as that of the `OFPBCT_OPEN_REQUEST` message.
- If the error code is `OFPBFC_MSG_UNSUP`, then it implies that the switch doesn't support this particular OpenFlow message in bundle processing. The controller could choose to send this OpenFlow message as a non-bundle message for normal switch processing.

- If the error code is OFPBFC_MSG_CONFLICT, then it implies that there is some inconsistency issue in the switch while processing this OpenFlow message, with the messages already stored in the bundle. The controller could choose to send this message as a non-bundle message for normal switch processing.
- If the error code is OFPBFC_MSG_BAD_LEN, then the controller should verify the length field present in the OpenFlow message and could choose to re-send the OFPT_BUNDLE_ADD_MESSAGE message with the proper length field.

Closing a bundle

When the controller wants to finish recording the bundle messages then it should send an OFPT_BUNDLE_CONTROL message with type field set as OFPT_BUNDLE_CLOSE_REQUEST.

Getting started

The controller should have created the bundle as described in the *Creation of a bundle* recipe, before sending the bundle add message to a switch.

How to do it...

The message format that should be used for bundle operations (OFPT_BUNDLE_CONTROL) is described in the *Introduction* section of this chapter.

The type field should be filled with the value OFPBCT_CLOSE_REQUEST.

The bundle close message is an optional message and the controller does not need to send this message. It can directly send the bundle commit message. For more information regarding the bundle commit message, refer to the recipe *Committing or executing all the operations inside a bundle*.

Once the controller sends the OFPBCT_CLOSE_REQUEST message to the switch, the controller should wait for the response message from the switch. The controller may either receive an OFPBCT_CLOSE_REPLY message or ofp_error_msg with the type as OFPET_BUNDLE_FAILED.

The controller should not send any OFPT_BUNDLE_ADD_MESSAGE once it sends the OFPBCT_CLOSE_REQUEST to the switch with the same bundle_id

The operations to be performed when the controller receives the error message are defined as follows:

- If the error code is `OFPBFC_BAD_ID`, then the controller should re-verify if the bundle_id sent in the `OFPBCT_CLOSE_REQUEST` message is proper.
- If the error code is `OFPBFC_BUNDLE_CLOSED`, then the controller can ignore this error message as the bundle is already closed by the switch.
- If the error code is `OFPBFC_BAD_FLAGS`, then the controller should verify that the `flag` field set in this message is same as that of the `OFPBCT_OPEN_REQUEST` message. If not, it could choose to send a new `OFPBCT_CLOSE_REQUEST` message with the same `flag` field as that of the `OFPBCT_OPEN_REQUEST` message.

Committing or executing all the operations inside a bundle

When the controller wants to execute/apply all the operations in the bundle, it should send an `OFPT_BUNDLE_CONTROL` message with the `type` field set as `OFPBCT_COMMIT_REQUEST`.

Getting started

The controller should have created the bundle as described in the *Creation of a bundle* recipe before sending the bundle add message to a switch. The controller could optionally choose to close the bundle before sending the bundle commit message.

How to do it...

The message format that should be used for bundle operations (`OFPT_BUNDLE_CONTROL`) is described in the *Introduction* section of this chapter.

The `type` field should be filled with the value `OFPBCT_COMMIT_REQUEST`.

Once the controller sends the `OFPBCT_COMMIT_REQUEST` message to the switch, the controller should wait for the response message from the switch. The controller may either receive an `OFPBCT_COMMIT_` REPLY message or `ofp_error_msg` with the type as `OFPET_BUNDLE_FAILED`.

The operations to be performed when the controller receives the error message are defined as follows:

- If the error code is `OFPBFC_BAD_ID`, then the controller should re-verify whether the bundle_id sent in an `OFPBCT_COMMIT_REQUEST` message is proper.
- If the error code is `OFPBFC_BAD_FLAGS`, then the controller should verify that the `flag` field set in this message is the same as that of an `OFPBCT_OPEN_REQUEST` message. If not, it could choose to send a new `OFPBCT_COMMIT_REQUEST` message with the same `flag` field as that of the `OFPBCT_OPEN_REQUEST` message.
- If the error code is `OFPBFC_MSG_FAILED`, then one or more operations inside the bundle have failed. The controller should take necessary action to reconfigure the switch.

Discarding a bundle

When the controller wants to discard all the operation/messages in the bundle then it should send an `OFPT_BUNDLE_CONTROL` message with the `type` field set as `OFPBCT_DISCARD_REQUEST`.

Getting started

The controller should have created the bundle as described in the *Creation of a bundle* recipe in this chapter before sending the bundle add message to a switch.

How to do it...

The message format that should be used for bundle operations (`OFPT_BUNDLE_CONTROL`) is described in the *Introduction* section of this chapter. The `type` field should be filled with the value `OFPBCT_DISCARD_REQUEST`.

Once the controller sends the `OFPBCT_DISCARD_REQUEST` message to the switch, the controller should wait for the response message from the switch. The controller may either receive an `OFPBCT_DISCARD_REPLY` message or `ofp_error_msg` with the type as `OFPET_BUNDLE_FAILED`.

The operations to be performed when the controller receives the error message are defined as follows:

- If the error code is `OFPBFC_BAD_ID`, then the controller should re-verify whether the `bundle_id` sent in `OFPBCT_DISCARD_REQUEST` message is proper.

Common OpenFlow Headers, Structures, and Error Code

This appendix talks about some of the common message headers, structures, and error code defined in the OpenFlow specification.

Common OpenFlow headers

This section covers the OpenFlow header formats that are common to one or more messages. This includes the following header information.

OpenFlow Header

Every OpenFlow message begins with the OpenFlow header, and the format is as follows:

```
/* Header on all OpenFlow packets. */
struct ofp_header {
uint8_t version;    /* OFP_VERSION. */
uint8_t type;       /* One of the OFPT_ constants. */
uint16_t length;    /* Length including this ofp_header. */
uint32_t xid;       /* Transaction id associated with this packet.
                       Replies use the same id as was in the
                       Request to facilitate pairing. */
};
```

The `version` specifies the OpenFlow protocol version being used. The `type` field represents the message type being sent, which can take any one of the following values:

```
enum ofp_type {
            /* Immutable messages. */
OFPT_HELLO = 0,               /* Symmetric message */
OFPT_ERROR = 1,               /* Symmetric message */
OFPT_ECHO_REQUEST = 2,        /* Symmetric message */
OFPT_ECHO_REPLY = 3,          /* Symmetric message */
OFPT_EXPERIMENTER = 4,        /* Symmetric message */

       /* Switch configuration messages. */
OFPT_FEATURES_REQUEST = 5,    /* Controller/switch message */
OFPT_FEATURES_REPLY = 6,      /* Controller/switch message */
OFPT_GET_CONFIG_REQUEST = 7,  /* Controller/switch message */
OFPT_GET_CONFIG_REPLY = 8,    /* Controller/switch message */
OFPT_SET_CONFIG = 9,          /* Controller/switch message */
           /* Asynchronous messages. */
OFPT_PACKET_IN = 10,              /* Async message */
OFPT_FLOW_REMOVED = 11,           /* Async message */
OFPT_PORT_STATUS = 12,            /* Async message */

          /* Controller command messages. */
OFPT_PACKET_OUT = 13,             /* Controller/switch message */
OFPT_FLOW_MOD = 14,               /* Controller/switch message */
OFPT_GROUP_MOD = 15,              /* Controller/switch message */
OFPT_PORT_MOD = 16,               /* Controller/switch message */
OFPT_TABLE_MOD = 17,              /* Controller/switch message */

          /* Multipart messages. */
OFPT_MULTIPART_REQUEST = 18,       /* Controller/switch message */
OFPT_MULTIPART_REPLY = 19,         /* Controller/switch message */

          /* Barrier messages. */
OFPT_BARRIER_REQUEST = 20,         /* Controller/switch message */
OFPT_BARRIER_REPLY = 21,           /* Controller/switch message */

      /* Controller role change request messages. */
OFPT_ROLE_REQUEST = 24,            /* Controller/switch message */
OFPT_ROLE_REPLY = 25,              /* Controller/switch message */
```

```
      /* Asynchronous message configuration. */
OFPT_GET_ASYNC_REQUEST = 26,      /* Controller/switch message */
OFPT_GET_ASYNC_REPLY = 27,        /* Controller/switch message */
OFPT_SET_ASYNC = 28,              /* Controller/switch message */

      /* Meters and rate limiters configuration messages. */
OFPT_METER_MOD = 29,              /* Controller/switch message */

      /* Controller role change event messages. */
OFPT_ROLE_STATUS = 30,            /* Async message */

       /* Asynchronous messages. */
OFPT_TABLE_STATUS = 31,           /* Async message */

       /* Request forwarding by the switch. */
OFPT_REQUESTFORWARD = 32,         /* Async message */

       /* Bundle operations */
OFPT_BUNDLE_CONTROL = 33,
OFPT_BUNDLE_ADD_MESSAGE = 34,
};
```

Common OpenFlow structures

This section talks about generic OpenFlow structures that are used by the controller and switch while processing OpenFlow messages.

Port structures

This section describes the port structures defined in the OpenFlow specification:

```
            /* Description of a port */
struct ofp_port {
uint32_t port_no;                 /* Unique identity of port */
uint16_t length;
uint8_t pad[2];
uint8_t hw_addr[OFP_ETH_ALEN];    /* mac addr field */
uint8_t pad2[2];                  /* Align to 64 bits. */
char name[OFP_MAX_PORT_NAME_LEN]; /* Null-terminated name field*/
uint32_t config;                  /* Bitmap of OFPPC_* flags. */
uint32_t state;                   /* Bitmap of OFPPS_* flags. */
/* Port description property list - 0 or more properties */
struct ofp_port_desc_prop_header properties[0];
};
```

The `port_no` field uses the following convention:

```
/* Port numbering. Ports are numbered starting from 1. */

enum ofp_port_no {
/* Maximum number of physical and logical switch ports. */
OFPP_MAX = 0xffffff00,

/* Reserved OpenFlow Port (fake output "ports"). */
OFPP_IN_PORT = 0xfffffff8, /* Send the packet out the input port.
                              This reserved port must be
                              explicitly used in order to send
                              back out of the input port. */
OFPP_TABLE = 0xfffffff9,   /* Submit the packet to first flow
                              Table. NB: This destination port can
                              only be used in packet-out message.*/

OFPP_NORMAL = 0xfffffffa, /* Process with L2/L3 switching. */
OFPP_FLOOD = 0xfffffffb,  /* All physical ports in VLAN, except
                             Input port and those blocked or link
                             down. */
OFPP_ALL = 0xfffffffc,    /* All phy. ports except input port. */
OFPP_CONTROLLER = 0xfffffffd, /* Send to controller. */
OFPP_LOCAL = 0xfffffffe,      /* Local openflow "port". */
OFPP_ANY = 0xffffffff /* Wildcard port used only for flow mod
                         (delete) and flow stats requests. Selects
                         all flows regardless of output port
                         (including flows with no output port). */
};
```

The `config` field indicates the behavior of the physical port, and is defined as follows:

```
enum ofp_port_config {
OFPPC_PORT_DOWN = 1 << 0, /* Port is administratively down. */
OFPPC_NO_RECV = 1 << 2, /* Drop all packets received by port. */
OFPPC_NO_FWD = 1 << 5, /* Drop packets forwarded to port. */
OFPPC_NO_PACKET_IN = 1 << 6 /* Do not send packet-in msgs for port. */
};
```

The `state` field represents the current state of the port:

```
enum ofp_port_state {
OFPPS_LINK_DOWN = 1 << 0, /* No physical link present. */
OFPPS_BLOCKED = 1 << 1, /* Port is blocked */
OFPPS_LIVE = 1 << 2, /* Live for Fast Failover Group. */
};
```

Table structures

This section describes the port structures defined in the OpenFlow specification:

```
/* Table Feature property types.
* Low order bit cleared indicates property for regular Flow Entry.
* Low order bit set indicates property for Table-Miss Flow Entry.
*/
enum ofp_table_feature_prop_type {
OFPTFPT_INSTRUCTIONS = 0, /* Instructions property. */
OFPTFPT_INSTRUCTIONS_MISS = 1, /* Instructions for table-miss. */
OFPTFPT_NEXT_TABLES = 2, /* Next Table property. */
OFPTFPT_NEXT_TABLES_MISS = 3, /* Next Table for table-miss. */
OFPTFPT_WRITE_ACTIONS = 4, /* Write Actions property. */
OFPTFPT_WRITE_ACTIONS_MISS = 5, /* Write Actions for table-miss. */
OFPTFPT_APPLY_ACTIONS = 6, /* Apply Actions property. */
OFPTFPT_APPLY_ACTIONS_MISS = 7, /* Apply Actions for table-miss. */
OFPTFPT_MATCH = 8, /* Match property. */
OFPTFPT_WILDCARDS = 10, /* Wildcards property. */
OFPTFPT_WRITE_SETFIELD = 12, /* Write Set-Field property. */
OFPTFPT_WRITE_SETFIELD_MISS = 13, /* Write Set-Field for table-miss.
*/
OFPTFPT_APPLY_SETFIELD = 14, /* Apply Set-Field property. */
OFPTFPT_APPLY_SETFIELD_MISS = 15, /* Apply Set-Field for table-miss.
*/
OFPTFPT_TABLE_SYNC_FROM = 16, /* Table synchronisation property. */
OFPTFPT_EXPERIMENTER = 0xFFFE, /* Experimenter property. */
OFPTFPT_EXPERIMENTER_MISS = 0xFFFF, /* Experimenter for table-miss. */
};

/* Common header for all Table Feature Properties */
struct ofp_table_feature_prop_header {
uint16_t type; /* One of OFPTFPT_*. */
uint16_t length; /* Length in bytes of this property. */
};

/* Instruction ID */
struct ofp_instruction_id {
uint16_t type; /* One of OFPIT_*. */
uint16_t len; /* Length is 4 or experimenter defined. */
uint8_t exp_data[0]; /* Optional experimenter id + data. */
};
```

```
/* Instructions property */
struct ofp_table_feature_prop_instructions {
uint16_t type; /* One of OFPTFPT_INSTRUCTIONS,
OFPTFPT_INSTRUCTIONS_MISS. */
uint16_t length; /* Length in bytes of this property. */
/* Followed by:
* - Exactly (length - 4) bytes containing the instruction ids, then
* - Exactly (length + 7)/8*8 - (length) (between 0 and 7)
* bytes of all-zero bytes */
struct ofp_instruction_id instruction_ids[0]; /* List of instructions
*/
};

/* Next Tables and Table Synchronise From properties */
struct ofp_table_feature_prop_tables {
uint16_t type; /* One of OFPTFPT_NEXT_TABLES,
OFPTFPT_NEXT_TABLES_MISS,
OFPTFPT_TABLE_SYNC_FROM. */
uint16_t length; /* Length in bytes of this property. */
/* Followed by:
* - Exactly (length - 4) bytes containing the table_ids, then
* - Exactly (length + 7)/8*8 - (length) (between 0 and 7)
* bytes of all-zero bytes */
uint8_t table_ids[0]; /* List of table ids. */
};
OFP_ASSERT(sizeof(struct ofp_table_feature_prop_tables) == 4);
/* Action ID */
struct ofp_action_id {
uint16_t type; /* One of OFPAT_*. */
uint16_t len; /* Length is 4 or experimenter defined. */
uint8_t exp_data[0]; /* Optional experimenter id + data. */
};

/* Actions property */
struct ofp_table_feature_prop_actions {
uint16_t type; /* One of OFPTFPT_WRITE_ACTIONS,
OFPTFPT_WRITE_ACTIONS_MISS,
OFPTFPT_APPLY_ACTIONS,
OFPTFPT_APPLY_ACTIONS_MISS. */
uint16_t length; /* Length in bytes of this property. */
/* Followed by:
* - Exactly (length - 4) bytes containing the action_ids, then
* - Exactly (length + 7)/8*8 - (length) (between 0 and 7)
* bytes of all-zero bytes */
```

```
struct ofp_action_id action_ids[0]; /* List of actions */
};

/* Match, Wildcard or Set-Field property */
struct ofp_table_feature_prop_oxm {
uint16_t type; /* One of OFPTFPT_MATCH,
OFPTFPT_WILDCARDS,
OFPTFPT_WRITE_SETFIELD,
OFPTFPT_WRITE_SETFIELD_MISS,
OFPTFPT_APPLY_SETFIELD,
OFPTFPT_APPLY_SETFIELD_MISS. */
uint16_t length; /* Length in bytes of this property. */
/* Followed by:
* - Exactly (length - 4) bytes containing the oxm_ids, then
* - Exactly (length + 7)/8*8 - (length) (between 0 and 7)
* bytes of all-zero bytes */
uint32_t oxm_ids[0]; /* Array of OXM headers */
};

/* Experimenter table feature property */
struct ofp_table_feature_prop_experimenter {
uint16_t type; /* One of OFPTFPT_EXPERIMENTER,
OFPTFPT_EXPERIMENTER_MISS. */
uint16_t length; /* Length in bytes of this property. */
uint32_t experimenter; /* Experimenter ID which takes the same
form as in struct
ofp_experimenter_header. */
uint32_t exp_type; /* Experimenter defined. */
/* Followed by:
* - Exactly (length - 12) bytes containing the experimenter data, then
* - Exactly (length + 7)/8*8 - (length) (between 0 and 7)
* bytes of all-zero bytes */
uint32_t experimenter_data[0];
};

/* Body for ofp_multipart_request of type OFPMP_TABLE_FEATURES./
* Body of reply to OFPMP_TABLE_FEATURES request. */
struct ofp_table_features {
uint16_t length; /* Length is padded to 64 bits. */
uint8_t table_id; /* Identifier of table. Lower numbered tables
are consulted first. */
uint8_t pad[5]; /* Align to 64-bits. */
char name[OFP_MAX_TABLE_NAME_LEN];
```

```
uint64_t metadata_match; /* Bits of metadata table can match. */
uint64_t metadata_write; /* Bits of metadata table can write. */
uint32_t capabilities; /* Bitmap of OFPTC_* values. */
uint32_t max_entries; /* Max number of entries supported. */
/* Table Feature Property list */
struct ofp_table_feature_prop_header properties[0]; /* List of
properties */
};

/* Body of reply to OFPMP_TABLE request. */
struct ofp_table_stats {
uint8_t table_id; /* Identifier of table. Lower numbered tables
are consulted first. */
uint8_t pad[3]; /* Align to 32-bits. */
uint32_t active_count; /* Number of active entries. */
uint64_t lookup_count; /* Number of packets looked up in table. */
uint64_t matched_count; /* Number of packets that hit table. */
};

/* Body of reply to OFPMP_TABLE_DESC request. */
struct ofp_table_desc {
uint16_t length; /* Length is padded to 64 bits. */
uint8_t table_id; /* Identifier of table. Lower numbered tables
are consulted first. */
uint8_t pad[1]; /* Align to 32-bits. */
uint32_t config; /* Bitmap of OFPTC_* values. */
/* Table Mod Property list - 0 or more. */
struct ofp_table_mod_prop_header properties[0];
};
```

Common OpenFlow error codes

This section talks about error types, error code for different error types, and the data values for each error code and error type combination:

```
/* Values for 'type' in ofp_error_message. These values are
 * immutable: they will not change in future versions of the
 * protocol (although new values may be added). */
enum ofp_error_type {
OFPET_HELLO_FAILED = 0,              /* Hello protocol failed. */
OFPET_BAD_REQUEST = 1,              /* Request was not understood.
*/
```

```
OFPET_BAD_ACTION = 2,                          /* Error in action
description. */
OFPET_BAD_INSTRUCTION = 3,          /* Error in instruction list. */
OFPET_BAD_MATCH = 4,                           /* Error in match. */
OFPET_FLOW_MOD_FAILED = 5,         /* Problem modifying flow entry. */
OFPET_GROUP_MOD_FAILED = 6,      /* Problem modifying group entry. */
OFPET_PORT_MOD_FAILED = 7,         /* Port mod request failed. */
OFPET_TABLE_MOD_FAILED = 8,        /* Table mod request failed. */
OFPET_QUEUE_OP_FAILED = 9,          /* Queue operation failed. */
OFPET_SWITCH_CONFIG_FAILED = 10, /* Switch config request failed. */
OFPET_ROLE_REQUEST_FAILED = 11, /* Controller Role request failed. */
OFPET_METER_MOD_FAILED = 12,      /* Error in meter. */
OFPET_TABLE_FEATURES_FAILED = 13, /* Setting table features failed. */
OFPET_BAD_PROPERTY = 14,              /* Some property is invalid. */
OFPET_ASYNC_CONFIG_FAILED = 15, /* Asynchronous config request failed.
*/
OFPET_FLOW_MONITOR_FAILED = 16, /* Setting flow monitor failed. */
OFPET_BUNDLE_FAILED = 17,          /* Bundle operation failed. */
OFPET_EXPERIMENTER = 0xffff        /* Experimenter error messages. */
};
```

For the OFPET_HELLO_FAILED error type, these codes are currently defined:

```
/* ofp_error_msg 'code' values for OFPET_HELLO_FAILED.
 * 'data' contains an
 * ASCII text string that may give failure details. */
enum ofp_hello_failed_code {
OFPHFC_INCOMPATIBLE = 0, /* No compatible version. */
OFPHFC_EPERM = 1,         /* Permissions error. */
};
```

For the OFPET_BAD_REQUEST error type, the following codes are currently defined:

```
/* ofp_error_msg 'code' values for OFPET_BAD_REQUEST.
 * 'data' contains at least the first 64 bytes of
 * the failed request. */
enum ofp_bad_request_code {
OFPBRC_BAD_VERSION = 0,    /* ofp_header.version not supported. */
OFPBRC_BAD_TYPE = 1,       /* ofp_header.type not supported. */
OFPBRC_BAD_MULTIPART = 2, /* ofp_multipart_request.type
* not supported. */
OFPBRC_BAD_EXPERIMENTER = 3, /* Experimenter id not supported
                              * (in ofp_experimenter_header or
                              * ofp_multipart_request or
                              * ofp_multipart_reply). */
```

```
OFPBRC_BAD_EXP_TYPE = 4, /* Experimenter type not supported. */
OFPBRC_EPERM = 5,        /* Permissions error. */
OFPBRC_BAD_LEN = 6,      /* Wrong request length for type. */
OFPBRC_BUFFER_EMPTY = 7, /* Specified buffer has already
                          * been used. */
OFPBRC_BUFFER_UNKNOWN = 8, /* Specified buffer does not exist. */
OFPBRC_BAD_TABLE_ID = 9,   /* Specified table-id invalid or
                            * does not exist. */
OFPBRC_IS_SLAVE = 10,    /* Denied because controller is slave. */
OFPBRC_BAD_PORT = 11,    /* Invalid port. */
OFPBRC_BAD_PACKET = 12, /* Invalid packet in packet-out. */
OFPBRC_MULTIPART_BUFFER_OVERFLOW = 13, /* ofp_multipart_request
                                        * overflowed the assigned
                                        * buffer. */
OFPBRC_MULTIPART_REQUEST_TIMEOUT = 14, /* Timeout during
                                        * multipart request. */
OFPBRC_MULTIPART_REPLY_TIMEOUT = 15,   /* Timeout during multipart
                                        * reply. */
};
```

For the `OFPET_BAD_ACTION` error type, these codes are currently defined:

```
/* ofp_error_msg 'code' values for OFPET_BAD_ACTION.
 * 'data' contains at least the first 64 bytes of the
 * failed request. */
enum ofp_bad_action_code {
OFPBAC_BAD_TYPE = 0,          /* Unknown action type. */
OFPBAC_BAD_LEN = 1,           /* Length problem in actions. */
OFPBAC_BAD_EXPERIMENTER = 2, /* Unknown experimenter id
                               * specified. */
OFPBAC_BAD_EXP_TYPE = 3, /* Unknown action for experimenter id. */
OFPBAC_BAD_OUT_PORT = 4, /* Problem validating output port. */
OFPBAC_BAD_ARGUMENT = 5, /* Bad action argument. */
OFPBAC_EPERM = 6,        /* Permissions error. */
OFPBAC_TOO_MANY = 7,     /* Cannot handle this many actions. */
OFPBAC_BAD_QUEUE = 8,    /* Problem validating output queue. */
OFPBAC_BAD_OUT_GROUP = 9,/* Invalid group id in forward action. */
OFPBAC_MATCH_INCONSISTENT = 10, /* Action can't apply for this
                                 * match, or Set-Field missing
                                 * prerequisite. */
OFPBAC_UNSUPPORTED_ORDER = 11,  /* Action order is unsupported for
                                 * the action list in an
                                 * Apply-Actions instruction */
```

```
OFPBAC_BAD_TAG = 12, /* Actions uses an unsupported tag/encap. */
OFPBAC_BAD_SET_TYPE = 13, /* Unsupported type in SET_FIELD action. */
OFPBAC_BAD_SET_LEN = 14,      /* Length problem in SET_FIELD
                               * action. */
OFPBAC_BAD_SET_ARGUMENT = 15, /* Bad argument in SET_FIELD
                               * action. */
};
```

For the `OFPET_BAD_INSTRUCTION` error type, the following codes are currently defined:

```
/* ofp_error_msg 'code' values for OFPET_BAD_INSTRUCTION.
 * 'data' contains at least
 * the first 64 bytes of the failed request. */
enum ofp_bad_instruction_code {
OFPBIC_UNKNOWN_INST = 0,  /* Unknown instruction. */
OFPBIC_UNSUP_INST = 1,     /* Switch or table does not support
                            * the instruction. */
OFPBIC_BAD_TABLE_ID = 2,   /* Invalid Table-ID specified. */
OFPBIC_UNSUP_METADATA = 3, /* Metadata value unsupported by
                            * datapath. */
OFPBIC_UNSUP_METADATA_MASK = 4, /* Metadata mask value unsupported
                                 * by datapath. */
OFPBIC_BAD_EXPERIMENTER = 5,    /* Unknown experimenter id
                                 * specified. */
OFPBIC_BAD_EXP_TYPE = 6,        /* Unknown instruction for
                                 * experimenter id. */
OFPBIC_BAD_LEN = 7,   /* Length problem in instructions. */
OFPBIC_EPERM = 8,     /* Permissions error. */
OFPBIC_DUP_INST = 9, /* Duplicate instruction. */
};
```

For the `OFPET_BAD_MATCH` error type, here are the currently defined codes:

```
/* ofp_error_msg 'code' values for OFPET_BAD_MATCH.
 * 'data' contains at least the first 64 bytes of the
 * failed request. */
enum ofp_bad_match_code {
OFPBMC_BAD_TYPE = 0, /* Unsupported match type specified by
                      * the match */
OFPBMC_BAD_LEN = 1,  /* Length problem in match. */
OFPBMC_BAD_TAG = 2,  /* Match uses an unsupported tag/encap. */
OFPBMC_BAD_DL_ADDR_MASK = 3, /* Unsupported datalink addr mask
                              * switch does not support
                              * arbitrary datalink address
                              * mask. */
```

```
OFPBMC_BAD_NW_ADDR_MASK = 4, /* Unsupported network addr mask
                              * switch does not support arbitrary
                              * network address mask. */
OFPBMC_BAD_WILDCARDS = 5,    /* Unsupported combination of fields
                              * masked for omitted in match. */
OFPBMC_BAD_FIELD = 6, /* Unsupported field type in the match. */
OFPBMC_BAD_VALUE = 7, /* Unsupported value in a match field. */
OFPBMC_BAD_MASK = 8,  /* Unsupported mask specified in the match,
                       * field is not dl-address or nw-address. */
OFPBMC_BAD_PREREQ = 9, /* A prerequisite was not met. */
OFPBMC_DUP_FIELD = 10, /* A field type was duplicated. */
OFPBMC_EPERM = 11,     /* Permissions error. */
};
```

For the `OFPET_FLOW_MOD_FAILED` error type, the following codes are currently defined:

```
/* ofp_error_msg 'code' values for OFPET_FLOW_MOD_FAILED.
 * 'data' contains at least the first 64 bytes of the failed
 * request. */
enum ofp_flow_mod_failed_code {
OFPFMFC_UNKNOWN = 0,      /* Unspecified error. */
OFPFMFC_TABLE_FULL = 1,   /* Flow not added because table was
                           * full. */
OFPFMFC_BAD_TABLE_ID = 2, /* Table does not exist */
OFPFMFC_OVERLAP = 3,      /* Attempted to add overlapping flow
                           * with CHECK_OVERLAP flag set. */
OFPFMFC_EPERM = 4,        /* Permissions error. */
OFPFMFC_BAD_TIMEOUT = 5,  /* Flow not added because of unsupported
                           * idle/hard timeout. */
OFPFMFC_BAD_COMMAND = 6,  /* Unsupported or unknown command. */
OFPFMFC_BAD_FLAGS = 7,    /* Unsupported or unknown flags. */
OFPFMFC_CANT_SYNC = 8,    /* Problem in table synchronisation. */
OFPFMFC_BAD_PRIORITY = 9, /* Unsupported priority value. */
};
```

For the `OFPET_GROUP_MOD_FAILED` error type, these codes are currently defined:

```
/* ofp_error_msg 'code' values for OFPET_GROUP_MOD_FAILED.
 * 'data' contains at least the first 64 bytes of the failed
 * request. */
enum ofp_group_mod_failed_code {
OFPGMFC_GROUP_EXISTS = 0, /* Group not added because a group
                           * ADD attempted to replace an
                           * already-present group. */
```

```
OFPGMFC_INVALID_GROUP = 1,/* Group not added because Group
                           * specified is invalid. */
OFPGMFC_WEIGHT_UNSUPPORTED = 2, /* Switch does not support
                                 * unequal load sharing with
                                 * select groups. */
OFPGMFC_OUT_OF_GROUPS = 3,  /* The group table is full. */
OFPGMFC_OUT_OF_BUCKETS = 4, /* The maximum number of action
                             * buckets for a group has been
                             * exceeded. */
OFPGMFC_CHAINING_UNSUPPORTED = 5, /* Switch does not support
                                   * groups that forward to
                                   * groups. */
OFPGMFC_WATCH_UNSUPPORTED = 6, /* This group cannot watch the
                                * watch_port for watch_group
                                * specified. */
OFPGMFC_LOOP = 7,           /* Group entry would cause a loop. */
OFPGMFC_UNKNOWN_GROUP = 8, /* Group not modified because a group
                            * MODIFY attempted to modify a
                            * non-existent group. */
OFPGMFC_CHAINED_GROUP = 9, /* Group not deleted because another
                            * group is forwarding to it. */
OFPGMFC_BAD_TYPE = 10,    /* Unsupported or unknown group type. */
OFPGMFC_BAD_COMMAND = 11, /* Unsupported or unknown command. */
OFPGMFC_BAD_BUCKET = 12,  /* Error in bucket. */
OFPGMFC_BAD_WATCH = 13,   /* Error in watch port/group. */
OFPGMFC_EPERM = 14,       /* Permissions error. */
};
```

For the `OFPET_PORT_MOD_FAILED` error type, here are the currently defined codes:

```
/* ofp_error_msg 'code' values for OFPET_PORT_MOD_FAILED.
 * 'data' contains at least the first 64 bytes of the failed
 * request. */
enum ofp_port_mod_failed_code {
OFPPMFC_BAD_PORT = 0,    /* Specified port number does not
                          * exist. */
OFPPMFC_BAD_HW_ADDR = 1, /* Specified hardware address does not
                          * match the port number. */
OFPPMFC_BAD_CONFIG = 2,  /* Specified config is invalid. */
OFPPMFC_BAD_ADVERTISE = 3, /* Specified advertise is invalid. */
OFPPMFC_EPERM = 4,         /* Permissions error. */
};
```

For the OFPET_TABLE_MOD_FAILED error type, the following codes are currently defined:

```
/* ofp_error_msg 'code' values for OFPET_TABLE_MOD_FAILED.
 * 'data' contains at least the first 64 bytes of the failed
 * request. */
enum ofp_table_mod_failed_code {
OFPTMFC_BAD_TABLE = 0,  /* Specified table does not exist. */
OFPTMFC_BAD_CONFIG = 1, /* Specified config is invalid. */
OFPTMFC_EPERM = 2,      /* Permissions error. */
};
```

For the OFPET_QUEUE_OP_FAILED error type, these codes are currently defined:

```
/* ofp_error msg 'code' values for OFPET_QUEUE_OP_FAILED.
 * 'data' contains
 * at least the first 64 bytes of the failed request */
enum ofp_queue_op_failed_code {
OFPQOFC_BAD_PORT = 0, /* Invalid port (or port does not exist). */
OFPQOFC_BAD_QUEUE = 1,/* Queue does not exist. */
OFPQOFC_EPERM = 2,    /* Permissions error. */
};
```

For the OFPET_SWITCH_CONFIG_FAILED error type, the codes currently defined are as follows:

```
/* ofp_error_msg 'code' values for OFPET_SWITCH_CONFIG_FAILED.
 * 'data' contains
 * at least the first 64 bytes of the failed request. */
enum ofp_switch_config_failed_code {
OFPSCFC_BAD_FLAGS = 0, /* Specified flags is invalid. */
OFPSCFC_BAD_LEN = 1,   /* Specified len is invalid. */
OFPSCFC_EPERM = 2,     /* Permissions error. */
};
```

For the OFPET_ROLE_REQUEST_FAILED error type, here are the currently defined codes :

```
/* ofp_error_msg 'code' values for OFPET_ROLE_REQUEST_FAILED.
 * 'data' contains at least the first 64 bytes of the failed
 * request. */
enum ofp_role_request_failed_code {
OFPRRFC_STALE = 0,    /* Stale Message: old generation_id. */
OFPRRFC_UNSUP = 1,    /* Controller role change unsupported. */
OFPRRFC_BAD_ROLE = 2, /* Invalid role. */
};
```

For the OFPET_METER_MOD_FAILED error type, the following codes are currently defined:

```
/* ofp_error_msg 'code' values for OFPET_METER_MOD_FAILED.
 * 'data' contains at least the first 64 bytes of the failed
 * request. */
enum ofp_meter_mod_failed_code {
OFPMMFC_UNKNOWN = 0,        /* Unspecified error. */
OFPMMFC_METER_EXISTS = 1, /* Meter not added because a Meter ADD
                           * attempted to replace an existing
                           * Meter. */
OFPMMFC_INVALID_METER = 2, /* Meter not added because Meter
                            * specified is invalid. */
OFPMMFC_UNKNOWN_METER = 3, /* Meter not modified because a Meter
                            * MODIFY attempted to modify a
                          * non-existent Meter. */
OFPMMFC_BAD_COMMAND = 4, /* Unsupported or unknown command. */
OFPMMFC_BAD_FLAGS = 5,   /* Flag configuration unsupported. */
OFPMMFC_BAD_RATE = 6,    /* Rate unsupported. */
OFPMMFC_BAD_BURST = 7,   /* Burst size unsupported. */
OFPMMFC_BAD_BAND = 8,    /* Band unsupported. */
OFPMMFC_BAD_BAND_VALUE = 9, /* Band value unsupported. */
OFPMMFC_OUT_OF_METERS = 10, /* No more meters available. */
OFPMMFC_OUT_OF_BANDS = 11,  /* The maximum number of properties
                             * for a meter has been exceeded. */
};
```

For the OFPET_TABLE_FEATURES_FAILED error type, these codes are currently defined:

```
/* ofp_error_msg 'code' values for OFPET_TABLE_FEATURES_FAILED.
 * 'data' contains at least the first 64 bytes of the failed
 * request. */
enum ofp_table_features_failed_code {
OFPTFFC_BAD_TABLE = 0,     /* Specified table does not exist. */
OFPTFFC_BAD_METADATA = 1, /* Invalid metadata mask. */
OFPTFFC_EPERM = 5,         /* Permissions error. */
};
```

For the OFPET_BAD_PROPERTY error type, the codes currently defined are as follows:

```
/* ofp_error_msg 'code' values for OFPET_BAD_PROPERTY.
 * 'data' contains at least the first 64 bytes of the failed
 * request. */
enum ofp_bad_property_code {
OFPBPC_BAD_TYPE = 0,  /* Unknown property type. */
```

```
OFPBPC_BAD_LEN = 1,    /* Length problem in property. */
OFPBPC_BAD_VALUE = 2, /* Unsupported property value. */
OFPBPC_TOO_MANY = 3,  /* Can't handle this many properties. */
OFPBPC_DUP_TYPE = 4,  /* A property type was duplicated. */
OFPBPC_BAD_EXPERIMENTER = 5, /* Unknown experimenter id
                              * specified. */
OFPBPC_BAD_EXP_TYPE = 6,     /* Unknown exp_type for experimenter
                              * id. */
OFPBPC_BAD_EXP_VALUE = 7, /* Unknown value for experimenter id. */
OFPBPC_EPERM = 8,         /* Permissions error. */
};
```

For the `OFPET_ASYNC_CONFIG_FAILED` error type, here are the currently defined codes:

```
/* ofp_error_msg 'code' values for OFPET_ASYNC_CONFIG_FAILED.
 * 'data' contains at least the first 64 bytes of the failed
 * request. */
enum ofp_async_config_failed_code {
OFPACFC_INVALID = 0,      /* One mask is invalid. */
OFPACFC_UNSUPPORTED = 1, /* Requested configuration not
                          * supported. */
OFPACFC_EPERM = 2,        /* Permissions error. */
};
```

For the `OFPET_FLOW_MONITOR_FAILED` error type, the following codes are currently defined:

```
/* ofp_error_msg 'code' values for OFPET_FLOW_MONITOR_FAILED.
 * 'data' contains at least the first 64 bytes of the failed
 * request. */
enum ofp_flow_monitor_failed_code {
OFPMOFC_UNKNOWN = 0,         /* Unspecified error. */
OFPMOFC_MONITOR_EXISTS = 1, /* Monitor not added because a
                             * Monitor ADD attempted to replace an
                             * existing Monitor. */
OFPMOFC_INVALID_MONITOR = 2,/* Monitor not added because Monitor
                             * specified is invalid. */
OFPMOFC_UNKNOWN_MONITOR = 3,/* Monitor not modified because a
                             * Monitor MODIFY attempted to modify
                             * a non-existent Monitor. */
OFPMOFC_BAD_COMMAND = 4,   /* Unsupported or unknown command. */
OFPMOFC_BAD_FLAGS = 5,     /* Flag configuration unsupported. */
OFPMOFC_BAD_TABLE_ID = 6, /* Specified table does not exist. */
OFPMOFC_BAD_OUT = 7,       /* Error in output port/group. */
};
```

For the `OFPET_BUNDLE_FAILED` error type, these codes are currently defined:

```
/* ofp_error_msg 'code' values for OFPET_BUNDLE_FAILED.
 * 'data' contains at least the first 64 bytes of the failed
 *  request. */
enum ofp_bundle_failed_code {
OFPBFC_UNKNOWN = 0,          /* Unspecified error. */
OFPBFC_EPERM = 1,            /* Permissions error. */
OFPBFC_BAD_ID = 2,           /* Bundle ID doesn't exist. */
OFPBFC_BUNDLE_EXIST = 3,     /* Bundle ID already exist. */
OFPBFC_BUNDLE_CLOSED = 4,    /* Bundle ID is closed. */
OFPBFC_OUT_OF_BUNDLES = 5,/* Too many bundles IDs. */
OFPBFC_BAD_TYPE = 6,         /* Unsupported or unknown message
                              * control type. */
OFPBFC_BAD_FLAGS = 7,       /* Unsupported, unknown, or inconsistent
                             * flags. */
OFPBFC_MSG_BAD_LEN = 8,     /* Length problem in included message. */
OFPBFC_MSG_BAD_XID = 9,     /* Inconsistent or duplicate XID. */
OFPBFC_MSG_UNSUP = 10,      /* Unsupported message in this bundle. */
OFPBFC_MSG_CONFLICT = 11,/* Unsupported message combination in this
bundle. */
OFPBFC_MSG_TOO_MANY = 12,/* Cant handle this many messages in bundle.
*/
OFPBFC_MSG_FAILED = 13,     /* One message in bundle failed. */
OFPBFC_TIMEOUT = 14,        /* Bundle is taking too long. */
OFPBFC_BUNDLE_IN_PROGRESS = 15, /* Bundle is locking the
                                 * resource. */
};
```

For the `OFPET_EXPERIMENTER` error type, the error message is defined by the following structure and fields:

```
/* OFPET_EXPERIMENTER: Error message (datapath -> controller). */
struct ofp_error_experimenter_msg {
struct ofp_header header;
uint16_t type;          /* OFPET_EXPERIMENTER. */
uint16_t exp_code;      /* Experimenter defined. */
uint32_t experimenter; /* Experimenter ID. */
uint8_t data[0];        /* Variable-length data. Interpreted based
                         * on the type and experimenter. No
                         * padding. */
};
```

Common OpenFlow multipart message types

This section talks about OpenFlow multipart message, and message types, as per the following code snippet:

```
enum ofp_multipart_type {
   /* Description of this OpenFlow switch.
    * The request body is empty.
    * The reply body is struct ofp_desc. */
OFPMP_DESC = 0,
  /* Individual flow statistics.
   * The request body is struct ofp_flow_stats_request.
   * The reply body is an array of struct ofp_flow_stats. */
OFPMP_FLOW = 1,
   /* Aggregate flow statistics.
    * The request body is struct ofp_aggregate_stats_request.
    * The reply body is struct ofp_aggregate_stats_reply. */
OFPMP_AGGREGATE = 2,
   /* Flow table statistics.
    * The request body is empty.
    * The reply body is an array of struct ofp_table_stats. */
OFPMP_TABLE = 3,
   /* Port statistics.
    * The request body is struct ofp_port_stats_request.
    * The reply body is an array of struct ofp_port_stats. */
OFPMP_PORT_STATS = 4,
   /* Queue statistics for a port
    * The request body is struct ofp_queue_stats_request.
    * The reply body is an array of struct ofp_queue_stats */
OFPMP_QUEUE_STATS = 5,
   /* Group counter statistics.
    * The request body is struct ofp_group_stats_request.
    * The reply is an array of struct ofp_group_stats. */
OFPMP_GROUP = 6,
   /* Group description.
    * The request body is empty.
    * The reply body is an array of struct ofp_group_desc. */
OFPMP_GROUP_DESC = 7,
   /* Group features.
    * The request body is empty.
    * The reply body is struct ofp_group_features. */
OFPMP_GROUP_FEATURES = 8,
   /* Meter statistics.
```

```
     * The request body is struct ofp_meter_multipart_requests.
     * The reply body is an array of struct ofp_meter_stats. */
  OFPMP_METER = 9,
    /* Meter configuration.
     * The request body is struct ofp_meter_multipart_requests.
     * The reply body is an array of struct ofp_meter_config. */
  OFPMP_METER_CONFIG = 10,
    /* Meter features.
     * The request body is empty.
     * The reply body is struct ofp_meter_features. */
  OFPMP_METER_FEATURES = 11,
    /* Table features.
     * The request body is either empty or contains an array of
     * struct ofp_table_features containing the controller's
     * desired view of the switch. If the switch is unable to
     * set the specified view an error is returned.
     * The reply body is an array of struct ofp_table_features. */
  OFPMP_TABLE_FEATURES = 12,
    /* Port description.
     * The request body is empty.
     * The reply body is an array of struct ofp_port. */
  OFPMP_PORT_DESC = 13,
    /* Table description.
     * The request body is empty.
     * The reply body is an array of struct ofp_table_desc. */
  OFPMP_TABLE_DESC = 14,
    /* Queue description.
     * The request body is struct ofp_queue_desc_request.
     * The reply body is an array of struct ofp_queue_desc. */
  OFPMP_QUEUE_DESC = 15,
    /* Flow monitors.
     * The request body is struct ofp_flow_monitor_request.
     * The reply body is array of struct ofp_flow_update_header. */
  OFPMP_FLOW_MONITOR = 16,
    /* Experimenter extension.
     * The request and reply bodies begin with
     * struct ofp_experimenter_multipart_header.
     * The request and reply bodies are otherwise
     * experimenter-defined. */
  OFPMP_EXPERIMENTER = 0xffff
  };
```

Index

A

action
about 89
Change-TTL 90
cookie field 92
drop 89
group 89
output 89
push-tag/pop-tag 90
set-field 90
set-queue 89
timeout 92
action list 89
action set 89
action, switch
OFPFMF_ADD 197
OFPFMF_INITIAL 197
OFPFMF_INSTRUCTIONS 197
OFPFMF_MODIFY 197
OFPFMF_NO_ABBREV 198
OFPFMF_ONLY_OWN 198
OFPFMF_REMOVED 197
performing 197
asynchronous events list
fetching 67
auxiliary connection
establishing 24-26
establishing, to controller 9-11

B

barrier message
handling, from controller 54
sending, to switch 75, 76
body field
about 146, 168
bucket_stat 165
byte_count 165
duration_nsec 160, 165
duration_sec 154, 160, 165
packet_count 165
port_no 159
properties 155, 160
queue_id 159
rx_bytes 154
rx_dropped 154
rx_errors 154
rx_packets 154
tx_bytes 154, 159
tx_dropped 154
tx_errors 154
tx_packets 154, 159
bundle
closing 229, 238, 239
creating 226, 227, 235, 236
discarding 231, 240
messages, adding to 227, 228, 236-238
operations, committing 239, 240
operations, executing 239, 240
bundle_id field 234, 235
Bundle message 225

C

command field 109
Command-line Interface (CLI) 2
config field 244

connection, from controller to switch
setting up, on TCP and TLS 18-20
TCP procedure 18
TLS procedure 20
connection, from switch to controller
interruption procedures 16
setting up, on TCP and TLS 2-5
setting up, with multiple controllers 5, 6
TCP procedure 3
TLS procedure 3, 4
controller
auxiliary connection, establishing 9-11
barrier message, handling from 54
controller role-status message, sending to 49, 50
flow removed message, sending to 45-47
handshake message, handling 11-13
packet-in message, sending to 41-44
packet-out message, handling from 53
port-status message, sending to 47, 48
request forward message, sending to 52
role of communication channel, setting 7-9, 22-24
switch configuration message, handling 14, 15
table-status message, sending to 51, 52
controller role-status message
processing, from switch 70
sending, to controller 49, 50
cookie field 108
cookie mask field 108
counter field 87

E

echo request
processing 35, 60
sending 35, 60, 61
entry
deleting, from flow table 111, 112
modifying, in flow table 112, 113
error codes, OpenFlow 248-257
error message
processing 37, 61, 62
sending 37, 61, 62
eviction 102
experimenter message
processing 38, 62, 63
sending 38, 62, 63
experimenter multipart messages 202, 223

F

fields, Ethernet ports
collisions 156
rx_crc_err 156
rx_frame_err 156
rx_over_err 156
flag field 146, 168, 235
flag field, controller
OFPFMF_ADD 222
OFPFMF_INITIAL 222
OFPFMF_INSTRUCTIONS 222
OFPFMF_MODIFY 222
OFPFMF_NO_ABBREV 222
OFPFMF_ONLY_OWN 222
OFPFMF_REMOVED 222
flow entry
adding, in flow table 95, 96, 106-110
deleting, in flow table 97
modifying, in flow table 98
flow entry statistics
obtaining, multipart messages used 171-173
flow monitor
configuring, multipart messages used 197-201, 219-223
flow removed asynchronous message
processing, from switch 69
flow removed message
sending, to controller 45-47
flow table
cookie 79
counter 79
entry, deleting from 111, 112
entry, modifying 112, 113
flow entry, adding 95, 96, 106-110
flow entry, deleting 97
flow entry, modifying 98
instructions 79
Match Fields 79

modifying, with eviction enabled 92, 93, 102-104
modifying, with vacancy enabled 94, 95, 104-106
priority 79
synchronizations 99
timeout 79
Vacancy_down 94
Vacancy_up 94
flow table entry
about 81
counter field 87
instruction set 87, 88
Match Fields 81
priority field 87
flow table entry statistics
multipart request message handling, for obtaining 150, 151
flow table statistics
multipart request message handling, for obtaining 151, 152
obtaining, multipart messages used 173, 174

G

Get Asynchronous Configuration message
handling, from controller 40
group description
obtaining, multipart messages used 205
group entry
adding, in group table 130-134
deleting, in group table 134, 135
modifying, in group table 135, 136
group feature
obtaining, multipart messages used 185, 186, 205, 206
group statistics
multipart request message handling, for obtaining 163-165
obtaining, multipart messages used 178
group table
about 129
group entry, adding in 130-134
group entry, deleting in 134, 135
group entry, modifying in 135, 136

H

handshake message
handling, from controller 11-13
sending, to switch 26, 27
Hard_timeout 92, 109
hello message
OFPT_HELLO message, receiving 34, 35
OFPT_HELLO message, sending 33, 34
processing 33-35, 58, 59
sending 33-35, 58, 59

I

Idle_timeout 92, 109
individual flow table entry statistics
multipart request message handling, for obtaining 147-150
obtaining, multipart messages used 169-171
information
obtaining, on switch 204
instruction field 96
instruction set 87, 89

K

KBPS (Kilo-Bits Per Second) 139

L

Link Aggregation Group (LAG) 43

M

Match Fields
about 81
Oxm_class 82
Oxm_field 82
Oxm_haskmask 82-87
messages
adding, to bundle 227, 228, 236-238
meter
applying, in meter table 136-141
meter configuration
obtaining, multipart messages used 186, 187, 206, 207

meter entry
deleting 141, 142
modifying, in meter table 142, 143
meter feature
obtaining, multipart messages used 188, 189, 207, 208
meter statistics
multipart request messages handling, for obtaining 161-163
obtaining, multipart message used 177, 178
meter table
about 129
meter, applying in 136-141
meter entry, modifying in 142, 143
multipart messages
about 145
used, for configuring flow monitor 197-201, 219-223
used, for defining switch 182, 183
used, for meter configuration 186, 187
used, for obtaining flow entry statistics 171-173
used, for obtaining flow table statistics 173, 174
used, for obtaining group description 183, 184, 205
used, for obtaining group feature 185, 186, 205, 206
used, for obtaining group statistics 178
used, for obtaining meter configuration 206, 207
used, for obtaining individual flow table entry statistics 169-171
used, for obtaining meter feature 188, 189, 207, 208
used, for obtaining meter statistic 177, 178
used, for obtaining port description 190-192, 217
used, for obtaining port queue statistic 175, 177
used, for obtaining port statistic 174, 175
used, for obtaining queue description 194-196, 218, 219
used, for obtaining table description 193, 194, 217
used, for obtaining table feature 189, 208-216
multipart message types, OpenFlow 258
multipart request message, handling
for obtaining group statistics 163-165
for obtaining meter statistics 161-163
for obtaining port queue statistics 158-160
for obtaining port statistics 153-158
for obtaining statistics, of flow table 151, 152
for obtaining statistics, of flow table entry 150, 151
for obtaining statistics, of individual flow table entry 147-150
multiple controllers
switch, managing with different roles 21, 22
switch to controller connection, setting up 5, 6

N

Nicira Extensible Match (NXM) 82

O

OFPM_CONTROLLER meter 138
OFPMP_FLOW request
byte_count 148
cookie 148
duration_sec 148
flag 148
hard_timeout 148
idle_timeout 148
importance 148
length 148
packet_count 148
table_id 148
OFPMP_METER_FEATURES
fields 188
OFPMP_METER request
band_stat 163
byte_band_count 163
duration_nsec 162
duration_sec 162

flow_count 162
packet_band_count 163
packet_in_count 162
OFPMP_QUEUE_DESC
fields 195
OFPM_SLOWPATH meter 138
OFPT_ECHO_REPLY message
processing 36, 61
OFPT_ECHO_REQUEST message
receiving 36, 61
sending 36, 60
OFPT_GROUP_MOD message 134, 135
OFPT_HELLO message
receiving 59
sending 58
OFPT_METER_MOD message 141, 142
OpenFlow bundle mechanism
stages 226, 233
OpenFlow channel 2
OpenFlow Extensible Match (OXM) 43, 81
OpenFlow headers 241, 242
OpenFlow specification
eviction 92, 102
eviction, based on importance field 93
eviction, based on remaining lifetime 93
eviction, based on switch criteria 93
vacancy 92, 102
OpenFlow structures
about 243
port structures 243, 244
table structures 245
OpenFlow switch pipeline processing 79
Open Networking Foundation (ONF) 2, 63
operations
committing, in bundle 230-240
executing, in bundle 230-240
optical ports
fields 157
Oxm_class
about 82
ONF member classes 82
ONF reserved classes 82
Oxm_field 82
Oxm_haskmask
about 82-87
fields 83-86

P

packet
constructing 75
packet buffer
using 75
packet-in asynchronous message
processing, from switch 68
packet-in message
sending, to controller 41-44
packet-out message
handling, from controller 53
sending, to switch 73, 74
port description
obtaining, multipart messages used 190-192, 217
port queue statistics
multipart request message handling, for obtaining 158-160
obtaining, multipart messages used 175, 176
port statistics
multipart request message handling, for obtaining 153-158
obtaining, multipart messages used 174, 175
port-status asynchronous message
processing, from switch 70
port-status message
sending, to controller 47, 48
port structures 243, 244
PPS (Packets Per Second) 139
priority field 87
properties field 235

Q

queue description
obtaining, multipart messages used 194-196, 218, 219

R

reply message
processing 35, 61
sending 35
request forward message
processing, from switch 72
sending, to controller 52

role, of communication channel
setting, towards controller 7-9
role, of controller's communication channel
setting 22-24
roles, controller
Role Equal (OFPCR_ROLE_EQUAL) 21
Role Master (OFPCR_ROLE_MASTER) 21
Role Slave (OFPCR_ROLE_SLAVE) 21

S

Set Asynchronous Configuration message
handling 39
state field 244
switch
barrier message, sending to 75, 76
configuring 64-67
controller role-status message, processing from 70
defining, multipart messages used 182-184
flow removed asynchronous message, processing from 69
handshake message, sending 26, 27
packet-in asynchronous message, processing from 68
packet-out message, sending to 73, 74
port-status asynchronous message, processing from 70
request forward message, processing from 72
switch configuration message, sending 27, 28
table-status asynchronous message, processing from 71
switch configuration message
handling, from controller 14, 15
OFPT_GET_CONFIG_REPLY 27
OFPT_GET_CONFIG_REQUEST 27
OFPT_SET_CONFIG 27
sending, to switch 27
sending, to the switch 28

T

table description
obtaining, multipart messages used 193, 194, 217
table feature
obtaining, multipart messages used 189, 208-216
table-status asynchronous message
processing, from switch 71
table-status message
sending, to controller 51, 52
table structures 245
TCP and TLS
connection from controller to switch, setting up 18-20
connection from switch to controller, setting up 2-5
TTL actions 91
type field 146, 168
type-length-value (TLV) 81

V

vacancy threshold 104
VLAN header 90

Thank you for buying
OpenFlow Cookbook

About Packt Publishing

Packt, pronounced 'packed', published its first book, *Mastering phpMyAdmin for Effective MySQL Management*, in April 2004, and subsequently continued to specialize in publishing highly focused books on specific technologies and solutions.

Our books and publications share the experiences of your fellow IT professionals in adapting and customizing today's systems, applications, and frameworks. Our solution-based books give you the knowledge and power to customize the software and technologies you're using to get the job done. Packt books are more specific and less general than the IT books you have seen in the past. Our unique business model allows us to bring you more focused information, giving you more of what you need to know, and less of what you don't.

Packt is a modern yet unique publishing company that focuses on producing quality, cutting-edge books for communities of developers, administrators, and newbies alike. For more information, please visit our website at `www.packtpub.com`.

About Packt Open Source

In 2010, Packt launched two new brands, Packt Open Source and Packt Enterprise, in order to continue its focus on specialization. This book is part of the Packt open source brand, home to books published on software built around open source licenses, and offering information to anybody from advanced developers to budding web designers. The Open Source brand also runs Packt's open source Royalty Scheme, by which Packt gives a royalty to each open source project about whose software a book is sold.

Writing for Packt

We welcome all inquiries from people who are interested in authoring. Book proposals should be sent to `author@packtpub.com`. If your book idea is still at an early stage and you would like to discuss it first before writing a formal book proposal, then please contact us; one of our commissioning editors will get in touch with you.

We're not just looking for published authors; if you have strong technical skills but no writing experience, our experienced editors can help you develop a writing career, or simply get some additional reward for your expertise.

Software Defined Networking with OpenFlow

ISBN: 978-1-84969-872-6 Paperback: 152 pages

Get hands-on with the platforms and development tools used to build OpenFlow network applications

1. Get to grips with the essentials of OpenFlow and its ecosystem features.
2. Thorough overview of OpenSource switches, controllers, and tools.
3. Build your own laboratory and develop your own networking apps.

Untangle Network Security

ISBN: 978-1-84951-772-0 Paperback: 368 pages

Secure your network against threats and vulnerabilities using the unparalleled Untangle NGFW

1. Learn how to install, deploy, and configure Untangle NG Firewall.
2. Understand network security fundamentals and how to protect your network using Untangle NG Firewall.
3. Step-by-step tutorial supported by many examples and screenshots.

Please check **www.PacktPub.com** for information on our titles

Kali Linux Network Scanning Cookbook

ISBN: 978-1-78398-214-1 Paperback: 452 pages

Over 90 hands-on recipes explaining how to leverage custom scripts, and integrated tools in Kali Linux to effectively master network scanning

1. Learn the fundamentals behind commonly used scanning techniques.
2. Deploy powerful scanning tools that are integrated into the Kali Linux testing platform.
3. A step-by-step guide, full of recipes that will help you use integrated scanning tools in Kali Linux, and develop custom scripts for making new and unique tools of your own.

Oracle Coherence Quickstart [Video]

ISBN: 978-1-84969-494-0 Duration: 01:43 hours

Build dynamic next-generation applications using the market leading in-memory datagrid

1. Step-by-step, and easy to follow instructions to leverage Coherence and provide real-time updates to client applications.
2. Detailed demonstrations with suggested best practices to build scalable websites and Enterprise applications using a tried and tested data grid product.
3. Structured examples and projects, with hands-on exercises and guidance.

Please check **www.PacktPub.com** for information on our titles

Made in the USA
Middletown, DE
08 November 2016